RURAL CONFLICT, CRIME AND PROTEST

Rural Conflict, Crime and Protest makes a major contribution to the historiography of nineteenth-century crime. The work presents a new analysis of several important and controversial themes: the concept of social crime, petty crime and protest in the English countryside between 1800 and 1860. The bulk of the research into rural crime has traditionally emanated from East Anglia, the south and the east; however, the bulk of the evidence for this book has come from Herefordshire, in the west of England, adding to the historiography of nineteenth-century rural crime. Based upon a rich vein of primary source material and liberally interspersed with court room revelations and newspaper reports, this work is both informative and scholarly and would make a useful addition to the bookshelves of academics and students alike, without excluding the casual reader.

Timothy Shakesheff is a lecturer in modern British social history at University College Worcester.

RURAL CONFLICT, CRIME AND PROTEST

Herefordshire, 1800 to 1860

Timothy Shakesheff

THE BOYDELL PRESS

First published 2003

Published by The Boydell Press
An imprint of Boydell & Brewer Ltd
PO Box 9, Woodbridge, Suffolk IP12 3DF, UK
and of Boydell & Brewer Inc.
PO Box 41026, Rochester, NY 14604–4126, USA
website: www.boydell.co.uk

ISBN 1 84383 018 3

A catalogue record for this book is available from the British Library

Library of Congress Cataloging-in-Publication Data
Shakesheff, Timothy, 1952–
Rural conflict, crime, and protest : Herefordshire, 1800 to 1860 /
Timothy Shakesheff.
p. cm.
Includes bibliographical references and index.
ISBN 1-84383-018-3 (alk. paper)
1. Rural crimes—England—Herefordshire—History—19th century.
2. Social conflict—England—Herefordshire—History—19th century.
3. Herefordshire (England)—History—19th century. I. Title.

HV6950.H47S53 2003
364.9424'2'09034—dc21
2003012674

Typeset by Keystroke, Jacaranda Lodge, Wolverhampton
Printed in Great Britain by
St Edmundsbury Press Limited, Bury St Edmunds, Suffolk

Contents

List of illustrations   vii

Introduction   1

1 Rebels without a clue? The nature of rural protest in
Herefordshire, 1800–60   7

2 'A painful scene of crime, depravity and misery': rural poverty
and crime   30

3 'To overawe those vagabonds who infest the county': policing
rural Herefordshire   54

4 Rustlers, social criminals or common thieves? Sheep-stealing in
rural Herefordshire   78

5 Criminal women, crop deprivators and crop-thieves   113

6 'Give him a good un': social crime, poaching and the Game Laws   141

7 'Vile' and 'evil-disposed persons': incendiarism and
animal-maiming   176

Conclusion: the rural poor in Herefordshire, c.1800–60 –
assertive criminals or silent victims?   201

Appendices   206
Bibliography   218
Index   227

To James (Mick) Shakesheff

Illustrations

Maps

1.1 England and Wales, c.1832, showing the location of Herefordshire   2
1.2 Herefordshire c.1832, showing the location of principal market towns   3

Figures

2.1 Petty Session Returns: Convictions for wood- and crop-theft, trespass, wilful or malicious damage and Game Law infringements: c.1822–60   35
2.2 Petty Session Returns: Convictions for rural crimes by type of offence: 1822–60   35
4.1 Committals for sheep-stealing and wheat prices, 1815–20   86
4.2 Committals and convictions for sheep-stealing, 1800–32   87
4.3 Convictions for sheep-stealing, 1800–60   98
4.4 Committals and convictions for sheep-stealing, 1833–60   101
4.5 Committals to Hereford Gaol on suspicion of sheep-stealing, by season, 1833–60   102
5.1 Petty Session Returns: Convictions for wood-theft, 1822–60   115
5.2 Petty Session Returns: Convictions for crop-theft, 1826–60   116
5.3 Petty Session Returns: Convictions for wilful or malicious damage, 1836–60   116
5.4 Petty Session Returns: Convictions for wood-theft, by session, 1822–60   122
5.5 Petty Session Returns: Convictions for crop-theft, by session, 1826–60   123
6.1 Petty Session Returns: Convictions for Game Law offences, 1822–60   146
6.2 Petty Session Returns: Convictions for trespass and Game Law offences, 1822–60   147
6.3 Convictions at Hereford Quarter Sessions for Game Law offences, 1816–21   152
6.4 Petty Session Returns: Convictions for Game Law offences, by session, 1822–60   153
7.1 Reported cases of rural incendiarism: Herefordshire, 1800–60   178
7.2 Rural incendiarism in Herefordshire, 1830–60   179

ILLUSTRATIONS

7.3 Targets of rural incendiarism in Herefordshire, 1800–60   183
7.4 Reported cases of incendiarism by season in Herefordshire,
    1800–60   189
7.5 Reported cases of animal-maiming in Herefordshire, 1800–60   195
7.6 Targets of animal-maimers in Herefordshire, 1800–60   198

Table

5.1 Sex of prisoners taken into custody at Hereford Gaol, 1841–52   127

Introduction

> In intellect he is a child, in position a helot, in condition a squalid outcast . . .
> his knowledge of the future is limited to the field he works in. . . . The Squire is
> his King, the parson his deity, the taproom his highest conception of earthly
> bliss.[1]

Although this was written in 1872, beyond the period with which this book
is principally concerned, the stereotype of the slack-jawed, straw-chewing
yokel was a commonplace picture throughout the nineteenth century.
Undoubtedly the rural labourer of Herefordshire was poorly educated and
quite often totally illiterate. Moreover, he was poorly paid and his horizon
rarely extended past his parish, but it is a mistake to confuse his illiteracy with
lack of intellect and his poverty with dumb obedience. Research for this
study has suggested that his intellect was far from childlike. To illustrate his
intelligence and assertiveness, however, is problematic. He rarely, willingly,
left any reason to suppose he even existed, and if we expect to find detailed
life histories written by the agricultural working class we will be disappointed.
Indeed, he had little inclination or the skills to leave such testimonies; this
was left to other, more official, bodies. Admittedly, his birth was documented;
as was his marriage and his death. It is possible that his name might appear
on a farmer's accounts book or on a Union Workhouse ledger; however,
they are merely names. Despite this we can glean some information from
these shaky signatures and scratched crosses. We can tell how long he lived,
at what age he married, we can discover how well, or how poorly, he was paid
and we can tell when he was not paid at all. Although these sources can
produce statistics and give an indication of his life-span, age of marriage
and average wage, they paradoxically tell us very little about their social
world. Their meetings with government and parish administrators were
but brief encounters and do little for the historian who wishes to reconstruct
the experiences of the rural working class. While the majority of the rural
working class lived and died undocumented lives, those who broke the law
often had more prolonged brushes with administrators and social observers.
Court records tell us the nature of the crime, the victim's name, the offender's
name and the date and parish in which the crime was committed. The local

[1] Lloyd Jones, editorial in the 'Beehive': January 1872, cited in Alan Armstrong,
Farmworkers: A Social and Economic History. 1770–1980, Batsford, London (1988).

1

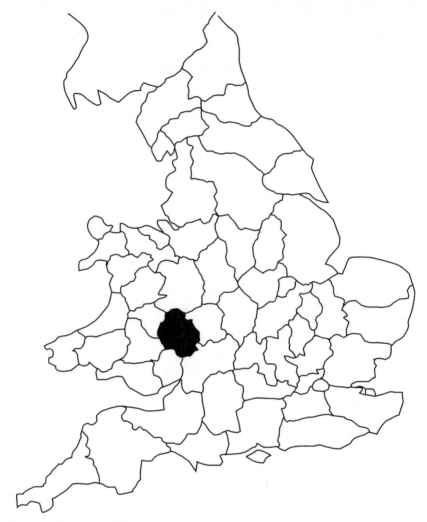

Map 1.1 England and Wales, *c.* 1832, showing the location of Herefordshire

newspapers of the period add flesh to the bare bones of the crime, often stating the value of the goods stolen or destroyed, the offender's and the victim's occupations. The press often reported if the offender was poor, old, unemployed or simply 'vicious'. Moreover, the press reflected the fears of the usual victims of crime in Herefordshire: the employing landowners and farmers. Using these sources it is possible to open a crack in a door through which the social historian can peer to capture a picture of labouring rural life in the nineteenth century. The study of crime, as a way into the lives of ordinary men and women, is not new and historical criminology is now seen

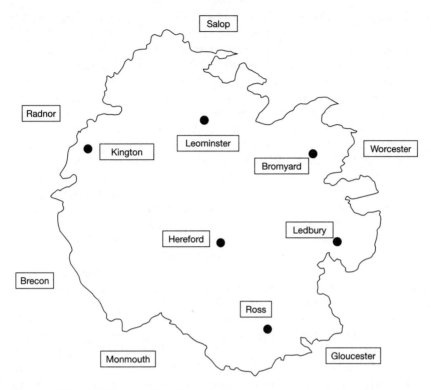

Map 1.2 Herefordshire, *c.* 1832, showing the location of principal market towns

as 'central to unlocking the meanings of . . . social history'.[2] Moreover, the field grows ever more diverse as historians begin to recognize the value of researching crime and the criminal.[3]

The study of rural crime in Herefordshire attempts to add to this diversity. Unlike East Anglia and the south and east of England, Herefordshire, although a rural county, has largely been ignored. This is not surprising, since

---

[2] D. Hay, P. Linebaugh and E. P. Thompson, *Albion's Fatal Tree: Crime and Society in Eighteenth Century England*, Allen Lane, London (1975). Preface. 13.
[3] The corpus of material pertaining to crime and criminality in the eighteenth and nineteenth centuries is now so far-reaching it would be impossible to list the full range of titles. There are, however, several articles and books that provide an overview of the historiography of crime. See e.g. Joanna Innes and John Styles, 'The Crime Wave: Recent Writings on Crime and Criminal Justice in Eighteenth Century England', *Journal of British Studies*, Vol. 25 (1986), J. A. Sharpe, 'The History of Crime in England, c1300–1914: An Overview of Recent Publications', *British Journal of Criminology*, Vol. 28 (1988), J. Briggs, *Crime and Punishment in England: An Introductory History*, University College London Press, London (1996) and Peter King, 'Locating Histories of Crime: A Bibliographical Study', *British Journal of Criminology*, Vol. 39 (1999).

the county never experienced any overt displays of agricultural discontent; moreover, the county was peripheral to the 'Swing' disturbances of 1830 to 1831. At first glance this may suggest that because the county's agricultural produce was more diverse the agricultural labourer of Herefordshire escaped the unemployment experienced by his wheat-reliant eastern and southern counterparts. Research, however, indicates that this was not the case. Herefordshire, especially the central plain and southern and eastern areas, similar to the eastern counties of England, was regarded as 'a great wheat-growing county'. Moreover, wheat accounted for over half of the county's produce during the first half of the nineteenth century. Admittedly there was 'a significant livestock interest in all parts of the county', and hops, apples, turnips, oats and beans and peas were also important to the prosperity of the county's farmers and went some way towards cushioning a succession of depressions.[4] However, as the following chapters will show, rural poverty, caused by unemployment, underemployment and low wages, was as much a fact of life on the rolling hills of the Welsh border areas as it was on the flat wheat fields of the east. Moreover, this book will also argue that agricultural discontent was not confined to years such as 1830 to 1831 but was present, to a greater or lesser extent, throughout the period.

While Herefordshire never experienced those criminal acts usually associated with rural protest to the same extent as East Anglia or Suffolk incendiarism, threatening anonymous letters and animal maiming did occur. Arguably these crimes were comparatively rare, not only in Herefordshire but throughout England. It would be safe to assume that for every incendiarist or animal maimer who passed through the courts, thousands of rural petty criminals had been committed and convicted of crimes that 'lack the his-toriographically attractive, protopolitical associations' of the rick burner.[5] Despite the petty nature of many of the crimes dealt with in this study these acts were often as assertive a message as a burnt rick. The thefts of sheep, game, wood and crops were clear statements of poverty, alienation and displacement. This is not to argue that the entire rural population resorted to crime to survive or protest; the majority of the rural population clearly did not. However, that Herefordshire, in 1857, was rated as 'one of the six counties in England having the greatest amount of crime in proportion to the population' shows that many did.[6]

---

[4] J. P. Dodd, 'Herefordshire Agriculture in the Mid-nineteenth Century', *Transactions of the Woolhope Naturalists Field Club*, Vol. XLIII (1979). 217.

[5] Innes and Styles, 'Crime Wave'. 397.

[6] Archdeacon Freere, using criminal returns, argued at a lecture that Herefordshire boasted a ratio of one criminal for every 471 of the population. The other counties were Middlesex, Gloucester, Worcester, Chester and Monmouthshire. See *Hereford Journal: 15 July 1857*.

Research has focused upon the conflict between two inherently hostile groups: those who owned the land and those who worked it. The conflict in Herefordshire was not the classic struggle between the industrial bourgeoisie and an emerging proletariat but between agricultural employers and rural communities. Indeed, the points of conflict between the agricultural labourer and his employer were more diverse than those of his urban industrial counterpart. While a factory master may have had control over wages and conditions the employers of agricultural labour exercised control over almost all aspects of a labourer's life. Not only did they set wages and control tied housing but, before 1834, they also sat in vestries dispensing welfare to those they deemed worthy. Moreover, many landowners sat as magistrates, setting wages and the price of bread, and enforcing laws that protected their property and interests.[7] Arguably Lloyd Jones was right in claiming that the squire was the agricultural labourer's king, and as employers, poor law administrators and magistrates they reigned over every aspect of rural society. They were the county's elite. Indeed, the power they wielded over the everyday lives of the rural labourer and his family meant that overt displays of discontent were rare. While factory hands could rely upon the solidarity of his fellow workers in striking for better pay or improved conditions this was not the case for the agricultural worker. Experiences of exploitation, alienation and proletarianization occurred on different farms, in different parts of the county at different times in Herefordshire. Within the period of study, class-consciousness had not developed sufficiently to present a united front to even try to improve their position and this is why they resorted to various criminal acts. Essentially they continued to act as a 'class in itself' rather than a 'class for itself'. This is not surprising, not only because of the county's labourers' disparate experiences, but also because the Herefordshire land owners had not entirely abdicated their patriarchal responsibilities to the rural poor. Evidence of this is illustrated by the pleas for clemency on the behalf of wayward employees at court, the winter gifts of coal and clothing for the parish poor and the continuation of harvest feasts. Admittedly such acts of charity reaped rewards in terms of fostering good relations with the bulk of the rural population but, as the following chapters will illustrate, beneath the velvet glove of paternal charity often lay the iron hand of the criminal justice system.

Arguably, it is a relatively simple task to record industrial discontent. One simply has to count the numbers of strikes, petitions for higher pay or the numbers of sabotaged machines. To gauge discontent among the rural workforce, however, is a more complex task. With a surplus of labour to choose from, with relief reserved for the deserving poor and, after 1834, the fear of the workhouse the agricultural labourer was forced to resort to more

---

[7] Magistrates still set the price of bread in Hereford as late as November 1834. For the last recorded Bread Assize see *Hereford Journal: 26 November 1834*.

cunning, covert methods of protest and survival. It is necessary, therefore, to turn to the court records and the contemporary local newspapers for evidence of discontent. These sources are often the only means available to illustrate their discontent and, imperfect as they are, they are one of the few ways in which this discontent may be studied. In many ways the literate sections of rural society have, perhaps unconsciously, illustrated the lives of the rural poor.

This book concerns itself only with rural crime and is seen as a means to reconstruct the life of the Herefordshire farm labourer. This is not to suggest that impoverished or discontented agricultural labourers only committed the crimes referred to in this work. Some clearly did not and agricultural labourers occasionally committed burglary, highway robbery and horse theft. Equally, not all rural crimes were carried out by members of the rural population, and town labourers, for example, occasionally made poaching forays into the countryside. Where possible, however, research has concentrated upon crimes that were particular to rural Herefordshire and crimes that were committed in an urban setting; that is, crimes committed in Hereford itself or in any of the surrounding market towns have been largely ignored. It has to be admitted that, given the fragmentary nature of the evidence, it has not always been easy to ascertain the occupation of many of those who stood accused. For example, the occupational status given to offenders by court clerks has not always been as sharply defined as the researcher would wish. Indeed, research suggests that court clerks, as well as magistrates and newspaper reporters, often described any unskilled worker, whether agricultural or urban, as a 'labourer'. Despite vigorous research it has been necessary, in several cases, to assume that a rural crime committed by a rural 'labourer' was in all probability a crime committed by an agricultural labourer.

This book challenges Lloyd Jones' view that the agricultural labourer was submissive and fatalistic and it will argue that despite his poverty, his illiteracy and his apparently servile demeanor, the agricultural labourer of Herefordshire fought to survive in a rapidly changing rural world. In many ways his survival depended upon his ability to mix overt deference with covert terrorism. As Thompson argued, the agricultural labourer 'who touches his forelock to the squire by day – and who goes down to history as an example of deference – may kill his sheep, snare his pheasants or poison his dogs at night'.[8] Essentially this study concerns men and women who reacted to agricultural change and unemployment by the only means open to them: crime, that most primitive form of insurrection.

---

[8] E. P. Thompson, 'Patrician Society, Plebeian Culture', *Journal of Social History*, Vol. 7 (1974). 399.

1

Rebels without a clue?

The nature of rural protest in Herefordshire, 1800–60

On 30 March 1831, before the opening of the Oxford Circuit Assize at Hereford, Justice Patterson remarked:

> I am happy to find this calendar does not contain any cases of arson, rioting or breaking machinery . . . it shows that the labouring classes in this county are more peaceable and contented . . . it is proof that they are treated by their employers with kindness and attention to their wants.[1]

The following day he proceeded to sit and pass judgment upon cases of rural vandalism, armed poaching and sheep-stealing. While this is not the evidence the historian would expect to find if seeking a 'peacable and contented' rural population, Herefordshire's elite, in the aftermath of Swing, was able to congratulate itself upon the lack of any open revolt in the countryside. Yet all was not well with this rural idyll. During the period 1800 to 1860 the sheer volume of Petty Session convictions and cases reaching the Assizes and the Quarter Sessions and, from time to time the very nature of the offences, suggests that Justice Patterson, like the majority of the county's agricultural employers, was deluding himself. Throughout the period the available evidence suggests that the rural labouring population of the county were far from 'peacable and content'. Indeed, why should they be? Economic hardship and social distress were as hard-felt in the county of Herefordshire as in any of the areas of overt rural protest.[2] Once the surface is scratched the evidence

---

[1] *Hereford Journal* (hereafter abbreviated to *HJ*): *31 March 1831.*
[2] The main body of research thus far into rural crime and protest has emanated from East Anglia, the south east and to a lesser extent the south. See e.g. A. J. Peacock, *Bread or Blood: The Agrarian Riots in East Anglia, 1816*, Victor Gollancz, London (1965), and 'Village Radicalism in East Anglia: 1800–1850', in J. P. D. Dunbabin (ed.), *Rural Discontent in Nineteenth Century Britain*, Faber, London (1974). E. Hobsbawm and G. Rudé, *Captain Swing*, London, Pimlico (1969), John Archer, *'By a Flash and a Scare': Arson, Animal Maiming and Poaching in East Anglia, 1815–1870*, Clarendon Press, Oxford (1990), P. Muskett, 'The East Anglian Riots of 1822', *Agricultural History Review*, Vol. 32 (1984). Roger Wells, 'Rural Rebels in Southern England in the 1830s', in C. Emsley and J. Walvin (eds), *Artisans, Peasants and Proletarians*, Croom Helm, Beckenham (1985), and

suggests that seeds of discontent were present in the county. These seeds grew not into open revolt, or even semi-overt protest, but were manifested via the medium of crime.

Much of what has been written about the history of crime has been based on sources created by those who made and enforced the law. Historians have tended to rely on calendars of prisoners and the rudimentary statistics that may be derived from lists of committals, convictions and sentences in seeking to assess the extent of crime. When dealing with the causes of crime, discursive sources, such as local newspapers, are generally more significant though there is clearly an inherent bias in the nature of such evidence. Prison governors, magistrates, judges and journalists were capable, by virtue of their literacy, of generating the kind of documentary evidence on which historians have conventionally relied. Their viewpoint was significantly different from that of the accused and convicted, who were drawn mainly from the largely illiterate labouring poor. Yet, as Innes and Styles have argued, it is possible to use the available sources imaginatively and thereby 'reconstruct the experiences of the inarticulate and dispossessed', those on the wrong end of the law who could not speak or write for themselves.[3]

As the title of this book suggests, it will be argued here that many crimes committed in rural Herefordshire between 1800 and 1860 were acts of social and political protest. This is not a new argument as such, though historians have tended to concentrate upon the arsonist and the animal maimer.[4] Such crimes, although often referred to as 'marginal', are clearly recognized as acts that were carried out by those who sought to convey a message of discontent.[5] Any study of rural crime as protest would undoubtedly be incomplete without their inclusion and the crimes of incendiarism and animal maiming will be discussed in relation to Herefordshire.[6] What, however, of the other rural criminals such as the sheep-stealer, the crop thief and the hedge-breaker? Were they all merely common thieves and mindless vandals, or were their crimes also motivated by a primitive ideology, or justified by a sense of what was morally 'right'?

John Rule and Roger Wells, *Crime, Protest and Popular Politics in Southern England: 1740–1830*, Hambledon Press, London (1997).

[3] Innes and Styles, 'Crime Wave'. 382.

[4] Hobsbawm and Rudé's *Captain Swing* remains the definitive study of the agrarian disturbances of 1830 to 1831, and David Jones' 'Thomas Campbell Foster and the Rural Labourer: Incendiarism in East Anglia in the 1840s', *Social History*, Vol. 1 (1976) deals with rural arson in the post-'Swing' era. John Archer's 'By a Flash and a Scare', and '"A Fiendish Outrage"?, A Study of Animal Maiming in East Anglia: 1830–1870', *Agricultural History Review*, Vol. 33 (1985) deals with the unusual and sadistic crime of animal maiming.

[5] George Rudé, *Criminal and Victim: Crime and Society in Early Nineteenth Century England*, Oxford University Press, Oxford (1985).

[6] See Chapter 7.

The purpose of this chapter, then, is twofold. First, it seeks to examine the concept of protest and to argue that the current framework used by historians to define 'protest' is too restrictive when applied to the early nineteenth-century agricultural labourer. Arguably, the number of types of crime that could be viewed as protest should be widened to encompass the more mundane rural criminal acts, as the following chapters on sheep-stealing and wood and crop theft will show. This chapter will also discuss the ideological motivation behind such crimes, arguing that while rural protest in the period was essentially pre-political and reactive in nature, protest acts often did have clearly defined ends – usually the defence of working practices, customs and relief, which had a political dimension.

The pitfalls in taking such a stance are clear. If care is not taken in the interpretation of the available sources, then certain types of criminal and criminal activity can become romanticized. The danger exists whereby all thieves could be reclassified as 'social' criminals, all sheep-stealers and poachers become proto-revolutionaries and all those who destroyed private property did so with the blessing of the whole working-class community. This would give credence to Sharpe's tongue-in-cheek comment that 'nobody has been as fond of bandits as the left-wing historian'.[7] Despite his reservations and the limitations of the sources it is important to try to see crime from the bottom up. Such an approach is not intended to elevate every sheep-stealer to the status of Robin Hood but it is necessary if we wish to illuminate the depth of conflict between two hostile camps, namely the rural labourers and the agricultural employing classes. Such an approach may also illuminate the anger felt by an increasingly proletarianized workforce when faced with often sweeping economic and social change. Essentially, this is a study of reaction and defence by individuals and communities who sought to protect what was seen as 'right' and 'just' when faced with events and innovations that were seen as 'wrong' and 'unjust'. Indeed, even Sharpe concedes that if crimes were committed with these ideas in mind then such actions were 'politically subversive' and, by definition, crimes of protest.[8]

George Rudé defined protest crime as a collective act, 'though it may not always be carried out in the company of others . . . (it is those) who generally protest within the context of a popular movement'.[9] It was easily recognizable in, for example, the actions of the mob, turnpike rioters, machine breakers and trade union militants, to name but a few. They were protest criminals and, according to this definition, members of collective interest groups who were seeking a defined and pre-set goal. Rudé's perception of what constituted a protest crime may, at first glance, seem contradictory, arguing that

[7] Sharpe, 'History of Crime'. 258.
[8] Ibid.
[9] Rudé, Criminal and Victim. 85–6.

it was a collective act which could be carried out by an individual. We can only deduce, however, that he meant it to be a criminal act, that, while carried out by an individual, was carried out in the name of a collective interest. Rudé's idea of a protest crime was clear-cut. He argued that it could not be a protest crime if it was an individual act; it had to represent some body of collective interest.

This definition seems too narrow. First, the concept is based upon the assumption that protest can only be collective, in both thought and action and the individual acting autonomously is excluded. Nevertheless, it takes but one man, or woman, to break a fence, light a rick or maim a farmyard beast. For such a criminal to have to belong to a specific movement before his or her actions can be classified as a protest means that much of what could be described as 'protest' has often slipped through the net merely to satisfy academic order. If a typical definition of a movement is 'a collective attempt to further a common interest, or secure a common goal', then this effectively discounts many protest movements.[10] 'Swing', or the events of 1830 to 1831, could, by using this definition, be discounted as a genuine expression of protest. The targets of 'Captain Swing' were, after all, diverse. The victims of the discontented ranged from the clergy, to landowners, to the threshing machine to poor law officials. The protesters were equally diverse and they were not all employed as farm labourers. For example, although 'Swing' only touched Herefordshire, the one person to be convicted in the county for his part in the disturbances was Henry Williams, a 20-year-old Welsh tailor, who also doubled as a 'ranting' preacher.[11] Arguably Williams, who would not have benefited from an increase in agricultural wages, or from the abandonment of the threshing machine, was not part of a general rural labourer's movement seeking improved conditions. Indeed, it is probable that Williams composed his threatening letter alone, although his actions were probably supported by the local labouring population. Similarly, in 1834, a woman named Milbourgh Brown was committed to Hereford Gaol for setting fire to her local overseer's wheat rick.[12] It was claimed that Brown had fired the rick because Mr Lane, the overseer, 'refused to comply to her unreasonable demands'. There are good reasons for classifying this as a crime of protest. Brown, a 'vile incendiary' according to the *Hereford Journal*, was protesting against an agent of a relief system which, she believed, had treated her badly.[13] She did not belong to any anti-poor law movement and she acted alone. Nevertheless, her actions, like those of Williams, were probably applauded, covertly if not overtly, by much of the rural working-class population. These were not isolated cases and, as the following chapters will

[10] Anthony Giddens, *Sociology*, Polity Press, Cambridge (1991). 624.
[11] *HJ: 8 December 1830*. See also Hobsbawm and Rudé, *Captain Swing*. 219.
[12] *HJ: 26 February 1834*.
[13] Brown was acquitted; see *Lent Assize, HJ: 26 March 1834*.

show, there were numerous individual protest acts which reflected prevailing working-class sentiment.

Protest action, either as part of a general movement or of a more localized dispute, is essentially made up of individuals. Collectivity of action is helpful when attempting to judge the mood of a community or a class. Arguably, protesters acting as individuals, or in small groups made up of two or three people, are as valid a subject of study as are the participants of the large-scale riot. Large-scale overt protests have been well reported by contemporaries and well researched since.[14] The small-scale rural criminal act, however, has been often overlooked as a vehicle of protest; yet, as research indicates, such acts may well have been prompted by some immediate cause for concern. Connections often exist between a recent enclosure and a spate of hedge-breaking in a particular parish, or, similarly, a rise in poaching at a time when labourers were being laid off. Peacock argues that the evidence is plentiful; it merely needs to be sifted to establish links between specific unpopular events and acts of criminal protest. Indeed, he goes further and suggests that crime was indeed the routine form of protest and that it was a continual feature of rural society during the early nineteenth century. He argues that:

> Only when conditions became really overpowering . . . did the labourers unite on a grand scale, then they appear in the pages of the history books. But they appeared all the time on the pages of the local press. . . . He (the agricultural labourer) protested all the time, and most of the time very effectively indeed.[15]

Peacock claims that protest about conditions, unemployment, wages and welfare was a perpetual feature of the early nineteenth century. The events of 1830 and 1831 and the East Anglia disturbances of 1816 and 1822 should be seen as merely the boiling points of a continually simmering kettle of agricultural discontent.

The second criticism that could be aimed at Rudé's definition involves the idea of collectivity. If collectivity is the prerequisite of protest, as Rudé claimed, then it could be argued that many individual acts of protest were indeed collective. Collectivity could be expressed via the medium of positive sanction or the support, often unspoken, of the criminal's community or class. This is not necessarily the collectivity of pursuing a common goal but reflects the collectivity of having a common enemy. Criminals who poached the local estates, or who vandalized turnpikes or fences did not, as far as we know, belong to any movement; yet their crimes were often sanctioned either at the time they were committed or in retrospect. Their crimes often articulated

---

[14] See e.g. Andrew Charlesworth, *An Atlas of Rural Protest in Britain: 1548–1900*, Croom Helm, London (1983), and John Stevenson, *Popular Disturbances in England: 1700–1832* (2nd edn), Longman, London (1992) for details of nineteenth-century overt protests.
[15] Peacock, 'Village Radicalism'. 27.

community or class grievances and as such received popular support. Such criminal actions, especially if an offender had escaped detection, may have been seen as small victories in a war against change.

It is difficult to measure the extent to which a particular crime would be sanctioned. One of the few ways we can attempt this is to assess the reaction of a community to a particular crime, especially when the authorities attempted to enlist help to discover the perpetrators. Villages were close-knit communities and were often reluctant to give up those who turned to crime. Rural people were often aware of the identity of local poachers and their presence was tolerated. Significantly, despite the absence of an effective rural police force for much of the period, the perpetrators of unsanctioned crimes, such as sexual offenders or murderers, were quickly discovered and delivered up to the authorities. Under such circumstances villagers were often eager to join in the 'hue and cry'. The authors of community sanctioned crimes, on the other hand, seemed to enjoy a certain degree of protection. When attempting to apprehend poachers the local law enforcement agencies often met a wall of silence. Often communities refused to inform upon criminals and, in the denial of all aid to the authorities, this constituted what Hopkins called 'the silence of protest'.[16] That a community could close ranks in this way is proof enough of collectivity, as well as displaying solidarity in the face of a class that sought social control using the rule of law.[17] Hobsbawm endorses this view, arguing that the criminal often enjoyed some prestige and protection if the victim was wealthy. In such circumstances, he explains, the criminal was naturally protected by the peasants and by the weight of local conventions which stood for 'our' law – custom, blood-feud or whatever it might be – against 'theirs', and 'our' justice against that of the rich.[18]

Herefordshire's newspapers in the nineteenth century often printed advertisements offering rewards by the landowning gentry and large tenant farmers, attempting to track down arsonists, animal maimers, stock thieves and vandals.[19] It seems clear, from the evidence of 'assize intelligence', that such methods had limited success. In 1840, following a spate of sheep thefts from near Ross, the editor of the *Hereford Journal* lamented that 'despite liberal rewards being offered in each case, offenders hitherto have escaped

---

[16] Harry Hopkins, *The Long Affray: The Poaching Wars in Britain*, Secker and Warburg, London (1983). 60.

[17] For a discussion on the criminal law being used as an agent of social control see Douglas Hay, 'Property, Authority and the Criminal Law', in Hay *et al.* (eds) *Albion's Fatal Tree*.

[18] Eric Hobsbawm, *Primitive Rebels*, Manchester University Press, Manchester (1963). 126.

[19] The advertising 'for information' which could lead to the apprehension of a criminal was not particular to Herefordshire, nor to the nineteenth century. See John Styles, 'Print and Policing: Crime Advertising in Eighteenth Century Provincial England', in D. Hay and F. Snyder (eds), *Policing and Prosecution in Britain: 1750–1850*, Clarendon Press, Oxford (1989).

detection'.[20] The rewards on offer were often substantial enough to make a very wealthy man of a labourer who was prepared to cooperate with the authorities. Such a reward was on offer in 1811 following an intensification of poaching on Lady Rodney's Berrington estate. After an anonymous letter was delivered threatening an incendiary attack on her home and an assassination attempt on the life of her gamekeeper, Lady Rodney took the step of placing the following notice in the *Hereford Journal*:

NOTICE IS HEREBY GIVEN, that a REWARD of ONE HUNDRED GUINEAS will be paid by Lady Rodney, upon the conviction of the person who wrote the said incendiary paper, and placed the same in the mouth of the said cannon, or caused it so to be placed.

And whereas, about nine o'clock on Saturday Evening, the Sixteenth of February 1811, some person discharged a gun, loaded with Duck Shot, at William Taswell, Gamekeeper to the said Lady Rodney, and slightly Wounded him, a further reward of ONE HUNDRED GUINEAS will also be paid by the said Lady Rodney to any Person or Persons (then in company) upon the Conviction of the person who actually Fired such Gun.[21]

At that time a Herefordshire farm labourer earned an average wage of 7s 6d per week.[22] Such a reward was the equivalent of approximately eleven years' hard work in the fields, yet despite the exceptional size of the reward no person, or persons, were ever brought to trial to face the above charges. We can only assume that the criminals in question enjoyed a degree of community protection from the local poaching community and the rural community in general. We have to be aware of the nature of village life in early nineteenth-century Herefordshire. The villages and hamlets that surrounded the Berrington estate were small worlds. The three nearest villages or hamlets to the Berrington estate were Eye, Moreton and Ashton which, even as late as 1867, boasted a combined population of only 302.[23] Despite improvements in transport most rural people still kept to the parish of their birth.[24] In such an environment neighbours would have been known intimately, enhancing a reluctance to inform.

---

[20] *HJ: 11 November 1840*.

[21] *HJ: 4 March 1811*. For the full contents of the anonymous letter see the chapter concerning poaching.

[22] John Duncumb, 'General View of the Agriculture of the County of Hereford' (1813), *The Board of Agriculture*. 136.

[23] *Littlebury's Directory and Gazetteer of Herefordshire (1867)*, Collingridge, London. 142.

[24] Herefordshire, as was much of the south and south west, characteristically late in developing what we would call a modern infrastructure. The Hereford to Gloucester canal was not completed until 1845, well after most sizeable cities, and towns, had a canal system. Similarly, the county of Herefordshire, along with Yeovil and Weymouth, 'remained unserved' by the railways as late as 1852, again well after the 'railway mania' of

Alternatively, to inform upon a criminal may have had violent consequences. An example of the hostility which rural communities sometimes expressed towards informers was illustrated at Shelwick in 1852. A 'correspondent' to the *Hereford Times* reported that 'a very discreditable sight met the traveller' near Burcott Farm:

> In an elevated part of a garden, belonging to a retail cider seller . . . stood a gibbet, upon which were suspended two figures, clothed in cast-off garments of some labourers, with an inscription painted on a board at the foot of the gibbet 'Shelwick Informers'. On Monday night last, the effigies were ceremonially shot, and then taken down and burnt, amid a crowd of persons.[25]

Admittedly Rudé did recognize the existence of what he called 'marginal protest' crimes.[26] It is into this category that he placed the animal maimer, the arsonist and the poacher. Their actions, he argued, belonged to 'that shadowy realm between crime and protest where it is not easy to tell them apart'.[27] For Rudé such acts of protest are relegated to 'marginal' because of the lack of any obvious signs of collectivity of purpose by the perpetrators. Nevertheless, such criminal action was often the only means available to them to express their displeasure. We also have to remember that during the period under study most forms of protest were essentially illegal. In these circumstances crimes which Rudé categorized as 'marginal' may have provided the only way in which powerless individuals could express their displeasure with their employers, landowners and the authorities in general.

Roger Wells has argued that from the 1790s overt protest was no longer an option for the agricultural labourer.[28] The old poor law, argues Wells, while subsidizing inadequate wages during periods of high prices and excusing farmers from paying a living wage, was also used as a form of social control. The old poor law system, by its very nature, allowed discrimination. To qualify for relief the claimant often had to be seen as of 'good character'. By cutting or withholding relief the drinker and idler could be forced to reform. Similarly troublemakers, both real and imaginary, those men who were, according to Hobsbawm, 'unwilling to bear the traditional burdens of

the 1830s. Trevor May, *An Economic and Social History of Britain: 1760–1970*, Longman, London (1987). 154. Also the roads of the county were imfamously poor. A visiting magistrate, in 1811, compared the roads of Herefordshire to those of Lincolnshire, 'the worse in England'. *HJ: 20 March 1811*.

[25] *Hereford Times* (hereafter abbreviated to *HT*): 29 May 1852.

[26] Rudé, *Criminal and Victim*. 86.

[27] Ibid.

[28] Roger Wells, 'The Development of the English Rural Proletariat and Social Protest: 1700–1850', in M. Reed and R. Wells (eds) *Class, Conflict and Protest in the English Countryside: 1770–1880*, Frank Cass, London (1990).

a class society', could be made to conform.[29] Wells argues further, claiming that from the 1790s on there was what he calls 'an extension of public authority', the increasing regulation of village life, notably in relation to those dens of iniquity the beer-house, the keeping of dogs and post-harvest gleaning.[30] There is Herefordshire evidence to support Wells' argument. By 1800 some magistrates in the county began to catalogue 'poor people who keep dogs' in an attempt to keep track of potential poachers.[31] In addition, in 1817, a particularly bad year for the agricultural labourer in the county, six 'paupers' were hauled before the City magistrate for refusing to work five days for their 3s dole. That the magistrate ruled in favour of the Breinton overseer and forced them to labour for less than half a week's wages is further evidence of tightening poor law administration.[32]

Because of this extension of public authority, overt protest against prices, relief payments, under- and unemployment, wages, enclosures and changing work practices became, according to Wells, 'a rare ephemeral experience'.[33] The only means to express discontent was through covert criminal action. Overt action, although it took place from time-to-time, was likely to bring potential victimization to those recognized in a crowd. To be seen in a protesting mob may have put not only opportunities for employment in jeopardy but also poor relief. The vestries were dominated by squires, parsons and the employing farmers; in other words the very people often deemed by the poor as responsible for their plight. Considering the powerless position of the agricultural labourer any action was not so much 'marginal' but should be seen as the only vehicle available to the rural labourer to express his discontent. Rudé did concede that the problem of interpreting criminal acts as acts of protest is beset with difficulties. He accepted that 'there is no easy blanket definition to fall back on . . . it all depends on the precise nature of the act and where and how and against who it was committed'.[34]

This suggests a certain uneasiness regarding the categorization of crime and a sense that each case should be judged in its particular context. Rudé's framework has its uses, especially when discussing riot and other forms of overt action. However, a more flexible concept, social criminality, provides a helpful tool for the analysis of crime as protest. The concept of social crime was first discussed in 1972 when Eric Hobsbawm asked if 'there were types of criminal activity which could be classified as "social" in the sense that they expressed a conscious, almost a political, challenge to the prevailing social

[29] Hobsbawm, *Primitive Rebels*. 13.
[30] Wells, 'The Development'. 38.
[31] HRO: BB/88/1. *Magistrates Examination Book of the Rev Henry Gorges Dobyns Yate (1801–03)*.
[32] *HJ*: 3 March 1817.
[33] Cited in J. G. Rule, *The Labouring Classes in Early Industrial England*, Longman, London (1986). 354.
[34] Rudé, *Criminal and Victim*. 86.

and political order and its values'.[35] Such a conceptual framework is not as restrictive as the model favoured by Rudé. Hobsbawm, however, has so far failed to follow his own line of enquiry. The concept, therefore, has never been, as Innes and Styles have argued, 'specified very tightly'.[36] Indeed, it is the very flexibility of Hobsbawm's concept which has led to some confusion. As Rule has pointed out:

> Several historians have used the term, but it is by no means certain that they all mean the same thing. Some view it as synonymous with protest crime; others as involving a wide grouping of collective as opposed to individual crime.[37]

Rule has attempted to bring order to this complex subject. He simply argues that a social crime is a 'criminal action legitimized by popular opinion'.[38] He argues further that social crimes fall into two categories. Criminal activities that are grouped under the umbrella of the first category consist of the 'classic' social crimes such as poaching, wrecking or smuggling. These activities, although illegal, were 'openly or tacitly' supported by the immediate local community.[39] These were the kinds of crime that Hobsbawm argued led to a 'conflict of laws'.[40] Poaching was such an activity. To take game without the necessary qualifications (qualifications that were essentially only possessed by the gentry) was illegal. Despite this, and despite a veritable mountain of draconian legislation, many continued to do so. There existed, then, a conflict of laws. The official system, which forbade poaching, was backed by statute, constructed in Parliament by the gentry and enforced by the courts. This was in conflict with folklore, which condoned poaching, deriving its authority from the argument that no private property could legitimately exist in wild animals and from a few lines in the Old Testament which claimed that wild animals were for the use of all men and not merely those fortunate enough to be born into landed wealth. As a correspondent for the *Hereford Journal* claimed in 1834, when arguing against the harshness of the Game Laws, 'our peasantry are apt to look upon all wild animals as their own . . . (and see) poaching as a very trivial offence'.[41] At its simplest, the unqualified continued to pursue game, aware that their actions were illegal, but they believed they were morally justified in doing so. Equally, while most criminals would be shunned by their respective communities if

---

[35] E. J. Hobsbawm, 'Distinctions Between Socio-Political and Other Forms of Crime', *Bulletin of the Society for the Study of Labour History*, No. 25 (1972). 5.
[36] Innes and Styles, 'Crime Wave'. 395.
[37] J. G. Rule, 'Social Crime in the Rural South in the Eighteenth and Early Nineteenth Centuries', *Southern History*, Vol. 1 (1979). 137.
[38] Rule, 'Social Crime'. 138.
[39] Ibid. 139.
[40] Hobsbawm, 'Socio-political Crime'. 5.
[41] *HJ: 5 February 1834.*

they had committed a crime that was socially unacceptable, the poacher and other social criminals would enjoy a degree of protection and support.

Rule's second category of social crime is that of 'criminal actions committed as acts of explicit protest which represent collective grievances'.[42] This type of criminal act needs little introduction and this is essentially a return to Rudé's ideal protest actions. For example, when in 1820 part of the common at Cradley was enclosed, the 'fences were torn down by people acting in the character of commoners'.[43] This action was clearly a protest in pursuit of a collective grievance, in this case the enclosure of the common. Similarly, in 1849, the inhabitants of Upton Bishop rioted after Hannah Goode's claim that she was assaulted by two men was thrown out of court by the magistrate on the recommendation of a local constable.[44] Again this was a clear-cut case of protest with the crowd overtly showing its collective displeasure at an unpopular judgment.

While Rule's work goes a long way in clarifying the concept of social crime there are distinctions between 'social' crime, a crime that is acceptable to plebeian culture, and 'protest' crime, an explicit protest against an unpopular event or innovation. Certain crimes, however, have characteristics that pertain to both categories. Poaching, the classic social crime, often carried an element of social protest. To poach in itself was a protest against the tyranny of the English Game Laws. The affrays between the landowner, his game-keepers and the poachers were often pitched battles that left men beaten, maimed or even dead. Arguably these were the expressions of class warfare. The Game Qualification Act of 1671, an act which remained on the statute books until 1831, did not state that it was illegal to take game but merely that it was illegal to take game without the necessary qualifications, which were based upon landed wealth. Herefordshire's unqualified, who made up the bulk of the rural population, however, not only continued to take game but believed they had the right to do so.

Equally poachers were not averse to a little animal maiming or arson. Rider Haggard's poacher reputedly shot and killed a bull, justifying his actions by arguing that the beast's owner had put the animal into a field to deter the local population from using a footpath, while, as we have seen, Berrington Hall was threatened with incendiarism by outraged poachers.[45] Poachers often took game because of their impoverished circumstances, but because they were reduced to skulking around the hedgerows at night for a meal does

[42] Rule, 'Social Crime'. 139.

[43] HJ: 9 August 1820.

[44] HJ: 4 July 1849. See also HRO: Q/SR/137. Hereford Quarter Sessions (hereafter abbreviated to HQS): Epiphany, 31 December 1849. For a further discussion of the Upton riot see Chapter 5.

[45] Rider Lilias Haggard, The King of the Norfolk Poachers, The Norfolk Library, Boydell Press, Woodbridge (1974).

not mean that their actions did not carry the message of discontent. There is little doubt that much of the rural labour force held the gentry and employing farmers responsible when their wages were reduced or stopped and believed that they had the moral right to take game from the preserves, wood from the hedgerows and crops from the fields.

The progressively repressive legislation which favoured those who wished to keep both the pleasures and profits of the countryside to themselves encouraged class conflict. Moreover, repressive legislation was not merely confined to the protection of game. During the eighteenth and the first half of the nineteenth centuries laws were continually being passed in an attempt to protect everything from peas to pheasants, and from wood to walnuts. Almost every means which a labouring agricultural family could avail itself of in order to supplement an inadequate income had become illegal by the mid-nineteenth century. It became increasingly difficult to retain some degree of independence or to escape the clutches of the workhouse. Yet what was seen as illegal by the dominant class was not necessarily seen as wrong by a large section of the rural population.

Innes and Styles have remarked that the concept of social crime, at its weakest, merely acknowledges that a great many activities that were illegal were not recognized as such. At its strongest they argue that the concept:

> implies that at least some activities were, either explicitly or implicitly, proto-political forms of resistance by the poor; a form of opposition, perhaps the only form of opposition, to their exploitation and subordination by the rich.[46]

Using such an approach makes it possible to understand criminality in terms of the conflict between the rural labouring poor and agrarian capitalism. Agrarian capitalism throughout the eighteenth and nineteenth centuries became progressively more rationalizing and intrusive. Conflict was assured, since the landowners and farmers pursued greater profits while the labouring poor sought to defend traditional working practices and employment. A great deal of property crime, as Peter Linebaugh has argued, was a direct challenge to capitalist innovation.[47] For capitalism to triumph in the countryside the destruction of customary work and payment practices was an absolute necessity. This was usually achieved by making such practices illegal.[48] An example of the changing legality of work customs may be illustrated

---

[46] Innes and Styles, 'Crime Wave'. 396.

[47] Peter Linebaugh, 'Eighteenth Century Crime, Popular Movements and Social Control', *Bulletin of the Society for the Study of Labour History*, No. 25 (1972). 12.

[48] See Linebaugh, 'Eighteenth Century Crime', Peter King, 'Gleaners, Farmers and the Failure of Legal Sanctions in England: 1750–1850', *Past and Present*, No. 122–5 (1989), Bob Bushaway, 'From Custom to Crime: Wood Gathering in Eighteenth and Early Nineteenth Century England: A Focus for Conflict in Hampshire, Wiltshire and the South', in J. G. Rule (ed.), *Outside the Law: Studies in Crime and Order*, University of

by the unfortunate conviction for felony of James Fidoe at the Hereford Assizes in 1826. Fidoe was charged with 'feloniously taking . . . cord wood and faggots . . . the property of John Gregg, his master'.[49] Fidoe had worked for several years on a contractor basis, cutting down trees on behalf of Mr Gregg and had claimed the wood chips, twigs and so on, as was the custom, for his own use. Gregg, no doubt wishing to maximize his profits, forbade Fidoe to take the wood and Fidoe in turn claimed his assumed 'customary' right to do so. The net result was a court appearance for both parties with Gregg being the victor and the unfortunate Fidoe being transported.[50] This case was an isolated one but it is an example of how landowners and farmers were able to ride roughshod over the customary perks associated with many rural trades, using the criminal law to do so.

Equally important for the triumph of agrarian capitalism was the creation of an untied mobile workforce and the removal of any means by which a man could support himself and his family by 'living on his wits', or 'without visible means of support'.[51] Poachers, or what Richard Jefferies later called 'mouchers', were those who could have survived without the need to submit to work discipline.[52] They may be seen as men who were 'unwilling to bear the traditional burdens of the common man in a class society'.[53] The majority of poachers, wood-thieves, sheep-stealers and crop-raiders, however, if they had the opportunity, worked. Poaching, along with wood-gathering and leasing, supplemented income and gave rural families a certain degree of independence, as well as an insurance against hunger. Customary rights to these practices often conflicted with an increasingly agrarian capitalist mentality, and as a result these practices were gradually outlawed.

The concept of social crime has received some criticism. The most common argument put forward is that historians have concentrated their efforts upon those crimes that lend themselves most easily to the concept. Poachers, wreckers, smugglers and all types of rioters have been, at one time or another, classed as social criminals. They were what Edward Thompson called the 'good' criminals.[54] Moreover, such criminal behaviour had what Innes and Styles call 'attractive proto-political associations'. However, they go on to comment that:

Exeter Press, Exeter (1982), E. P. Thompson, 'Custom, Law and Common Right', in *Customs in Common*, Penguin, Harmondsworth (1991).

[49] *Lent Assize 1826. HJ: 22 March 1826.*

[50] The severity of the sentence was probably due to Fidoe having a previous conviction for felony.

[51] Linebaugh, 'Eighteenth Century Crime'. 12.

[52] Richard Jefferies, 'The Gamekeeper at Home' (1880), in E. G. Walsh (ed.) *The Poacher's Companion: An Anthology*, Boydell Press, Woodbridge (1983). 17.

[53] Hobsbawm, *Primitive Rebels*. 13.

[54] Thompson in Hay *et al.* (eds) *Albion's Fatal Tree*. 14.

While historians working with this approach have spawned several armies of 'social criminals', there exists no detailed studies of petty larcenists, burglars, horse stealers etc who make up the bulk of business of the courts of Quarter sessions and Assizes.[55]

The crimes of burglary and horse-stealing were not wholly rural crimes and are outside the scope of this book. The 'bulk of business of the courts' at Hereford, after drunkenness and assault, were the crimes of poaching, sheep-stealing, crop-raiding and wood-theft. All of these crimes, as the following chapters will make clear, had an element of protest about them. It will also become clear that these crimes were often a community sanctioned means to an end, an accepted way to feed a family in times of economic hardship. Such crimes quite often also carried messages of discontent. It is important for social historians to view, as much as possible, the agricultural labourer's social reality. During the first half of the nineteenth century the labourer was undoubtedly pauperized, alienated and exploited. He had few, if any, means to express his sense of injustice and anger towards those whom he saw as responsible for his plight. In such a situation the labourer often resorted to rural terrorism and theft.

It has also been argued that many social crimes, far from rejecting capitalism, actively embraced it. Sharpe, for example, has argued that:

Eighteenth century poachers and smugglers operating large organised networks aiming at supplying the growing consumerism of the period seem to reflect the spirit of an increasingly capitalist and market-orientated world rather than offering any challenge to it.[56]

Sharpe would have a point if the poachers of Herefordshire – and one suspects other counties – were 'organized' to the extent he suggests. While the county's farmers and landowners sometimes appear to have believed this was so, it seems clear that it was the exception rather than the rule. The theft of a single sheep, a hare or a few chickens was the norm. Such crimes did not require or suggest a high degree of organization or professionalism. Undoubtedly, a few poachers were professional enough to have contact with higglers, or other middlemen, who in turn sold on game to meet consumer demand, but to suggest that the courts were clogged up with professional bandits is to glamorize the criminal's impoverished situation. The vast majority of men and women who stood before a magistrate or assize judge to answer charges under the game laws poached for their own consumption.

The field labourer of the early nineteenth century had little understanding of such concepts as capitalism. In all probability, they merely understood that

---

[55] Innes and Styles, 'Crime Wave'. 397.
[56] Sharpe, 'History of Crime'. 250.

changes were taking place, changes that affected their everyday lives. Agricultural workers had for many years laboured under such an economic system and were content to continue to do so, as long as their needs were met. It is doubtful if the criminal protester consciously sought to reject capitalism through his actions. The point of rebellion, or display of discontent, arose when certain limits were breached such as the removal of relief, employment or customary rights. Capitalism was neither rejected, nor renounced, by the mass of the rural working class; indeed, 'Ludd' and 'Swing' did not reject capitalism and the later trade unions merely sought to limit its excesses.[57] This is exactly, either consciously or unconsciously, what Herefordshire's rural terrorists and social criminals sought to do. To suggest that a crime should seek to change an economic system before it can be classified as an act of protest is a nonsense. Capitalism, as far as it was understood by the rural labourer, was largely acceptable. It ceased to be so when aspects of agrarian capitalism became unacceptable, by changing a way of life or causing hardship, that those affected acted. Camus may be instructive here:

> In every act of rebellion, the man concerned experiences . . . a feeling of revulsion at the infringement of his rights. . . . Up to this point he has, at least, kept quiet and, in despair, has accepted a condition to which he submits even though he considers it unjust.[58]

Crime, poverty and protest are the by-products of capitalism. Indeed, according to Zehr, crime is a sign of 'modernity'.[59] Despite Victorian protestations that the rising rates of crime reflected a rejection of society's values, urban criminals were accepting an ideology based upon aggressive self-interest. In the countryside, however, as Zehr points out, 'expectations were low and property was protected by village traditions and by informal controls upon behaviour'.[60] Rural traditions and customs were being, albeit slowly, dismantled in the Herefordshire countryside and the erosion of these practices goes some way towards explaining the increase in criminal activity in the county between 1800 and 1860.

Mankoff, writing about modern-day America, argued that 'crime represents a primitive pre-political form of protest against powerlessness, alienation and class society'.[61] Comparing modern-day America with western

---

[57] The only movement in the English countryside to reject capitalism were the short-lived Diggers, who advocated a society free of class distinctions, money or property, with land being held, and exploited communally.
[58] Albert Camus, The Rebel, Penguin, Harmondsworth (1962). 19.
[59] Harold Zehr, Crime and the Development of Modern Society: Patterns of Criminality in Nineteenth Century Germany and France, Croom Helm, London (1976). 106.
[60] Zehr, Patterns of Criminality. 106.
[61] M. Mankoff, 'Introduction to Perspectives on the Problem of Crime', in M. Haralambos (ed.) Sociology: Themes and Perspectives, Unwin Hyman, London (1988). 450.

Europe, he argues that crime is not so prevalent in the latter continent because it is 'offset'.[62] The provision of welfare, which acts as a safety-net for society's poorest members, the protection of trade unions and the available representation by socialist political parties acts as a safety-valve against working-class discontent. Their very existence, he argues, diffuses 'open hostility'. If we place Mankoff's thesis in a historical context we can understand why crime increased in the first half of the nineteenth century, and why so much of it was protest. The mesh of the welfare net was getting wider and more of the poor either slipped through or were excluded altogether. The non-option of overt demonstration, or regulating protest, coupled with no serious political representation or unionization, effectively meant that criminal activity was the only means available for the agricultural labourer to express his frustration.

It would be naive to imagine that all rural crime was protest crime. The professional poacher and sheep-stealer did exist; yet the majority of rural thieves stole to meet their immediate needs rather than being filled with a desire to become rich. Their actions were legitimized by circumstances and were often legitimized further by choice of victim. All poachers took game from the gentry and the vast majority of sheep-stealers took their booty from employing farmers and landowners. From the point of view of the labourer, he took from the cause of his hardship or simply those who could sustain the loss. Hobsbawm sees this victim selection as a feature of social banditry and points out that:

> He (the bandit) will almost certainly try to conform to the Robin Hood stereotype in some respects; that is; he will try to be 'a man who took from the rich'. . . . He is virtually obliged to, for there is more to take from the rich than the poor, and if he takes from the poor . . . he forfeits his most powerful asset, public aid and sympathy.[63]

Though it would be equally naive to assume that all thieves stole from agricultural employers this Robin Hood mentality is important.[64] The criminal who stole from his own class can be discounted as a protester; also, as Hobsbawm suggests, if he did so he could expect little community sympathy or sanction. Indeed, this kind of criminal activity even horrified the usual victims of rural crime, the propertied classes. A graphic example of this

---

[62] Mankoff, 'Problem of Crime'. 450.

[63] Hobsbawm, *Primitive Rebels*. 20.

[64] See e.g. Peter King, 'Decision-Makers and Decision-Making in the English Criminal Law: 1750–1800', *Historical Journal*, No. 27 (1984), and Rudé, *Criminal and Victim*, who clearly show that inter- as well as intra-class crime was commonplace. However, as Chapter 2 will argue, the majority of cases reaching the Quarter Sessions. c.1849 to 1860 were brought by farmers.

was the comment made by the editor of the *Hereford Journal* after the theft of some potatoes from a poor man's garden in 1827. He wrote that 'to rob from the rich is bad, but to steal from the poor is degrading'.[65] Undoubtedly poor men's gardens and other chattels were plundered, but to either class a crime such as this was socially unacceptable. To steal from the rich was without doubt frowned upon, especially by those who had property to lose, but the crime was understandable to a certain extent, especially in times of hardship. The editor's comment suggests that he understood the morality of stealing from the rich and the immorality of stealing from the poor. Such comments inadvertently lend a certain nobility to the poacher, hedge-breaker and the sheep-stealer, unlike those who chose to grub up the potato patches of the poor.

Theft was a positive reaction when faced with material deprivation and, at its simplest level, a primitive redistribution of wealth. Although the usual victims of crime may be seen as worthwhile targets by virtue of the fact that they had something to steal, we cannot doubt the criminal was often consciously selective. Indeed, if we accept that the motivation behind the majority of property theft was want, we merely have to scan the court records and newspaper reports to see that the victims were not impoverished.[66] Equally as important, the tendency to steal from the rich illustrated the power of community sanction. It was the power of community sanction that encouraged the thief to steal the sheep and game from the wealthy, rather than the pig from a neighbour's yard.

Although in the broadest sense many rural criminal protesters were politically subversive they were never, at any time, a revolutionary force waiting in the wings for an opportunity to tear down agrarian capitalism and build a rural utopia based upon 'three acres and a cow'. Marx's analysis of the rural population was undoubtedly right. The rural working class of Herefordshire were never a revolutionary class, nor could they be. Kimmel elaborates on Marx's behalf and argues that they were either an incoherent mass, or potentially counter-revolutionary to be enlisted by the 'old regime'; they were also, at once, isolated and separate and collective and communal, thus making solidarity difficult.[67] Indeed, this is another clue as to why protest in the Herefordshire countryside took the criminal form it did. The agricultural labourer tended to look backwards to days that were, in his imagination at least, better than they really were. They wished for a return to a golden age of pastoral harmony when stomachs were full, cottages were

---

[65] *HJ: 22 July 1827.*

[66] For a full discussion of the extent of rural crime in Herefordshire, and of the social status of the victims, see Chapter 3 concerning law and order in rural Herefordshire. c.1800 to 1860.

[67] M. S. Kimmel, *Revolution: A Sociological Interpretation*, Polity Press, Cambridge (1990). 121.

warm and family employment was assured. Indeed, most protest concerned itself with what was, rather than what was to be.

Swing was, superficially at least, the result of the introduction of mechanical innovation, but, if the threshing machine was the spark, then the wind that fed the flames of 1830 to 1831 was unemployment and low wages. While the disturbances did, in some areas, bring a temporary respite for some of the protesters, Swing was a backward-looking phenomenon. The movement, if it could be called thus, was more regulatory in nature than revolutionary in intent. Although the events of 1830 to 1831 were, as Rule has suggested, 'touched lightly in places and at the edges by the brush strokes of political radicalism, their aspirations were fundamentally limited'.[68] 'Swing', and arguably similar outbreaks of discontent, sought to retain a way of life rather than seeking to instigate social change. Attacks, on recently completed or part completed enclosures, especially on common land, sought the same ends. Fences were torn down in often futile attempts to halt the erosion of customary rights. These rights not only concerned land use but also, indirectly, offered many the means of supplementing inadequate wages, as well as giving the user a degree of independence. Such usage was often crucial to the physical and psychological well-being of those who lived a hand-to-mouth existence. While such rights were often assumed, rather than having been any actual legal basis, they were nevertheless important and cannot be underestimated.[69] As we have seen, those deprived of such rights, or affected by new work practices, often tried to continue as before, as the contemporary local court records and reports in the press indicate. What was once legal, or at least tolerated, became illegal, and those who continued to exercise their right to glean, take wood, graze geese and so on, became criminals. Yet such criminal action was often community sanctioned by the rural working class. These actions became acts of protest, and as the employing class sought to maximize agrarian profits the rural labourer often fought a rearguard action to defend his, or a community's, assumed rights.

The ideology behind many rural criminal protest acts was an unsophisticated mixture of what Rudé termed the 'inherent' or 'traditional' and the 'derived'.[70] A sense of the 'traditional' was derived from 'direct experience', 'oral tradition' and 'folk memory'.[71] It supplied the rationale for the defence of common rights, gleaning rights and the right to collect wood. This

---

[68] Rule, *The Labouring Classes*. 354.

[69] See e.g. J. M. Neeson, *Commoners: Common Right, Enclosure and Social Change in England, 1700–1820*, Cambridge University Press, Cambridge (1993), Graham Rogers, 'Custom and Common Right: Waste Land Enclosure and Social Change in West Lancashire', *Agricultural History Review*, Vol. 41 (1994), and J. Humphries, 'Enclosures, Common Rights and Women: The Proletarianization of Families in the Late Eighteenth and Early Nineteenth Centuries', *Journal of Economic History*, Vol. 50 (1990).

[70] George Rudé, *Ideology and Popular Protest*, Lawrence and Wishart, London (1980). 28.

[71] Ibid.

inherent ideology was based upon customs that had been in place and practised since 'time immemorial'. Such customs, through usage, had become, regardless of the legal position, fact and therefore 'legal' to those who benefited from them. Both Bushaway and Thompson have argued the importance of plebeian culture, a culture that placed great emphasis upon the notion of customs and customary rights.[72] Despite the late Victorian notion that many rural practices were little more than quaint customs, they often served an important function. Indeed, rural plebeian culture was active throughout the nineteenth century and not merely used to keep alive usage rights but was also used to police their own communities. 'Riding the Stang', the public ridiculing of wife-beaters, was being employed as a means of expressing community feeling in neighbouring Monmouthshire as late as 1845 and in Herefordshire itself until the 1870s.[73] Similarly in 1811 the almost medieval punishment of 'ducking a scold' was used against an unfortunate woman 'not ten miles west of the city' and tried again near Leominster in 1817.[74] The 'sale of wives', while no longer common in the nineteenth century, continued in the county with a case being reported in the local press in 1818.[75]

The customary right to lease and gather wood had been under attack from farmers before 1800 but these rights had been important to the domestic economy of the rural poor.[76] When it was legally no longer possible to pick post-harvest crops or gather wood the families of rural workers were forced to look for other ways to supplement inadequate wages. Custom, and the idea of customary rights, were tenaciously adhered to by the labouring poor who were prepared to defend them, if not through the courts, then through covert action by continuing as before.

Although the rural working-class population of the county clung to these ideas their arguments had little in the way of legal credibility. Consequently

[72] See Bob Bushaway, By Rite: Customs, Ceremony and Community in England, 1700–1880, Junction Books, London (1982), Thompson, Customs in Common, and King, 'Gleaners'.

[73] HJ: 4 June 1845, under the heading 'Lynch-Law at Tintern Abbey', reported on a community's rough justice handed out to a wife-beater. Jones, the wife-beater, was 'placed astride a pole and, amidst the shouts of the boys, swearing of men and derision of some dozens of honest women, was conveyed on the shoulders of four or six men along the roads . . . while some tried to shame him by pointing the finger of scorn – some showed their contempt of his conduct by handing him a little mire, while others tried to cool his cowardly courage by frequent applications of cold water'. H. L. V. Fletcher, Herefordshire, Robert Hale, London (1948) 64, claims 'Riding the Stang' continued in rural Herefordshire until the end of the nineteenth century.

[74] HJ: 13 March 1811, and E. J. Burford and Sandra Shulman, Of Bridles and Burnings: The Punishment of Women, St Martin's Press, New York (1992). 102.

[75] HJ: 23 October 1818. See also Thompson, 'The Sale of Wives' in Customs in Common, Chapter 7.

[76] King, 'Gleaners'.

it was necessary to use political ideas to justify attacks to private property. This was the 'derived' ideology, gleaned from 'a more structured system of ideas'.[77] Such ideas could have been absorbed through the written word, produced by the likes of Spence, Cobbett and the earlier Paine, radicals who were reputedly widely read, if not fully understood. There can be little doubt that such authors were populists, attempting to reach as wide an audience as possible. Indeed, some of their arguments must have been heard even in the remotest parish. There has to be, however, a question mark hanging over the amount of influence their work had upon the rural workforce.

First, for these tracts to be assimilated a certain level of literacy is necessary. The standard of literacy, in rural Herefordshire at least, was not high even in 1860. Edward Thompson was confident in the reading skills of the working class and argued that 'two out of every three working men were able to read after some fashion in the early part of the century'.[78] When we study the literacy figures in Herefordshire this figure is seen to be optimistic. A typical newspaper statement printed in the *Hereford Journal* on 12 July 1826 shows the reader that 'of the twenty-six prisoners under sentence in our gaol, three can read and write, and nine can read only'.[79] A sample, taken from the Calendar of Prisoners held at Hereford Gaol between 1849 and 1851, shows that just over 60 per cent of the inmates were illiterate and only 38 per cent could 'either read or write imperfectly'. Only one prisoner during this period was classified as literate.[80] This seems fairly typical of the prison population at that time and, at less than 50 per cent, it is somewhat short of the two-thirds quoted by Thompson. The differences in figures, one suspects, is of using the averages for the country rather than individual counties. Literacy levels would, through necessity, be higher in the urban industrializing areas than in the countryside where the ability to read and write was of less importance. Admittedly Hereford's prison population may not have been typical of the whole county but the prisoners were overwhelmingly from the poorer section of society. Moreover, the prison population would have comprised those who were most vulnerable to changes in the levels of agricultural employment or food prices and were perhaps more sensitive to radical ideas – or they would have been if they had the skills to take these ideas on board.

Second, while the level of literacy was an important factor it was not the only one. As Thompson himself pointed out, the ability to read and write was not necessarily enough. The ability to handle abstract and consecutive arguments was also important and this was not necessarily

[77] Rudé, *Ideology.* 28.
[78] E. P. Thompson, *The Making of the English Working Class*, Penguin, Harmondsworth (1991 edition). 783.
[79] *HJ: 12 July 1826.*
[80] HRO: Q/Smc/1. *Calendar of Prisoners, 1849–51.*

'inborn'.[81] Opportunities for the study of radical tracts were limited, especially when we consider that the average agricultural labourer (if he was fortunate enough to be employed) often worked from dawn until dusk. Even then he may have found the cost of study prohibitive. Candles, books and newspapers were expensive purchases on a labourer's wage. Indeed, even if he overcame all these difficulties misinterpretation of the texts must have been commonplace. The Pentridge rebels (1817), for example, thought a 'Provisional Government' would literally mean that provisions, notably food and drink, would be made available for all. Similarly, during an election riot at Ross in 1853 many of the placards waved by the crowd showed a certain degree of political naivity. One simply demanded 'A Large Loaf of Bread and Plenty of Everything'.[82] These were the ideas that would have occurred naturally to the Herefordshire labourer. They came directly from everyday experience rather than indirectly from the radical press, and reinforce the idea that food rather than revolution was on their minds.

It would appear that the radicals themselves were not particularly concerned with the plight of the rural labourer. Their efforts were usually concentrated upon the industrial worker. Cobbett, who arguably was more inclined to seek a return to paternalism rather than any real improvement in the rural labourer's life, did play a part in mobilizing ideas in the countryside, but, even in 1830 to 1831, derived political ideas formed only a small part of the ideology that motivated the 'Swing' activists. 'Agitators' were blamed for many of the incidents but if agitators were active their influence was peripheral to the incendiarists' essentially conservative, perceived ends. Indeed, Cobbett himself was tried, but later acquitted, for instigating the movement and, although he was touring and lecturing during the disturbances, fires had been lit before his arrival in the south east.

It is, of course, difficult to judge the interest the county's agricultural labourers expressed in political radicalism, or indeed to judge the interest the radicals expressed in the rural working class. If Monmouth, in 1830, was to be held up as an example of rural working-class radicalism, then the answer would be slight. On 1 May of that year, the first year of 'Swing', Cobbett lectured before thirty people at the King's Head Hotel, charging an admission of 2s.[83] Although he gave the small audience value for money, speaking in typical Cobbett fashion for two hours, the entrance fee, the equivalent of a quarter of a rural labourer's weekly wage, would have excluded those whom he sought to reach. This raises questions as to the audience Cobbett wished to preach to. The small attendance also raises questions of his popularity as a reformer who championed the cause of the rural poor. A month later he

---

[81] Thompson, The Making. 783.
[82] HT: 19 November 1853.
[83] Clifford Tucker, 'William Cobbett's Monmouthshire', Presenting Monmouthshire: Journal of Monmouthshire Local History Council, Vol. 35, No. 5. 42.

lectured at Hereford and seemed almost desperate for respectability, arguing he was a 'son of the Church' and wished to 'preserve the three estates of King, Lords and Commons', while seeing those who branded him a 'Jacobin' or a 'Radical' as 'slanderous'.[84] Admittedly Cobbett did mention the 'state' of the rural working class but while he was one of their few allies, he was against the agricultural labourer employing direct action. At his trial one of the most important pieces of evidence in his defence was an article written in the *Political Register* in 1816, where he condemned machine-breaking.[85] While this is not the place to debate the rural radical platform it was not until 'Swing' that notice was taken of the labourer's plight. Cobbett may have elected himself as the spokesman of the revolt and wrote the 'flames produced good, and great good too', but he was effectively jumping on the band-wagon.[86] Cobbett was not alone in retrospectively approving the labourers' actions but the fires were started without the radicals' consent.[87]

The transformation of the Herefordshire peasantry into a rural proletariat during the period under study was a gradual phenomenon. Whereas industrial workers shared and discussed ideas and experiences of exploitation and alienation this may not have been so for those whose lives were confined within the boundaries of a rural parish. Proletarianization in the countryside occurred in a piecemeal fashion. Experiences were different from parish to parish. If enclosure was one criteria for the making of a rural class totally reliant upon wage labour for its survival then we only have to be aware that enclosure occurred in a very gradual and often haphazard manner throughout most counties to see that experiences would be different. Between 1783 and 1878 there were fifty-eight enclosures, by act and agreement, of commons, waste and open fields in Herefordshire. Farming practices, then, were often very different from village to village.[88] A farm labourer's experiences of work in one village could have been of a more traditional nature than his neigh-bour's, who could have been employed in a more profit-orientated context. The situation existed, therefore, that rural labourers from the latter type of parish, or farm, may have gained little sympathy from the former, who may still have had a say in how the land was used. The relationship between labourers and employers on the smaller, unenclosed farms may have been less strained than with those farmers who had enclosed land. Ideas and experiences differed, and although there may have been 'Thomas Hardys in every town and in many villages throughout England, with a Kist or shelf

---

[84] *HJ: 2 June 1830.*

[85] Ian Dyck, 'William Cobbett and the Rural Radical Platform', *Social History*, Vol. 18 (1993). 197.

[86] Ibid.

[87] For an alternative view see Roger Wells, 'Mr William Cobbett, Captain Swing, and King William IV', *Agricultural History Review*, Vol. 45 (1998).

[88] HRO: Q/R1/1-59. *Herefordshire Enclosures: 1783–1878.*

full of radical books', the radical message may have fallen upon deaf ears. [89] This was probably true if the labourer still retained a claim, no matter how tentative, to the land and his rights to land use still remained intact. Although poverty and conditions played a part in forming ideas, alienation also played a large part, a part that has often been overlooked. Indeed, a great deal of rural protest crime may be seen as an attempt to defer this alienation; as a rearguard action to retain a say in agricultural production.

Although the likes of Francis Place saw the agricultural labourer as an ideological void, a dull 'Hodge', the idea can be discredited. Cobbett himself was aware of an ideology based more on the 'inherent' than the 'derived'. As Dyck explains:

> The politics of rural workers, as Cobbett said many times, was largely derived from the 'great teacher, experience'; these experiences were communicated orally as well as by print; they tended to be cast in a local context before a national one; and they were rendered more informed and more radical by the tendency of farm workers to compare their own life and labour with that of their parents and grandparents.[90]

Despite this tendency to rely upon the 'derived' it must be assumed that the radical word did reach even the remotest areas of the county by the end of the period. It would seem likely, however, that such ideas would have been used to bolster more primitive ideas of what was right and wrong. The traditional, inherent and derived elements of the ideology which motivated criminal protest came to the fore at different times in different circumstances. People used them, either singly or in combination. These folk memories and the erosion of customary law might well have been linked with Cobbett's identification of England before the 'Norman Yoke' when resisting the painful process of economic change. It made for an ideology that was not especially neat or coherent. Criminal protest and criminal action was often motivated and sanctioned by a mishmash of ideas and experiences which formed a rough-and-ready ideology over the course of the first half of the nineteenth century.

---

[89] Thompson, *The Making*. 201.
[90] Dyck, 'Cobbett'. 195.

2

'A painful scene of crime, depravity and misery'

Rural poverty and crime

Many nineteenth-century observers believed that crime was an increasing problem. A contributor to *Blackwood's Edinburgh Magazine* in 1844 argued that crime had risen by 700 per cent since 1805.[1] Engels, writing in the same year, agreed that the available statistical evidence showed a dramatic increase in criminal activity.[2] And writing from a totally different ideological stand-point, Sir Archibald Alison, the Tory Sheriff of Lanarkshire, commented, again in 1844, that 'destitution, sensuality and crime advance with unheard of rapidity'.[3] Despite their ideological differences they not only agreed that crime was on the increase but also that it was an urban phenomenon, a result of the manufacturing system. The idea that crime was predominately urban was commonplace. In 1842, Justice Erskine commented at the Hereford summer Assizes that:

> The circumstances under which the inhabitants of this county are placed, happily exempts you from many of those evils which attend the more crowded population of manufacturing districts, where the contagion of evil example has a most mischievous effect upon the morality of the population in general . . . which leads to the commission of many crimes.[4]

This view was understandable; it reflected the commonsense notion that the cramming together of humanity in towns led to a disintegration of morality with sexual impropriety, disease and crime running rife. While disease and promiscuity undoubtedly caused concern it was the increase in crime that worried contemporaries the most. Urban Victorians of substance were not only fearful for their property but also for their own safety, and their

---

[1] *Blackwood's Magazine*, Vol. 56 (1844), *The Working Class in the Victorian Age*, Vol. 11. Gregg International, Farnborough (1973). 1.
[2] Friedrich Engels, *The Condition of the Working Class in England* (1844). Penguin Classics, Harmondsworth (1987). 154–155.
[3] Cited in David Philips, *Crime and Authority in Victorian England: The Black Country, 1834–1860*, Croom Helm, London (1977). 147.
[4] HRO: BG/11/8/9. *Summer Assize 1842. HJ: 3 August 1842.*

fears resulted in 'moral panics' and theories of an emerging criminal class that lurked in dark alleys ready to prey upon respectable society.

Judging by the above comments one could easily believe that rural areas such as Herefordshire, with not a 'satanic mill' in sight, were virtually crime-free. Yet the link between crime and social and economic deprivation was not confined merely to the manufacturing districts. It was true that during the first half of the nineteenth century the rural labourer was untroubled by polluted air and water. Moreover, his place of work may have been more pleasant but he was as likely as his urban counterpart, perhaps more so, to experience lengthy periods of unemployment. His home, often little better than a hovel, was famously poor. His wages could be, and often were, reduced at a stroke and his existence was often one precarious step away from the workhouse. Although the labourer of urban Manchester, Birmingham and London often worked under appalling conditions, life for the field labourer of Herefordshire was far from idyllic. Indeed, throughout the first half of the nineteenth century the crime rate for Herefordshire increased rapidly. This chapter is concerned with the growth of crime in this rural setting and argues that a great deal of the increasing criminal activity was linked to the declining social and economic condition of the county's agricultural labour force; in short, that much of the property crime committed was either a consequence of, or a response to, poverty.

The respectable Victorian's fear of becoming a victim of crime has been well documented and subsequently the field of nineteenth-century urban crime has been well researched.[5] There have also been general studies of nineteenth-century crime which have encompassed both rural and urban communities.[6] This chapter, however, seeks merely to evaluate the extent of rural crime in Herefordshire. A number of studies of nineteenth-century rural crime have already been completed yet these have either concentrated upon the more proto-politically attractive crimes, such as incendiarism or poaching, or have focused on events such as the 'Swing' disturbances of

[5] The list of publications relating specifically to urban crime is quite extensive. The following, therefore, are but a sample of the most influential: D. Philips, *Crime and Authority in Victorian England*, J. Tobias, *Crime and Industrial Society in the Nineteenth Century*, Batsford, London (1967), J. Davis, 'The London Garroting Panic of 1862: A Moral Panic and the Creation of a Criminal Class in Mid-Victorian London', V. A. C. Gatrell (ed.), *Crime and the Law: The Social History of Crime in Western Europe Since 1500*, Europa Press, London (1980) and David Jones, *Crime, Protest, Community and Police in Nineteenth Century Britain*, Routledge & Kegan Paul, London (1992).

[6] For more general works relating to nineteenth-century crime see Rudé, *Criminal and Victim*, David Jones, *Crime in Nineteenth Century Wales*, University of Wales Press, Cardiff (1992), Clive Emsley, *Crime and Society in England: 1750–1900*, Longman, London (1987) and V. A. C. Gatrell and T. B. Hadden, 'Criminal Statistics and their Interpretation', in E. A. Wrigley (ed.) *Nineteenth Century Society: Essays in the Use of Social Data*, Cambridge University Press, Cambridge (1972).

1830 and 1831.[7] With a few notable exceptions the more mundane rural crimes, the type of crime that filled the dock at every Petty and Quarter Session, have been largely ignored.[8]

Before any detailed analysis of crime between 1800 and 1860 can take place it is necessary to examine the extent of criminal activity in rural Herefordshire. This task is not a simple one. The researcher soon becomes aware that the figures gleaned from court records, magistrates returns and other official documents are likely to understate the extent of crime. Court records, for example, do not give details of unrecorded crime nor do they expose criminal acts that were unknown or unreported. They also fail to tell us how much wood was stolen or game was taken or when the victim was unaware of his loss, or quite simply could not be bothered to pursue or report the crime. In short, for a crime to figure among the court records, one had to be committed, a prisoner charged and a conviction lodged against his or her name. We can only guess at the true figure.

Even when a crime had been committed and the criminal had been identified, the victim did not always seek a prosecution. David Jones argued that 'many people (victims of crime) looked for compensation, compromise, and apologies rather than strict punishment'.[9] In 1814 James Hooke, a servant to John Charles, 'barbarously beat a horse belonging to his master' to the extent that the horse was 'so cruelly treated that it would have died, if immediate assistance had not been applied'.[10] There is little doubt that Charles could have taken his servant to court and even seen him transported for this act of cruelty, but Charles was content to let the matter drop because 'Hooke expressed his sorrow and agreed to pay the expenses'.[11] Similarly, in

---

[7] See Hobsbawm and Rudé's *Captain Swing*, and Peacock's *Bread or Blood* for works pertaining to specific agrarian disturbances. The literature on specific rural crimes is quite large, and to list all the publications would be a chapter in itself. The most influential, however, are David Jones, 'Thomas Campbell Foster', which deals with arson. David Jones, 'The Poacher: A Study in Victorian Crime and Protest', *History Journal*, No. 22, Vol. 4 (1979), and P. B. Munche, *Gentlemen and Poachers: The English Game Laws, 1671–1831*, Cambridge University Press Cambridge (1981), deals with infringements to the Game Laws, and John Archer's 'A Fiendish Outrage?' deals with the unusual and sadistic crime of animal maiming.

[8] The exceptions are King in 'Gleaners', who discusses the theft of post-harvest grain. Bob Bushaway, 'Grovely, Grovely, Grovely and all Grovely: Custom, Crime and Conflict in the English Woodland', *History Today*, Vol. 31 (1981) and 'From Custom to Crime' deals with wood-theft. More generally see Roger Wells, 'Crime and Protest in a County Parish: Burwash, 1790–1850, in Rule and Wells, *Crime, Protest and Politics*.

[9] Jones, *Crime in Nineteenth Century Wales*. 7.

[10] *HJ: 27 July 1814*.

[11] Animal maiming was a transportable offence, if the prosecution could prove 'malice' towards the beast's owner was intended, until 1823. Leon Radzinowicz, *A History of the English Criminal Law and its Administration from 1750, Volume One: The Movement for Reform*, Stevens and Son, London (1948). 66–68.

1838, two unnamed journeymen masons 'were detected in stealing turnips' from a field farmed by a Mr Matty of Holmer and 'upon begging Mr Matty's pardon and promising not to offend again . . . (they) were discharged'.[12] A compromise in this case had clearly been reached between the masons and Matty. These two cases are unusual because they were reported by the local press; however, it is probable that many such compromises were made and apologies accepted. It was often easier and cheaper, in both time and money, to be charitable towards criminals, especially if compensation could be extracted from the miscreant without the trouble of a court appearance. For rich and poor alike, especially during the first quarter of the nineteenth century, the court room was avoided if at all possible. The victims of fence- and hedge-breaking and crop thefts who brought prosecutions often seemed to be motivated by exasperation rather than a desire for retribution. Reporting the case of William Griffiths, charged in 1840 with stealing apples, the *Hereford Journal* reported that:

> the complainant stated that deprivations to a great extent had been committed on his property, and he had been at considerable expense in setting persons to watch; all that he wanted was protection – The boy, having been in gaol since Saturday, was liberated.[13]

The problem of attempting to determine the true extent of crime during parts of this period is complicated further by the variations in the legal process. Poachers, for example, were not always dealt with by a magistrate at the Quarter Sessions, or by a judge at the Assizes. A Justice of the Peace before 1831 could, with one 'creditable witness', convict a poacher; moreover, he was not obliged to record the conviction. [14] Similarly, not all wood and crop thieves made an appearance at the Hereford courts. Evidence of convictions, away from the city courts, derived from summary trials on charges of wood-theft, poaching and crop-theft are available after 1822; moreover, a few rural magistrates' note books still survive, though these cover but a few years from a few hundreds.[15] Not only were disputes and com- pensations settled out of court and cases went unrecorded but quite often court records have, quite simply, been either lost or destroyed. Nevertheless, using the evidence that does exist it is possible to gain some insight into the

---

[12] HJ: 28 November 1838.

[13] HJ: 16 September 1840.

[14] See Chapter 6, concerning poaching and the game laws.

[15] The only Magistrate's Minute Books of Magistrates Meetings that survive for rural Herefordshire are from the Wormlow Hundred, c.1810 to 1811 (HRO: AF/67), and Bromsberrow, c.1801to 1803 (HRO: BB/88/1). Summary offences were, as the title suggests, tried summarily by several magistrates, without a jury, at a local Petty Session. The verdict, and sentence, was decided by them, the magistrates, alone, on the evidence presented to them.

extent of rural crime in the county, although the picture will be far from complete.

Court rolls of indictable offences to be dealt with by Herefordshire Quarter Sessions are incomplete for the period 1800 to 1848.[16] The poor condition of these records and their partial nature before 1848 renders them unreliable as a means to ascertain the extent of the court's business. Despite their shortcomings before this date, however, they have been used throughout this thesis either to provide evidence or to illustrate an argument.

It is possible to arrive at more accurate figures for rural petty crime between 1822 and 1860 when details of convictions were recorded in two ledgers.[17] From 1822 Herefordshire's magistrates began to make regular returns each quarter which recorded the number of convictions from their particular hundred. These ledgers have proved to be valuable documents. Not only do they give the type of crime committed but also the name of the offender, the parish the crime was committed in, the date the crime was committed and occasionally the penalty or fine handed out to the offender. In short, by referring to these ledgers the researcher is able to compile a reasonably accurate picture of the extent of petty rural crime in the Herefordshire countryside between 1822 and 1860.

Between the above dates a total of 9,924 petty crime convictions were returned by the county's magistrates to the Herefordshire Quarter Sessions. Obviously not all of these convictions were for crimes that were particular to the countryside. Crimes such as drunkenness, assault, using threatening language, infringements of the Turnpike Acts and weights and measures offences made up 63.43 per cent of all the convictions.

A substantial amount of the crimes tried at the rural Petty Sessions, however, were for offences that were particular to the countryside (See Figure 2.1). Indeed, convictions for poaching, trespass, wood-theft, crop-theft and wilful or malicious damage amounted to 3,630, 36.57 per cent of the total convictions. Of these rural crimes poaching undoubtedly made up the bulk with 1,381 convictions, or 38.04 per cent, of all rural crime convictions. Wilful and malicious damage was the next most common rural crime, with 947 or 26.08 per cent of rural crime convictions. This was followed by 469 (12.93 per cent) convictions for trespass, 438 (12.06 per cent) for wood-theft and 395 (10.88 per cent) convictions for crop-theft (see Figure 2.2).

---

[16] Indictable offences had to be tried before a magistrate at the Quarter Sessions, or a judge at the Assizes, where a jury decided upon the prisoner's guilt. The Assizes tried the more serious trials on indictment where the prisoner could expect, if found guilty, to forfeit his life, or where the sentence of transportation for life for a first offence could be handed down. Night poaching, sheep-stealing and arson were a few crimes that could be judged thus. The Quarter Sessions tried the less serious of the more serious offences. The Quarter Sessions sat upon petty felonies, such as larceny, fraud and assault, etc.

[17] HRO: Q/CM/4. *Petty Session Returns: Convictions, c1822–51* and HRO: Q/CE/1. *Petty Session Returns, c1852–60.*

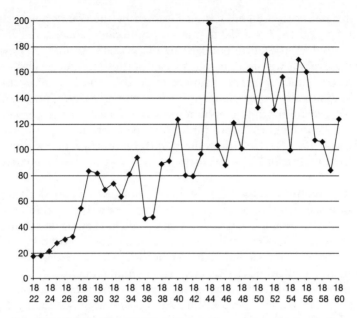

Figure 2.1 Petty Session Returns: Convictions for wood- and crop-theft, trespass, wilful or malicious damage and Game Law infringements, 1822–60[18]

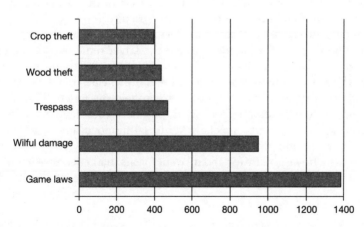

Figure 2.2 Petty Session Returns: Convictions for rural crimes by type of offence, 1822–60[19]

[18] HRO: Q/CM/4. *Petty Session Returns: Convictions, c1822–51* and HRO Q/CE/1: *Petty Session Returns, c1852–60.*
[19] Ibid.

It is the steady rise of convictions returned by the county's magistrates during the period 1822 to 1860 that is most noticeable. Indeed, the 700 per cent rise cited by the correspondent to *Blackwood's* is quite a conservative increase when we see that the conviction rate, for petty rural crimes alone, for the county of Herefordshire between 1822 and 1844 rose by 1,111 per cent. Admittedly we are comparing a peak with a trough. The year 1844, which saw 198 rural crime convictions, was the peak of the period, and 1822, with eighteen convictions for all rural petty crimes, was the trough. Nevertheless, there can be little doubt that the conviction rate was rising as rapidly in the Herefordshire countryside as it was in the manufacturing districts.[20]

Although the reasons for much of this criminal activity are dealt with in other chapters in terms of protest, other factors were also important, notably poverty related to unemployment, low wages, high food prices and changes in working practices. The rationalization of criminal court procedure and the establishment of a professional body to combat crime also have to be taken into account in explaining the apparent rise in rural crime.[21]

The plight of the early nineteenth-century agricultural labourer has been well documented.[22] Herefordshire was a county that was totally dependent on the land and what it produced to provide employment. This was fine while agriculture prospered but had a detrimental effect upon the working population when it fell into depression. Indeed, throughout much of the period under study, the latter was the case. Ernle argued that 'between 1813 and the accession of Queen Victoria falls one of the blackest periods of English farming'; indeed, the fortunes of agriculture rose and fell until the mid-nineteenth century.[23] Although the first thirteen years of the century had been a boom time, for landowners and the larger tenant farmers alike, the termination of hostilities with France in 1815 saw their prosperity decrease. It was the farmers who concentrated on wheat, grown to cash in on the inflated wartime prices, who were first to feel the pinch. The whole of the county's central, eastern and southern areas were devoted to grain production, with the centre especially 'a virtual monoculture of wheat'.[24] The price of wheat and other cereals crashed in 1813 and by 1815 a general depression, which was to last for about twenty years, had encompassed both arable and pasture farmers. Prosperity revived briefly in the mid-1830s. By

---

[20] For petty crime conviction figures for the county of Herefordshire see Appendix I and Appendix II.

[21] See Chapter 3, for a discussion on policing and the courts.

[22] See Hobsbawm and Rudé, *Captain Swing*, J.L. Hammond and B. Hammond, *The Village Labourer*, Longman, London (1966), Reed and Wells (eds), *Crime, Protest and Politics* and Armstrong, *Farmworkers* (chs 2 and 3).

[23] Lord Ernle, *English Farming: Past and Present* (6th edn), Frank Cass, London (1961). 319.

[24] Dodd, 'Herefordshire Agriculture'. 206.

that time the rents paid by tenant farmers had been adjusted in line with their reduced incomes and their overheads were reduced by the Poor Law Amendment Act of 1834 and the Tithe Communication Act of 1836. Tithes had been a heavy burden in Herefordshire costing tenants between 3s 6d to 4s in the pound. The improvements for farmers, however, proved to be short-lived as agricultural depression once more tightened its grip in 1837 – a grip that would not be relaxed until the early 1850s.

For the workforce the net result of these periods of agricultural depression was unemployment or, where a labourer was fortunate to retain his job, reduced or static wages. Many farmers during this black period in English agriculture went to the wall and, as bankruptcy struck, farms went vacant and workers became idle. It is difficult to ascertain exactly how many farms lay unworked in the county although the pages of the local press, in the 1820s especially, were liberally littered with advertisements offering tenancies that were 'immediately available'. Ernle noted at neighbouring Worcestershire that 'seizures, arrests and imprisonment for debt multiplied. Farmhouses were full of sheriff's officers . . . and the numbers of writs and executions' (in Worcester) rose from 640 to 890 in 1815.[25]

Because no unemployment statistics exist for this period it is impossible to know exactly what impact the agricultural depression between 1815 and 1850 had on the demand for agricultural labour. In England and Wales the expenditure for poor relief rose from £2m in 1784 to nearly £8m in 1818, suggesting a dramatic rise in the number of applicants.[26] Although the numbers of people applying for relief clearly grew, poor law expenditure is an inadequate guide when attempting to determine the extent of unemployment in the countryside. First, not all of the claimants during the period, especially between 1800 and 1815, were unemployed, and second, the figures do not take into account the rapid rise of the rural population. To illustrate the first point it would be possible to show that a labourer earning 8s per week, but burdened with a large family, would be entitled to relief, alongside the aged, the crippled and 'respectable' poor. As Duncumb pointed out in 1813:

The labourer, who cannot earn more than the value of as much wheat as the demands of a wife and three or four children require (and unfortunately his utmost exertions will not always produce as much,) must apply to the humiliating resource of parochial aid for the supply of other wants.[27]

Relief was not simply linked to unemployment but was also paid to those who worked but were unable to sustain a family by what was earned, a

[25] Ernle, *English Farming*. 323.
[26] B. R. Mitchell and P. Deane, *Abstract of British Historical Statistics*, Cambridge University Press, Cambridge (1962). 410.
[27] Duncumb, *General View*. 137.

common occurrence especially in times of high food prices. Moreover, the population of the county between 1801 and 1861 grew from 88,436 to 123,712, an increase of 40 per cent.[28] Proof that poor law expenditure was linked more to food prices and population increase is shown during the years of the French wars when despite relatively full rural employment in the county the bill for relief continued to rise. As Duncumb pointed out, 'the net expenses for maintaining the poor throughout the county of Hereford' rose from £10,393 7s 2d in 1776, to £16,727 18s 2d in 1785, to £20,000 in 1813.[29] Unemployment undoubtedly existed, especially during the winter and spring months, and it contributed to the rising costs of providing relief. Yet before the agricultural depression set in relief was granted as a supplement to wages, rather than a wage in itself. Nevertheless, that labourers had to apply for 'parochial aid' at all is a clear illustration of their poverty, even when in work. After 1813 the situation for the rural labourer deteriorated rapidly and work became scarce as farmers cut back on their wage bills by sacking their staff and reducing production. As early as 1815 the pauper population of the county stood at 10.5 per cent and, apart from a few good years in the mid-1830s, the numbers of those claiming relief grew steadily.[30] Even as late as 1849 the pauper population of the county was reputed to be 15.4 per cent.[31]

Not all farms went to the wall but those that did survive often did so at the expense of their labour force. It was not only the tenant farmers who made economies; even the large landowners were forced to reduce their wage bills. On the large Arkwright estate in the north of the county the labour bill was reduced by almost two-thirds, from £1,012 in 1814 to £344 in 1815.[32] Unemployment was not inevitable but where workers were kept on, their wages were often reduced in line with their employer's declining prosperity. The wage rate for the Herefordshire farm worker, while always poor when compared to many other counties, rose and fell during the period. Dodd argues that between 1818 and 1852 the weekly wage for an agricultural labourer in Herefordshire never fell below 8s but never exceeded 10s.[33] It is clear that the Herefordshire farm labourer, if he was lucky enough to have employment, was poorly paid and, according to Lord Ernle, the Herefordshire farm labourer between 1824 and 1860, on average, earned 2s 6d less than a Monmouthshire labourer and 2s less than a Norfolk labourer.[34] As Frederick Law Olmsted noted when he toured England in 1850, the Hereford labourer's

---

[28] *Littlebury's Directory*. 1.

[29] Duncumb, *General View*. 41.

[30] Hobsbawm and Rudé, *Captain Swing*. 76.

[31] *HT: 21 February 1852*.

[32] HRO: E41/75/110. *Hampton Court Estate Accounts*, Dodd, 'Herefordshire Agriculture'. 219.

[33] Dodd, 'Herefordshire Agriculture'. 220.

[34] Ernle, *English Farming*. Appendix IX. 525.

'wages were seven shillings – sometimes eight – a week. It was a common thing that they had nothing to eat but dry bread.'[35]

According to the census of 1851, 75 per cent of Herefordshire's population were employed in agriculture; however, from the early 1840s alternative forms of employment became available.[36] Indeed, by 1845 farmers were briefly in competition with the railway companies for the pool of surplus labour that was so necessary at harvest time. 'So great is the scarcity of labourers in some agricultural districts' reported the *Hereford Journal* in October 1845:

> That the Crier has been sent round to announce an increase in wages; with the drain upon the labour market, consequent upon the railways being laid down, labour will be exceedingly valuable next year, if it not be scarce enough to retard or prevent the gathering in of the fruits of the earth.[37]

Labourers benefited from the competition for their labour and often took the opportunity to raise their earning capacity. In 1846 the *Hereford Journal* reported that hay-mowers were asking 'as much as 7s per acre . . . the ordinary rates being 3s 4d, 3s 8d and 4s'.[38] Similarly, in 1845, some of the county's hop-growers were forced to increase the wages offered to female pickers from 1s to 1s 6d per day in order to get the number of workers necessary for a successful harvest.[39] Two years later, in 1847, the farmers of Eaton Bishop were forced to raise the wage for labourers at harvest time from 8s to 10s, to tempt workers away from the building of the Hereford to Brecon railway.[40] Generally these were short-term rises paid by desperate farmers. Once the crisis was dealt with and the harvest gathered in, wages returned to their previous low rate. The few years of railway-building in the county provided only short-term benefits and, as the lines were completed, labourers were forced to return to the farms as a source of employment.

Having acquired the taste for higher wages many abandoned the Herefordshire countryside altogether and left for the industrial areas of Wales and the North of England. Dodd estimated that by the mid-nineteenth century migration from the county 'was flowing at the rate of 19,000 per annum'.[41] Despite this exodus the steady growth in population suggests that

---

[35] Frederick Law Olmsted, 'Walks and Talks of an American Farmer in England', cited in Pamela Horn, *Life and Labour in Rural England: 1750–1850*. Macmillan, Basingstoke (1987). 166.
[36] British Parliamentary Papers (hereafter BPP): *1851 Census of Great Britain* (1852), Vol. 6, Irish University Press, Dublin.
[37] *HJ: 29 October 1845*.
[38] *HJ: 29 July 1846*.
[39] *HJ: 22 October 1845*.
[40] *HJ: 2 June 1847*.
[41] Dodd, 'Herefordshire Agriculture'. 220.

the numbers leaving the county would do little to ease the employment situation for those who remained and this is especially true when we remember that farmers kept a tight rein on their wage bills by restricting the numbers of labourers they employed.

A further blow to the farm worker's security and earning power came with the demise of the 'living-in' system. Traditionally farm workers were hired annually, usually at the Hereford May and Mop fairs, where contracts of employment were agreed upon and a wage for the year settled to the satisfaction of both parties. Bond labour was important for the agricultural worker for several reasons. Not only did 'living in' provide employment and food and lodgings, but it also relieved the stretched resources of the labourer's family. For married labourers such a system provided a cottage, tied though it was, and the opportunity to bring up a family. For the farmer, however, the living-in system was inflexible. As the contract between the worker and the employing farmer was legally binding the farmer was obliged to keep the labourers on, a potentially expensive overhead if profit margins fell. For the farmer casual labour became more attractive, as he could hire and fire men at will to meet his immediate needs. There is also evidence to suggest that farmers and their families, following the Napoleonic wars, no longer wished to share their table or home with labourers. The inflated wartime wheat prices not only swelled the farmers' purses but also their pride. The boom prices of the wartime years made many farmers better off than they had ever been and their rise in income encouraged them to assimilate the habits of the gentry. As a contemporary local ballad, 'The New Fashioned Farmer', argued:

> A good old-fashioned long great coat
> The farmers us'd to wear, sire
> And an old Dobbin they would ride
> To market and to fair, sir;
> But now fine geldings they must mount
> And all join in the chase, sire,
> Dress'd up like any lord or squire,
> Before their landlord's face, sir.[42]

With this enhanced view of their social standing some farmers 'came to find intimacy with their co-residing farm servants a social embarrassment'.[43] However, although it may have become unfashionable among farmers to have their workers living in, economic considerations speeded up the decline of the practice. While the convenience of hiring day labour has already been

---

[42] Roy Palmer, 'Herefordshire Street Ballads', *Transactions of the Woolhope Naturalists Field Club*, Vol. XLVII (Part 1) (1991). 72.
[43] Armstrong, *Farmworkers*. 59.

mentioned there were other factors involved. When food prices were high, as in 1817, farmers may have been forced to spend more on food for their workers than they had bargained for. Indeed, during some weeks of that year food prices probably outstripped the servant's productivity. Equally, before 1834, farmers, as ratepayers, were aware that a twelve-month period of employment in a parish could give the worker right of settlement, consequently becoming chargeable to the parish.

As with all changes in the countryside, living in did not cease overnight. Dodd points out somewhat vaguely that the practice in Herefordshire continued well into 'Victorian times' and there is recent evidence to suggest that the practice continued elsewhere in England.[44] According to the census of 1851 there were 1,170 male 'in-door farm servants' in the county aged 20 or over, which made up nearly 11 per cent of the agricultural labouring population.[45] By 1871 the percentage of male indoor farm servants aged 20 or over had fallen further to just under 10 per cent.[46] Using these figures, the evidence suggests that while living in was no longer commonplace by the middle of the century it still continued, although it was in slow decline. Farm servants were not prominent among the court records and, where occupation is given, notably in the Calendar of Prisoners c.1849 to 1860, they appear only three times and then for theft from their masters. On 26 June 1854, John Jones and Edward Rogers, two 18-year-old farm servants, were found guilty and sentenced to six months' hard labour for relieving their master of 'six pecks of potatoes' and William Preece, a 23-year-old servant, was found guilty and gaoled for one month for 'stealing a bushel of pease'(sic) on 1 January 1855. These are the only convictions for theft by farm servants to come to light.[47] While their absence from the courts may suggest that farm servants had no need to resort to crime we must also be aware that bad employers existed. Jones, Rogers and Preece may have been inadequately fed and forced to supplement their diet on pilfered food. Several of the labourers charged with 'deserting his master's service' complained of overwork and poor food and the existence of an (unnamed) popular ballad suggests such complaints were not unusual:

> Old Skin 'em-alive was my master last year,
> He allowed me neither ale nor small beer;
> The cheese was bad and full of eyes,

---

[44] Dodd, 'Herefordshire Agriculture'. 220. Stephen Caunce, 'Farm Servants and the Development of Capitalism in English Agriculture', *Agricultural History Review*, Vol. 45 (Part 1) (1997).

[45] BPP: *Population*, Vol. 45 (1851), Part 1. Irish University Press. 485–93.

[46] BPP: *Population*, Vol. 18 (1871–1873). Irish University Press. 30.

[47] HRO: Q/SMc/1. *Calendar of Prisoners: Trinity, 26 June 1854 – Epiphany, 1 January 1855.*

And rusty fat bacon was made into pies.
The bread was bad, the flesh was scarce,
These are the reasons for leaving my place.[48]

The pretentious penny-pinching by the employing farmers, though, played a key role in turning many young unmarried farm workers to crime. No longer could he leave the family home but he was forced to compete with his father and brothers for day work in an ever-shrinking job market. Indeed, even in the struggle to find work his youth and strength did not necessarily give him the advantage as employers often gave preference to family men. To employ men with wives and children was to reduce the poor rate. For example, when the Commissioners of the 1834 Poor Law Report were asked if there was any difference in the wage rates paid to married and single men, Charles Share, the Vestry Clerk and Acting Overseer for Ledbury, replied that there was 'no difference in wages, but a preference (is) given to married men with families, for the obvious reason, to keep them off the parish'.[49]

Cast into the ranks of the day labourers the young farm worker became a vulnerable figure. Not only was he disadvantaged when seeking work but he was, after the 1834 Amendment Act, 'unfailingly subject to the workhouse test'.[50] One way to survive without taking the dreaded test was to turn to crime, and the significant proportion of young men listed in the Calendar of Prisoners shows that many did just that, indeed young adults clearly predominate.[51] Of the 313 prisoners convicted of, or awaiting trial for, rural crimes at Hereford Gaol between 1849 and 1860 over 38 per cent were male labourers aged between 16 and 30. While the age group of the convicted males is not unusual, nor particular to Herefordshire, that they needed to resort to crime at all goes some way towards illustrating their vulnerability.[52] The decline of living in was mirrored by the decline in the relationship between the farmers and the rural workforce. That the farmers, in the name of economy, could so easily discard a practice that had existed for centuries undoubtedly encouraged a lack of deference and ultimately hatred towards the farmers themselves. Hobsbawm and Rudé's study of the 1830 to 1831 rural insurrection clearly shows a link between disaffected young men and rural arson, noting that 'the average age of the prisoners sent (for their part in the insurrection) to New South Wales was a little over twenty-seven'.[53]

---

[48] Palmer, 'Herefordshire Ballads'. 72.
[49] BPP: *Royal Commission on the Poor Laws* (1834), Vol. XXVII, Question 29, Irish University Press. 210.
[50] Armstrong, *Farmworkers*. 82.
[51] HRO: Q/SMc/1. *Calendar of Prisoners: Michaelmas, 15 October 1849 – Epiphany, 31 December 1860*.
[52] King, 'Decision-Makers'. 36.
[53] Hobsbawm and Rudé, *Captain Swing*. 247.

Archer agrees with this and, writing of East Anglia in the period 1815 to 1870, indicates that:

> Incendiaries were, in general, local, very often young and single men. Many of them had worked for, or were working for, the employers on whose property the fires were lit.[54]

Of course day labour was nothing new and as long as employment was assured it would be unlikely to affect the crime rate. Day labourers, however, were not only vulnerable to the farmer's fortunes, or misfortunes, but were also at the mercy of seasonal unemployment in the winter months and in competition with Welsh imported labour during the harvest months. If, for the arable farming workforce, summer was a time of employment, the winter was very often a time of enforced idleness. After the harvest was gathered in, the farmer, ever with an eye on profit or survival, shed his workers, perhaps only keeping on a skeleton force to maintain his property and thresh his corn. The rest of the workforce were cast upon the mercy of parish overseers or compelled to face the workhouse test. Again, it seems that the alternative to this humiliation, quite often, was crime. Criminality was at its height during the months of winter, a phenomenon reflected in the court calendars for the January and April sessions which were invariably heavier than at any other times of the year. For example, between 1822 and 1860, 68.72 per cent of all wood-theft convictions and 58.87 per cent of game convictions were dealt with at the winter and spring magistrates' sittings.[55] Similarly, between 1800 and 1834, just over 71 per cent of all the committals to Hereford Gaol for sheep-stealing, took place in the six-month period November to May.[56] Arguably, the labourer's position during the whole of the period was one of general misery but this was exacerbated in the winter months when the demand for labour fell away. Since most agricultural work was performed in the open air he was often at the mercy of the weather. Moreover, as many were paid by the task, by day or even by half-day, the labourer often took home a poor wage until the weather relented. The winter of 1839 was particularly harsh, and not only prevented men from working but the freezing conditions also pushed up the price of basic foods. As the editor of the Hereford Journal noted:

> the unprecedented continuance of bad weather, which seems to have paralyzed all out of door occupations, (has) destroyed immense quantities of potatoes, now a

---

[54] Archer, 'By A Flash and a Scare'. 196.

[55] HRO: Q/CM/4. Petty Session Returns: Convictions. Epiphany, 1822 – Michaelmas 1851.

[56] Details of Sheep-Stealing committals taken from HJ: 1 January 1800 – 31 December, 1834.

most important article of food to the labouring classes. The poor were so badly prepared to encounter the privations incidental to winter.[57]

Although employment was more plentiful and the weather was kinder in the summer, the Herefordshire agricultural labourer still faced competition for employment. This competition came not only from a growing indigenous population but from Welsh migratory labour. According to Charles Heath in 1808, these 'frontier Welchmen' (sic) migrated because the hay and corn harvest in Herefordshire was earlier 'than in South Wales'.[58] Although the use of Welsh labour at harvest was beginning to die off, by the time of Heath's journey it was still commonplace until the 1830s in some of the border areas. Gangs of Welsh harvesters comprising four or five men and a horse descended upon the fields of the county every summer to cash in on the bounty their own poor hillsides could not produce.[59] Their labour was attractive to local farmers as they were not only reputedly quicker, with each man capable of reaping 'one statute acre in a day', but also cheaper, charging only 2s per acre.[60] However, Duncumb, writing in 1813, noted that the practice was gradually dying out and observed that 'wheat is generally reaped by parties of Welshmen from Cardiganshire and other parts of Wales; but it is now gradually becoming a branch of labour amongst our natives'.[61] Welsh agricultural labourers in need of work were seeking it elsewhere by the first quarter of the nineteenth century, notably in the mining and manufacturing districts of Glamorgan and Monmouthshire. Despite this change Herefordshire labour was still partly in competition with migratory labour, at least until 1831. The evidence given before a Select Committee on Agriculture in 1833 clearly shows this was the case when it was pointed out by a witness that Welsh harvesters were 'flocking' into Worcestershire and that a 'good many' were visiting Herefordshire.[62] Although the effect of migrant labour on the employability of the indigenous workforce can be overstated it was, nevertheless, yet another downward pressure on wages and provided further competition to the county labourer in his struggle to find employment.

Asked by the Select Committee on Agriculture in 1833 if the farm worker was better off than previously, one witness, a farmer named Stallard, from Red Marley, Worcestershire, answered 'those that are employed'.[63] He was, in some respects, right. After 1817, the final year of the inflated grain prices,

---

[57] *HJ: 18 December 1839.*
[58] Charles Heath, *Down the Wye from Ross to Monmouth.* Heath (1808). 36.
[59] Duncumb, *General View.* 64.
[60] Ibid. 65.
[61] Ibid. 64.
[62] Cited in E. J. T. Collins, 'Migrant Labour in British Agriculture in the Nineteenth Century', *Economic History Review,* No. 29 (1976). 46.
[63] Cited in Armstrong, *Farmworkers.* 67.

the price of bread settled down and even began to fall in price. This made the cost of basic provisions cheaper. A 1s loaf bought at Hereford market on 4 June 1817 would have weighed 2lb 6oz, yet by 6 December 1820 the weight of a loaf, for the same price, had increased to 6lb 11oz and by 26 November 1834 a 1s loaf weighed 7lb 13oz.[64] Bread prices stabilized at affordable levels, making an inadequate wage go further for those who were fortunate enough to earn one. There is also evidence to suggest that the diet of the average farm labourer and his family changed over the period. At the beginning of the century a diet based on wheaten bread was normal but by the mid-1830s potatoes played a more prominent part in the Herefordshire labourer's daily nutritional intake.[65] That the county labourer had come to rely more and more on potatoes is clearly shown during the years after 1845 when the potato blight arrived in England. While the blight's effect in the county paled into insignificance when compared to the damage it wreaked upon the Irish population it undoubtedly caused hardship for Herefordshire's rural poor. On 1 January 1845 the *Hereford Journal* announced that the charitable classes intended to begin 'soup distribution' (sold at one penny per quart) to the 'working-classes, every Tuesday, Thursday and Saturday, between eleven a.m. and one p.m.'. This was prompted by the hardships caused by the failure of the potato crop.[66] That the labouring population of the county relied upon the potato is further illustrated by the need to repeat the distribution in 1846, 1847 and 1848. Indeed, by February 1848, owing to 'the poor potato crop and the intense coldness of the weather', soup was being sold every day.[67] And in the same year, the *Hereford Journal* reported that potatoes became more expensive to buy than wheat.[68] There was no shortage of the poor working class to buy the soup either, and consumption rose from 600 quarts on 12 January 1848 to 11,302 quarts per day on 2 February the same year.[69] Although the soup was available only in the city it is quite likely that some unemployed farm labourers made the journey into town to take advantage of this charitable offering.

Food prices aside, there is evidence to suggest that employment in agriculture, paradoxically, increased during the period of depression, although this increase was slight. Armstrong, using Wrigley's work as a source, argues that during the period 1811 to 1821 agricultural employment in England rose by 5 per cent, by 2.7 per cent between 1821 and 1831, by 1.5 per cent between 1831 and 1841, by 1.4 per cent between 1841 and 1851 and by 2 per

---

[64] *Assize of Bread* as reported in the HJ: *4 June 1817, 6 December 1820 and 26 November 1834.*
[65] Dodd, 'Herefordshire Agriculture'. 220.
[66] *HJ: 1 January 1845.*
[67] *HJ: 2 February 1848.*
[68] *HJ: 7 January 1848.*
[69] *HJ: 19 January 1848 and 2 February 1848.*

cent during the period 1851 to 1861.[70] Despite Armstrong's and Wrigley's assurances, the evidence suggests that the agricultural labouring population fell after 1851, in Herefordshire at least. The 1851 census counted 10,944 indoor and outdoor male labourers over the age of 20 in the county yet the census of 1871 indicated a slight drop in their numbers to 8,867.[71] Armstrong does concede, however, that during the period 1861 to 1871 the agricultural labouring population of England and Wales fell by 16 per cent, suggesting that employment opportunities for rural labourers peaked about the 1860s. Other historians put the date a decade earlier.[72]

This slight rise in agricultural employment is a redeeming factor in an otherwise depressed period; moreover, this rise is further put into perspective when we remember that the population grew by 40 per cent between 1800 and 1860. Although Armstrong argues that some of the surplus rural population was absorbed by 'an expansion of village trades and crafts', he notes that 'a degree of mismatch between the demand for and potential supply of wage-paid employment in agriculture was virtually bound to occur'.[73] Indeed, he argues elsewhere that 'the situation of the labourers, in general, was declining relative to that of the other agrarian classes, that is, landlords and farmers'.[74] Evidence from Herefordshire seems to support this view. The Herefordshire farmer not only paid poor wages and had a pool of available and willing workers at his disposal but they also benefited from the movement to enclose remaining wastes and commons; and the enclosure of commons and wastes continued throughout the period.

The debate concerning the impact of enclosure on the agricultural working class has been ongoing for many years and, generally, historians have stood at one of two poles. Some have argued that enclosure was beneficial for all sections of rural society, while others have claimed that enclosure was detrimental to the rural worker and his family; a phenomenon that destroyed a way of life.[75] It is unfortunate that the Herefordshire labourer's thoughts and

---

[70] Armstrong, *Farmworkers*. 63 and 95. Citing E. A. Wrigley, 'Men on the Land in the Countryside: Employment in Agriculture in Early Nineteenth Century England', in R. M. Smith and K. Wrightson (eds) *The World We Have Gained: Histories of Population and Social Structure*, Blackwell, Oxford (1986). 332.

[71] BPP: *Population: 1851 (Part 1)*, Vol. 45. Irish University Press. 485–93, and BPP: *Population: 1871–3*, Vol. 18. Irish University Press.

[72] Armstrong, *Farmworkers*. 95. David Grigg, *English Agriculture: An Historical Perspective*, Blackwell Press, Oxford (1989), states: 'after 1851 . . . the number of farmworkers has declined dramatically.' 137.

[73] Armstrong, *Farmworkers*. 63.

[74] Alan Armstrong, 'The Influence of Demographic Factors on the Position of the Agricultural Labourer in England and Wales: 1750–1914', *The Agricultural History Review*, Vol. 29 (1978). 78.

[75] For the 'optimists' see J. D. Chambers and G. E. Mingay, *The Agricultural Revolution: 1750–1850*, Batsford, London (1966). For the 'pessimists' see the Hammonds, *The Village*

experiences of enclosure have gone unrecorded but it could be argued that the enclosure of the wastes and commons deprived many of a means of supplementing their incomes. The prime agricultural land of the county had been, by the start of the century, already enclosed. Indeed, Wordie argues that this had been the case for some time and he noted that 59 per cent of the county had already been fenced in by 1600.[76] Thus by the time of the parliamentary enclosure 'boom' of the Napoleonic wars all that was left to enclose were the wastes and commons. The enclosure of such land favoured the few, notably the landowners and tenant farmers. For the majority, however, enclosure meant loss of employment, underemployment and loss of rights.[77] This is not to suggest that there was a huge loss of land for the rural working class during the years of parliamentary enclosure, nor in the previous century. The mass of the rural population had been essentially landless for many years.[78] While enclosure and the depression forced many small tenant farmers, freeholders and cottagers off the land the greatest social and economic damage was committed to those who were already poor. This was especially true when it came to fencing off the commons and wastes.

Common and waste ground supported some and supplemented the wages of more of the rural poor. This would have been especially true during the post-war crisis in agriculture when employment was difficult to find and the cost of food was often difficult to meet. With the removal of the common, however, common rights were also removed and commoners, cottagers and squatters were reduced to mere wage labour. Furthermore, as we have seen, wage labour alone was often inadequate when it came to supporting a labourer's family. More importantly labourers, as a class, became wholly dependent on the employing classes for their very existence. It was during the early nineteenth century that the rural labourer lost the very last vestiges of independence as land which, although inferior, could support a few animals and provide firewood was taken from him. The removal of such rights from the rural population was, to quote Thompson, 'social violence'.[79] These acts of social violence were carried out by the prosperous country elite and,

Labourer and W. E. Tate, *The English Village and the Enclosure Movements*, Victor Gollance, London (1967).

[76] J. R. Wordie, 'The Chronology of English Enclosure: 1500–1914', *Economic History Review*, Vol. 36, No. 4 (1983).

[77] For the farmer, if he could survive the depression, enclosure brought a greater tillage and thus greater profits, and for the landowner enclosure brought higher rents from his tenants.

[78] Roger Wells, 'The Development of the Rural Proletariat and Social Protest'. 29. Wells argues: 'England had relatively few peasants in 1700 and virtually none by 1800.' 29. However, for an alternative view see Mick Reed, 'The Peasantry of Nineteenth Century England: A Neglected Class?', *History Workshop Journal*, No. 18 (1984).

[79] Thompson, *The Making*. 238.

as the contemporary poet John Clare pointed out in 1820, the landowner's greed added to the labourer's poverty:

> Accursed wealth o'er bounding human laws
> Of every evil thou remanist the cause
> Victims of want those wretches such as me
> Too truely lay their wretchedness to thee
> Thou art the bar that keeps from being fed
> And thine our loss of labour and of bread.[80]

Duncumb, writing in 1813, suggested that wastes and commons were but 'a very inconsiderable proportion of Herefordshire', confined largely to the area bordering the Black Mountains.[81] This is misleading. Between 1779 and 1878 there were fifty-eight Herefordshire enclosures, forty-five of which related to commons, wastes or open fields.[82] Enclosure activity in that case was far from complete at the time Duncumb was writing. The spread of these mainly nineteenth-century enclosures, from Wigmore in the north of the county to Ganarew in the south, suggests that the negative impact on the supplementary incomes of labouring families was more widespread than Duncumb's account would suggest.

It is possible to overstate the importance of such land and the economic effect its removal had upon the rural poor, but enclosure, as Hobsbawm and Rudé have pointed out, made their poverty 'nakedly visible'.[83] Commons and waste ground did provide a certain amount of independence, both symbolic and real, and one of the reasons behind the enclosure movement, apart from increased tillage, was to destroy this independence. Indeed, by claiming that those who lived in unenclosed areas became marginal to mainstream society the advocates of enclosure probably won a great deal of support. This marginality, they argued, bred lack of deference, disorder and idleness, the inevitable by-product of which was crime. A Committee on Waste Land in 1795 argued that the commons and wastes supported the 'idle, crime and disease ridden animals'.[84] Equally, Clarke, writing about the state of agriculture in Herefordshire in 1794, had little good to say about those who lived on, or by, such land. They were all, it seems, either idle or potential criminals:

> The most extensive districts of waste lands, in this county are situate at the foot of the Black Mountains, above the Golden Valley. I do appeal to such gentlemen as

[80] Merryn and Raymond Williams (eds), *John Clare: Selected Poetry and Prose*, Methuen English Texts, London (1986). 28.
[81] Duncumb, *General View*. 46.
[82] HRO: Q/R1/1–59. *Herefordshire Enclosures*.
[83] Hobsbawm and Rudé, *Captain Swing*. 35.
[84] Cited in May, *An Economic and Social History*. 29.

have often served on grand juries in this county, whether they have not had more felons brought before them from that (area) than any other quarter of the county. . . . A cottage . . . gives the occupier a right to turn stock to these common hills. The profit of that stock is expected to supersede the necessity of labour . . . should these hopes, however, not be realised, any method of providing for the demands of the day is preferred to the drudgery of labour.[85]

These were the views of men who wished to change a way of life. Common and waste land, however, were often sorely missed by the rural poor. As a contemporary local ballad 'My Old Hat' lamented:

Now the commons they are taken in, and cottages pulled down,
And Molly has no wool to spin her linsey woolsey gown;
The winter cold, and clothing thin, and blankets very few,
Such cruelty did n'er abound, when this old hat was new.[86]

Although the likes of Clark mistook the lack of ambition for idleness they got their way, and the commons and wastes of the county slowly disappeared. While the local population were often able to protect their commons from encroachers they frequently lacked the financial capital to repel the men with money. Encroachers however were regularly on the receiving end of some 'rough justice'. For instance, the villagers from Cradley in 1820, 'acting in the character of commoners', destroyed the fences of an encroacher named Rochester who, in turn, sued one of the villagers, a man named Smith, for trespass. Smith won his case, a symbolic small victory for the villagers.[87] Similarly, in 1850, thirteen villagers from Wellington appeared before the magistrates charged with riot and assault after demolishing the house of Thomas Llewellyn who had encroached upon the common.[88] Again the villagers secured a small victory, although at the cost of a 2s 6d fine each.

The land 'improvers', the agricultural depression, the tight-fisted farmers and the high food prices impoverished the rural working classes and forced them either to seek assistance or to resort to theft for survival. 'The court this morning', remarked the *Hereford Journal* on 9 October 1844:

presented a painful scene of crime, depravity and misery, the dock being too small to accommodate the numbers of young and old, male and female persons charged with various offences.[89]

[85] John Clarke, 'General View of the Agriculture of the County of Hereford (1794)', *Board of Agriculture*. 27.
[86] Roy Palmer, 'Herefordshire Ballads'. 72.
[87] *HJ: 9 August 1820.*
[88] HRO: Q/SR/138. *HQS: Trinity, 1 July 1850.*
[89] HRO: Q/SR/132. *HQS: Michaelmas 1844. HJ: 16 October 1844.*

Indeed, the list of names, offences and punishments does represent a 'painful scene'. Eliza Element and Mary Higgins, found guilty of 'stealing a quantity of wheat, out of the sheaves', were sentenced to five weeks and fourteen days' hard labour respectively and John Williams, who stole a quantity of wheat valued at 1s 6d, was given three weeks' hard labour. William and Robert Lane were each fined £3, plus £2 costs, for poaching. John Davies was gaoled for six weeks for stealing four ducks, and Benjamin Skerme was gaoled for three months and ordered to be whipped twice for stealing two rabbits.[90] The complete list was much longer but these examples serve as useful illustrations to show the extent of their 'misery'. These were the petty crimes of the poor and miserable. Convictions for the theft of foodstuffs from the countryside were common and prisoners appeared before the county's magistrates, at one time or another, for stealing everything from asparagus to walnuts. That such commodities were targeted by thieves, however, suggests theft for immediate consumption rather than any desire to become wealthy. In 1840 the Hereford Journal reported that 'John Norgrove, a lad, was sentenced to two days hard labour for stealing pease (sic) from the field of Mr Hooper at Putson. (The) Prisoner in his defence said he had no victuals to eat and he plucked a few pease to satisfy the cravings of his hunger.'[91] In 1846 Noel Jones, after being fined 6d, plus 9s 4d expenses for damaging a fence while gathering firewood, 'declared that he had not a bit of bread in the house, nor money left to buy any'.[92] Similarly, Thomas Meek, after being found guilty of stealing turnips, in 1839 claimed that 'I was passing through the field and I took five turnips, and I should not have . . . only my wife and family were starving at home'.[93] Other examples could be cited to illustrate not only the pettiness of the crimes, but also the motives of the criminals.

Engels argued that 'what a man has he does not steal'.[94] Or, as Marcus elaborated later, crime is often 'driven by need and desperation . . . (it is) an incomplete but not altogether mistaken response to a bad situation'.[95] The response to poverty was often, in the absence of employment or a living wage, a criminal response. Although early nineteenth-century contemporaries were loath to admit it and clung tenaciously to the notion that poverty was the result of personal failings, many could, by the 1840s, see a link between want and crime. In 1848 the Hereford Journal reported that:

---

[90] HRO: Q/SR/132. HQS: Michaelmas 1844.
[91] HRO: Q/SR/128. HQS: Trinity 1840. HJ: 5 August 1840.
[92] HRO: Q/SR/134. HQS: Easter 1846. HJ: 18 February 1846.
[93] HRO: Q/SR/127. HQS: Michaelmas 1839. HJ: 20 November 1839.
[94] Engels, The Condition. 155.
[95] Steven Marcus, 'Engels': Manchester and the Working Class, Weidenfeld & Nicolson, London (1974). 223.

On Monday se'nnight a very able lecture on crime and punishment was delivered by Jelinger C Symmons esq, to the members of the *St Peter's Reading Institution.* . . . The increase in crime in 1847 (in Herefordshire) was shown to be 14.83 per cent over the previous year. The lecture embraced a variety of statistical details, including the cost of crime and pauperism . . . which Mr Symmons thought closely connected; rising and falling together. . . . In 1847 £45,363 was expended in the relief of the poor in this county alone, being an increase of £913.[96]

Arguably, by 1848, Symmons was preaching to the converted, as a year earlier Henry Horn Esq., the Recorder at the County Sessions, remarked that there had not been 'any great diminution of crime' as there had been a 'considerable want of employment, during the last quarter'.[97] Indeed, 'an abundance of employment' combined with 'a sound religious and moral education' was, he argued, necessary for the eradication of crime.[98]

The connection between unemployment, low wages and high food prices – the main causes of the rural worker's poverty – and crime is not difficult to illustrate. Indeed, the chapters which concern sheep-stealing and poaching will clearly indicate this link by showing an increase in these activities during periods of economic hardship. Similarly, through research of the contemporary Herefordshire press, we can compare, where possible, the extent of the gaol population during times of hardship and during times of relative prosperity. In 1822, a good summer in an otherwise depressed period, the *Hereford Journal* boasted proudly in June that there were 'no prisoners in Hereford Gaol'.[99] This, happy state of affairs should be compared with the prison population of 1817, when the agricultural depression in the county was at its deepest, unemployment was commonplace and the price of bread was inflated due to a poor harvest. The prison population, prior to the Easter Assize in 1817, numbered 111 inmates.[100] This situation was mirrored across the Welsh border in Monmouthshire, and Kissack notes that in 1808 'there were only four criminals and one debtor in Monmouth Gaol'. Yet in 1818, amidst 'great, unexampled and increasing distress in rural Monmouthshire the numbers had risen to forty criminal and thirty-three debtors'.[101]

The equation, that poverty equals crime, has not been confined merely to rural Herefordshire, or indeed to the nineteenth century.[102] Crime was a

---

[96] *HJ: 27 December 1848.*

[97] *HJ: 14 July 1847.*

[98] *HJ: 14 July 1847.*

[99] *HJ: 9 July 1822.*

[100] *HJ: 26 March 1817.*

[101] Kissack, *Monmouthshire*, 217.

[102] See Gatrell and Hadden, *Criminal Statistics*, for an explanation of the relationship between criminal activity and socio-economic conditions during the nineteenth century, and see D. Hay, 'War, Dearth and Theft in the Eighteenth Century: The Record of the

response, perhaps the only response, which the rural working class could make when faced with poverty, or even starvation. Their hunger and poverty were very real and from time to time it claimed victims. In 1839 an unemployed labourer, Francis Swan, walked into the city and broke a window with the sole intention of being taken into custody and, he hoped, get transported.[103] A year later, in 1840, under the headline 'Death From Destitution', the *Hereford Journal* reported that an unnamed man who wandered into Leominster, 'exhausted, apparently from want', had died despite a passing policeman 'assisting him to the workhouse'.[104]

Although the agricultural working class during this period were essentially victims when compared to the other agrarian classes, their illegal actions displayed a remarkable degree of resistance to the social and economic changes that impoverished them. Indeed, considering their poverty, it is remarkable that so few people turned to crime. Their actions may have been, to quote Hobsbawm and Rudé, 'a defence against hunger' but the thefts of crops, wood, game and sheep were positive acts when faced with a negative situation.[105] Equally, these acts were, or should be seen as, 'a primitive assertion of social justice and rebellion'.[106]

Property crimes against their own class were relatively rare. Indeed, that they targeted the source of their misfortune is further evidence that rural criminals often combined the relief of their poverty with a symbolic act of revenge. Trying to establish the socio-economic class of the victims, however, has been difficult. While the contemporary press often state the criminal's name, occupation or class it has been almost impossible to determine, in many cases, the victim's social status. Equally, the court records prior to 1849 do not always reveal the victim's occupation. The Calendar of Prisoners c.1849 to 1860, however, does give the victim's name, and by comparing these with contemporary directories it has been possible to present a picture of those who were the usual targets of criminal activity. In addition, this material shows who used the courts to seek compensation or justice.

There is no doubt that the farmers and gentlemen of the county bore the brunt of criminal activity between 1849 and 1860. Excluding game law offences, they made up 62 per cent of the victims of all prosecution at Quarter Sessions level, while 'respectable tradesmen' made up a further 11.6 per cent.[107] Although it could be argued that they were the obvious targets in that they had something to steal, it is conceivable that they were selected

English Courts', *Past and Present*, No. 95 (1982) and J. M. Beattie, 'The Pattern of Crime in England: 1660–1800', *Past and Present*, No. 62 (1974).

[103] *HJ: 16 January 1839.*

[104] *HJ: 22 April 1840.*

[105] Hobsbawm and Rudé, *Captain Swing.* 77.

[106] Ibid. 73.

[107] Names of victims taken from the *Calendar of Prisoners* c.1849–1860. HRO: Q/SMc/1. Occupational status of victims taken from *Littlebury's Directory*, 1830, 1845 and 1867.

because they were also seen as the cause of the labourer's poverty. The theft of game, wood and farm crops from those with plenty, by those with nothing, justified their actions. In short, the theft from the rich by the poor in rural society satisfied a primitive sense of social justice.

The numbers of criminal convictions between 1800 and 1860 involving rural crimes increased rapidly. It is also clear that the agricultural labourer in Herefordshire was poorly paid, subjected to often lengthy periods of unemployment and at the mercy of fundamental social and economic change. That criminal activity should increase under such circumstances is, perhaps, not surprising. Such an argument would suggest that the rural working class were not an inert mass, willing to be at the mercy of the employing classes, but assertively seeking survival. By resorting to poverty-driven theft they either consciously or unconsciously rebelled against a rural society that had cast them aside.

3

'To overawe those vagabonds who infest the county'

Policing rural Herefordshire

If the rural working class reacted to their poverty by resorting to crime, the county's elite, failing compromise or compensation, sought to bring offenders to court. This chapter seeks to examine the methods employed to achieve this end. It will identify ways in which Herefordshire was policed between 1800 and 1860 and assess the extent to which the growth of policing contributed to a rise in recorded crime. Attention will also be given to the criminal justice system as it applied to the county. In itself, more intensive policing was not enough to deter the rural criminal; for examples to be made punishment had to follow apprehension. This chapter will therefore also review those innovations made in the criminal justice system which appeared to contribute significantly to the rising conviction rate.

We will be disappointed if we expect to find an orderly transition from the village constable to a professional police force in rural Herefordshire. Different systems of policing existed throughout the period and, by the 1850s, the traditional village constable coexisted with a more modern professional police. The development of a professional police force for the county of Herefordshire was a gradual process, as it was elsewhere in England.[1] Both before and after the 'New Police' made an appearance in Hereford in 1835 the county's law enforcement was the responsibility of JPs and parish

[1] The historiography relating to the evolution of the police in England is now quite extensive. The following are but a sample of the most relevant to this chapter: J. Tobias, *Crime and Police in England: 1700–1900*, Gill & Macmillan, London (1972), Stanley Palmer, *Police and Protest in England and Ireland: 1750–1850*, Cambridge University Press, Cambridge (1988), Hay and Snyder (eds), *Policing and Prosecution in Britain*, T. Critchley, *A History of Police in England and Wales: 900–1966*, Constable, London (1967), V. A. C. Gatrell, 'Crime, Authority and the Policeman-State', in F. L. M. Thompson (ed.) *The Cambridge Social History of Britain: 1750–1950*, Vol. 3, Cambridge University Press, Cambridge (1993), Anthony Brundage, 'Ministers, Magistrates and Reformers: The Genesis of the Rural Constabulary Act of 1839', *Parliamentary History*, Vol. 5 (1986), Jones, *Crime, Protest, Community and Police*, Clive Emsley, 'The Bedfordshire Police, 1840–1856: A Case Study in the Working of the Rural Constabulary Act', *Midland History*, Vol. 7 (1982) and R. E. Foster, 'A Cure for Crime? The Hampshire Rural Constabulary: 1839–1856', *Southern History*, Vol. 12 (1990).

constables. While justices sat in court during the early nineteenth century they also fulfilled a wide range of administrative tasks as well as playing an active part in bringing law-breakers to court. JPs not only granted search warrants and warrants of arrest; they were also responsible for maintaining public order and quelling riots. Furthermore, they questioned suspects, witnesses and those already arrested. According to Tobias, many JPs arrived at the scene of a crime to carry out their own detective work; an active justice 'would take charge of the investigation, directing his subordinates to make inquiries and to bring before him those whom he wished to question'.[2] While this may occasionally have been the case the usual business for justices was questioning suspects and dealing with the administrative tasks associated with prosecutions. It was his subordinate, the parish constable, who carried out the most of the leg-work.

While the office of JP held some prestige, since only 'gentlemen' were permitted to serve as justices, the post of parish constable was less than glamorous. The parish constable was usually recruited from the ranks of tenant farmers, shopkeepers and other respectable, hard-working members of rural society. Although men from this section of society had a vested interest in maintaining law and order some magistrates believed that constables were 'generally chosen from the lowest class of tradesmen without any regard for their fitness for the office'.[3] That the 'better sort' evaded the office, however, is understandable when we consider that the post was one of those unpaid yearly duties left over from Tudor times. It was the parish constable who was expected to confront and attempt to halt public disorders, bearing little but his staff of office for protection. He was responsible for the unpleasant tasks of 'passing on' vagrants and discouraging begging, as well as carrying out warrants of search and arrest. Moreover, he was responsible for those he arrested, either by himself or via a citizen's arrest, and for delivering suspects to the local lock-up or to the county gaol. His duties as constable did not stop there. Among other tasks he was further expected to attend the four Quarter Sessions of his year of office, to present the affairs of his parish, such as the state of the roads, as well as give evidence against those accused of criminal offences.

The post was a full-time duty carried out on a part-time basis for expenses only. The parish constable did receive fees for some of his services but he was often out of pocket by the end of his term. Understandably, some constables refused to act unless payment was assured. Richard Munn, the constable of Tarrington, was fined 6s 6d in 1850 'for refusing to serve a summons which

---

[2] Tobias, *Crime and Police*. 27.

[3] BPP, 'Report of the Commissioners Appointed to Inquire as to the Best Means of Establishing an Effective Constabulary Force in the Counties of England and Wales (1839)', *Crime and Punishment: Police*, Vol. 8 (1839–53). Irish University Press. 102.

had been placed in his hands for service'. His 'excuse was, that he thought he should not get paid'.[4] Generally they did get paid, but as Tobias points out:

> All (his) duties had to be performed in addition to whatever the constable did as a means of gaining a livelihood, and though fees were payable for many of them, it must often have been the case that the labour involved was much greater than the fee would justify. In any event, the interruption to the daily routine must have been very trying.[5]

Indeed, the post was so trying that there is a substantial body of evidence to suggest that constabulary duties were avoided at all costs. There were, however, several ways in which a selected parish constable could dodge his turn. Those selected may have believed it cheaper and less time-consuming to pay a fine, of up to £10, to evade their duties. Alternatively they may have sought to obtain a certificate of exemption, by buying the necessary 'Tyburn Tickets'.[6] Probably the most common method, however, was simply to accept the post but to employ somebody else as deputy constable to perform the duties on his behalf. The magistrates of the Newnham district, of Gloucestershire, informed the Commissioners of the Rural Constabulary Report in 1839 that 'when persons who may be considered qualified in respect of station for the office are chosen, they almost all pay for substitutes, and avoid serving'.[7] Tobias argues that through this system of paying substitutes to carry out constabulary duties the post became the permanent employment of an individual, as successive appointees often delegated their duties to the same man. He further suggests that the semi-permanent nature of the post led to some degree of professionalism, through familiarity with court and judicial proceedings if nothing else.[8] Magistrates themselves, however, generally felt that delegation led to a debasement of the duty because it encouraged the less desirable elements of rural society to accept the post. The magistrates of Newcastle and Ogmore, Glamorganshire, pointed out to the Commissioners of 1839 that:

---

[4] HT: 1 June 1850.

[5] Tobias, *Crime and Police*. 30.

[6] An Act of 1699 (10 & 11 Will. 3, c. 23, s. 2.), which was passed to encourage the 'better apprehending, prosecuting and punishing of Felons', granted a free certificate to those who brought a criminal to justice. The certificate exempted the holder from having to serve in any office of the parish or ward where the crime had been committed. These certificates, later known as Tyburn Tickets, were bought and sold, sometimes at high prices, by people wishing to evade their civic duties. See Radzinowicz, *A History of the English Criminal Law*, Vol. 1. 192–4.

[7] BPP: *Crime and Punishment*, Vol. 8. Evidence given by the magistrates of the Newnham district, Gloucestershire. 109.

[8] Tobias, *Crime and Police*. 32.

The office of constable is one which, in rural districts, the hardworking, industrious labourer most earnestly shuns, and it (the post of constable) is taken by the indolent and lazy only; by such as prefer earning a shilling or two, by serving a warrant or summons, rather than attending to their work.[9]

An additional reason why the post was often accepted reluctantly, if at all, was that it could make the holder of the office unpopular in the locality. The court rolls and contemporary newspapers pertaining to early nineteenth-century Herefordshire occasionally reported cases of assaults on parish constables as they attempted to carry out their duties. For example, on 12 April 1826, a man named Williams was fined £2, plus 10s costs, for assaulting 'a constable at Ross whilst in the execution of his duty, on November 5th last'. Williams, and others who escaped detection, set about the constable because he was 'endeavoring to prevent the blamable and dangerous practice of making a bonfire and letting off fireworks'.[10] In a more sinister vein two constables, in 1810, had their effigies burnt and were later themselves thrown into the river at Chepstow (in neighbouring Monmouthshire) for fightingoff a mob who attempted to rescue some debtors.[11] Similarly, in 1850, the constable of Wellington, a man named Llewellyn, brought a charge of assault against Amelia Gunter, Henry Preece and Thomas Watkins. It would seem from the *Hereford Times* that these three were just a few of 'the good people of the village (who) were indulging in a little private spleen by carrying an effigy of the said constable'.[12] Popular feeling against Llewellyn triumphed and the magistrates advised the constable to withdraw his complaint, probably knowing that prosecution was likely to make the situation worse. These three incidents illustrate that the constable could become the focal point of people's anger when he was attempting to carry out his duties.

Most assaults on parish constables occurred when they attempted to intervene in a drunken dispute or in 'the execution of their duty' as arresting officers. A reluctance to be injured in the interests of public order is understandable and it is likely that many constables stood back, watched a drunken affray, then merely picked up the pieces afterwards. Even serious crimes could, through a constable's inaction, escape detection. In Newland (Monmouthshire) a constable's lethargy, or fear, aided the escape of a murderer, as the evidence to the Commissioners of 1839 indicated:

---

[9] BPP: *Crime and Punishment*, Vol. 8. Evidence given by the magistrates of Glamorganshire. 101.
[10] *HJ: 12 April 1826.*
[11] *HJ: 24 October 1810.*
[12] *HT: 6 March 1850.*

In the case of a man who committed a murder at midnight, the constable of the tything of Colgive refused to get up from his bed, though repeatedly and urgently called upon. In consequence the murderer got clear off.[13]

Generally the post of village or parish constable was one to be avoided, unless the appointee had a great sense of public duty. To accept the post, even for twelve months, was likely to prove both costly and time-consuming; moreover, the appointment could also be dangerous.

Despite the disadvantages of the post there is some evidence to suggest that not all parish constables were inept, lazy and unwilling to accept their responsibilities. Some sought actively to solve crimes and went to great lengths in arresting those responsible. In 1830, the constable for Tupsley displayed not only initiative but also determination by following the footprints of two sheep-stealers and the blood from the carcass for several miles 'on a dark night' before apprehending the criminals responsible.[14] A year earlier another constable, from the village of Dewchurch, tracked three sheep-stealers for a distance of some ten miles to the outskirts of the city to make an arrest.[15] Although Palmer argues that the effectiveness and efficiency of the parish constable is currently being reappraised we can be fairly certain that their crime-fighting abilities were limited. Indeed, the cases cited above were the exceptions rather than the rule.[16] Quite simply, if the farmers of Herefordshire had believed that the parish constable could cope with the levels of rural crime they would not have called for change. Policing, under the old system, was based upon 'bonds of kinship, friendship and neighborliness'.[17] Constables knew the villagers of their particular parish, and vice-versa. The result was that the constable was inclined to issue warnings and make compromises rather than risk the anger of his parish. In short, it was policing that was out of step with the rapid rise in rural crime. The farmers of Herefordshire occasionally wanted examples to be made. They were not always satisfied with compromise but sought compensation and justice through the courts. While the village constable could provide this, the county's agricultural employers and other frequent victims of crime clearly felt he could not deliver enough criminals for punishment to deter the rise in rural crime.

The enforcement of law and order in the Herefordshire countryside was not left to village constables alone. All prosecutions were the result of private initiatives and the defence of property was the responsibility of the individual. Property owners and farmers were aware that the responsibility

---

[13] BPP: *Crime and Punishment*, Vol. 8. Evidence of the magistrate of Newland. 43.
[14] HJ: *20 January 1830*.
[15] HJ: *18 February 1829*.
[16] Palmer, *Police and Protest*. 74.
[17] Ibid.

for taking a case to court lay with them and formed associations, both to protect their property and to prosecute those who stole from fellow association members. The idea behind Associations for the Prosecution of Felons was simple, although it is difficult to judge their effectiveness in dealing with rural crime. For an annual fee, fixed or otherwise, associations undertook to pay the expenses incurred by their members in prosecuting crime.[18] Or, to quote the Articles of the County of Herefordshire Association for the Discovery and Prosecution of Felons and Other Offenders, published in 1825:

> That all and every sum and sums of money, which shall from time-to-time be deposited as aforesaid, shall be employed in defraying the Expenses of this Society, in the Discovery, Apprehension, Prosecution, and bringing to justice, all and every person and persons, who have or hath, since the 28th day of January last, committed, or shall at any time hereafter, commit any Murder, or other Felonious offence, against the person, or persons, of any member, or members, of this Association, or any inmates or Inmate of their, his, or her, . . . (property), or any Felony, Theft, or Misdemeanor, upon or against the Property of any or either of the said Parties hereto.[19]

Hay and Snyder point out that to successfully prosecute a felon in the eighteenth century – and the system changed little until the mid-1820s – the victim had to negotiate, or complete, ten different tasks.[20] From the time the crime was committed until a prosecution had been achieved the victim had to give evidence to a magistrate, thereby being bound, with two others, as sureties, in a recognizance to prosecute; to conduct the proceedings himself, or employ a solicitor for that purpose; to interview the witnesses, and to bring them before a magistrate to be questioned; to decide upon the charge the criminal, or suspect, was to face; to attend the Court Clerks to draw up an indictment (which could take up to three days in the early nineteenth century); to ensure the witnesses turned up at the Grand Jury hearing, to make sure the charge could go ahead as a 'True Bill'; to ensure the witnesses

---

[18] While members of all the county's associations charged a fee there was by no means a fixed rate. For instance, The United Parochial Association for the Prosecution of Felons and the Prevention of Crime (established 1841), which covered fourteen parishes throughout the county, charged an annual subscription of 10s (50p), while the County of Herefordshire Association for the Discovery and Prosecution of Felons and Other Offenders (established 1825) charged £1. Other associations adopted other methods; for example, the Stoke Edith Association for the Prosecution of Felons (established 1841) had a scale of fees based upon the amount of land the member farmed: 10s with less than 300 acres, 15s with less than 500 acres and £1 with more than 500 acres.

[19] HCL: Local Collections, Pamphlets, Vol. 21. Articles of the County of Herefordshire Association for the Discovery and Prosecution of Felons and Other Offenders.

[20] Hay and Snyder, 'Using the Criminal Law, 1750–1850: Policing, Private Prosecution, and the State', in Hay and Snyder (eds) Policing and Prosecution. 25–6.

appeared at the trial and to present the prosecution in open court. If the prosecution was a success it was necessary to apply for any rewards, for expenses, and finally, if the prosecutor obtained a conviction he or she could intervene if the sentence appeared too harsh in relation to the crime committed. Prosecution also meant laying out sums of money with little guarantee of the victim recouping the initial outlay, either from the rewards system or from any costs awarded by the magistrate at sessions. Associations usually employed a solicitor to act on their member's behalf, relieving victims of the trouble and expense of prosecutions. Any rewards and costs granted to the prosecution went into the association's coffers but it seemed that there were significant advantages to be gained from membership for those who regarded themselves as likely victims of sheep-stealers, incendiarists, wood-thieves or indeed any type of rural crime.

Some areas of the county which set up associations did so in retrospect and had often already suffered at the hands of criminals. The association formed at St Weonards in 1841, for example, was a response to a recent spate of sheep-stealing:

> In consequence of the alarming extent to which this crime (sheep-stealing) has been carried (out) in several parishes, in the neighbourhood, an association has been formed in the parish of St Weonards, for the purpose of endeavoring to suppress it by offering a reward of £100 for the detection, and bringing them to justice. . . . We sincerely hope this praiseworthy and spirited association will meet with general support, and be the means of checking crime and rendering property more secure.[21]

It was not unusual for associations to offer rewards to encourage the local population to inform on law-breakers. The Herefordshire Association had a sliding scale of payments made to informers, ranging from £10 for the successful prosecution of animal maimers and incendiarists, to £2 for those who 'stole corn out of a field', to 10s for stealers of hop poles and fencing.[22] Although the posting of rewards, usually in the local press and by handbill, were not new phenomena, the existence of a table of financial inducements illustrates that the association members were highly organized and had some confidence in this method of controlling rural crime.[23] It is, however, difficult to judge the amount of success such a tactic had in the apprehension of criminals, although it would be safe to assume that rewards were sometimes claimed.

They did, however, enjoy some success from time to time. In 1842, a year after its formation, The United Parochial Association boasted that:

[21] *HJ: 6 January 1841.*
[22] *Herefordshire Association*, op. cit.
[23] See Styles, 'Print and Policing', in Hay and Snyder (eds), *Policing and Prosecution.*

Since the association was formed . . . an ingenious and notorious gang of thieves had been dispersed, and also that sheep, wheat, and poultry stealing had greatly decreased in the united parishes.[24]

However, such well-publicized success stories were rare. Indeed, some associations had a short life and were merely formed to halt a particular crime or as an immediate response to a particularly violent offence, such as murder.[25] Once these minor 'moral panics' had died down or were halted, membership may well have slackened off. In neighbouring Monmouthshire, for instance, the annual general meeting, in 1842, of the Monmouthshire Association for the Prosecution of Felons was reported as 'only thinly attended', suggesting, perhaps, that the Association may have served its purpose despite having been formed only the previous year.[26] In 1851, the *Hereford Times*, reported that:

We understand that in consequence of the numerous robberies and deprivations, now almost nightly occurring in different parts of the county, the farmers in some parishes have determined to band themselves together for the protection of (their) property and to devise means to ensure the detection of the daring marauders.[27]

The short life-span of some of the county's associations may have been due to their inefficiency in apprehending criminals. Indeed, judging by the rise in rural crime, it seems likely that these associations were an ineffective deterrent. Moreover, farmers and landowners would be unlikely to subscribe to an association for any length of time unless they were frequent victims of criminal activity. That associations existed at all, however, suggests that potential victims of crime – and in rural Herefordshire this was usually the farmers and landowners – were aware that village constables alone were inadequate when it came to protecting their property. Property owners and tenants, as association members, did not wish to replace the village constables but, in several cases, they supplemented them by providing paid officers and by attempting to ensure that existing constables attended their posts conscientiously. The success of the United Parochial Association in 1842 was put down to the strict enforcement of 'the twenty seventh rule', namely that: 'On the occasion of the annual appointment of parish constables, the members of the association shall exert themselves to get proper persons sworn

[24] HJ: 12 January 1842.
[25] David Philips, 'Good Men to Associate and Bad Men to Conspire: Associations for the Prosecution of Felons in England, 1760–1860', in Hay and Snyder (eds) *Policing and Prosecution*. 126.
[26] HJ: 12 October 1842.
[27] HT: 27 December 1851.

in for office.'[28] This association went further than most and, in the absence of a professional police force, employed their own 'special constables' to patrol the parishes where its members resided. Even here the association's committee, made up of a prominent figure from each of the fourteen parishes, selected officers carefully. Their rule book stated that the chief constable should, 'if possible, be elected from the yeomen of the neighbourhood' and the special constables from 'the leading farmers in the united parishes, or persons above the labouring class'.[29] This private police force was not intended to 'relieve the parish constables from their usual duties' but they were intended 'to be assistants, and they should act in unison together'.[30]

Professional policing in early nineteenth-century Herefordshire was not solely a matter for the associations. When the Municipal Corporations Act of 1835 was passed the opportunity, under clause 76, was taken by the Hereford City magistrates to establish a 'new police'.[31] Although this force was small in number, and was concerned with urban rather than rural crime, the new police eventually extended its operations to the countryside. Initially the force, made up of a superintendent named Adams along with several constables, notably two men named Bowler and Evans, policed the city, rounding up drunks, prostitutes and breaking up affrays. The *Hereford Journal*, a paper which reflected Tory views, argued that the ratepayer's money was being wasted, and wrote, in April 1836, that 'since the establishment of the New Police in this city they have apprehended nearly 130 persons, of whom about three quarters were taken up in a state of intoxication'.[32] A month later the same paper reported that 'at our Guildhall on Monday, sixteen cases were brought before the magistrate by the police; of these no less than ten were charged with drunkenness'.[33] Although the local press may have criticized the new police for carrying out tasks that were previously carried out by unpaid constables they, as well as the judiciary, were also quick to praise them when they solved cases arising from genuine criminal acts. It is equally clear that their police work was not confined to the city limits. The Recorder at the autumn Assize was quick to pay constable Evans 'a merited compliment for the intelligence and activity' he displayed in detecting and apprehending

---

[28] HJ: 12 January 1842.

[29] HCL: The Davies Collection, Vol. 3. *The United Parochial Association for the Prosecution of Felons and the Prevention of Crime in the Parishes of Bishopstone, Bredwardine, Bridge Sollers, Brobury, Byford, Kinnersley, Letton, Mansell Gamage, Moccas, Monnington, Norton Canon, Staunton on Wye and Yazor.*

[30] *The United Parochial Association.*

[31] Clause 76 suggested it was necessary for each borough council to form a Watch Committee, with paid constables and watchmen, which were to be financed by the ratepayers of the said borough.

[32] HJ: 13 April 1836.

[33] HJ: 25 May 1836.

a sheep-stealer at the village of Holmer in 1836.[34] Furthermore, in 1838, Superintendent Adams himself received a mention in dispatches when his 'active exertions' secured yet another sheep-stealer at Yarkhill.[35] Although Holmer is just outside the city limits, Yarkhill is some ten miles distant, showing that the range of operations was quickly extended to the surrounding countryside.

Some urban ratepayers objected to the new police acting outside their boroughs and felt that the police should keep to the city or town they were paid to patrol. Indeed, the requests by farmers from the south of the county, who were frequent victims to crime, for an investigation by the new police led a correspondent to the *Hereford Journal* to suggest that:

> The farmers within a few miles of Ross should subscribe a small sum to remunerate the police when required at a distance, as it cannot be supposed the ratepayers of the town will pay the officers for their services in the country.[36]

Ross was particularly blessed with a conscientious superintendent named George Colley who, like the Hereford police, was only too willing to extend his range of operations. This 'indefatigable police officer', together with his constables, fought crime of all descriptions and it prompted the *Hereford Journal* to recall, in 1839, that 'before the Ross police was established farmers in the neighbourhood were robbed nightly'.[37]

The opportunity to provide a rural constabulary for Herefordshire came in 1839 to 1840, under the County Police Act. This Act permitted, but did not compel, magistrates to establish a police force for the whole county. The Herefordshire magistracy, however, chose not to take advantage of this act, but elected to adhere to the rather haphazard system that was already in place. Despite calls from some areas within the county for a rural police force the majority of the county's magistracy successfully fought off the opportunity for change. The reasons for this refusal to have the county policed by an effective professional force are complex.

First, Herefordshire was a Tory stronghold which resisted any form of centralization, and the elite clearly believed that local affairs should remain in the hands of the county's magistrates. While the magistrates generally agreed that a rural constabulary was desirable they also believed that power over that force should remain with them. As the *Hereford Journal* reported in 1839:

[34] *HJ: 2 November 1836.*
[35] *HJ: 3 January 1838.*
[36] *HJ: 12 June 1839.*
[37] *HJ: 11 September 1839.*

The magistrates assembled at our County Sessions have expressed their concurrence in Lord Russell's (the Home Secretary) views as to the necessity of a more efficient rural constabulary force, but at the same time have given their decided opinion that such (a) force might be appointed by, and under the control of, the local magistrates.[38]

Although the 1839 Commission recommended the establishment of a national police force, based upon the 1829 Metropolitan model and under the authority of the Home Secretary, the idea was eventually abandoned in favour of a more palatable offer to the provincial magistrates. The Act itself stated that the county's magistrates had the power, but were not required, to set up a police force for either the whole county, or part of it, paid for by a rate. Although the Home Secretary's permission to set up a force was to be sought beforehand and the ratio of police to population was not to exceed 1:1000, the appointment of officers was left to the discretion of the local magistrates. However, the magistrate's fears of creeping centralization were not entirely groundless. The Bill gave the Home Secretary the power to choose the Chief Constables, as well as to set the pay rates of officers. Thus, 'from the start the county constabularies were to be under greater Home Office authority than the borough forces'.[39]

Opposition to this was inevitable but following the Chartist insurrection at Newport (Monmouthshire), in November 1839, some Herefordshire magistrates began to feel that a rural police would be an advantage. On the first day of 1840 at the County Sessions, the Chairman, a Mr Barnaby, read out three letters he had received in favour of establishing a rural police in the county. The most influential of these letters was written by the Lord Lieutenant of the county, Earl Somers, who argued 'that in consequence of the disturbed condition of (neighbouring) Monmouthshire, and the unprotected state of Herefordshire, it would be desirable to have an effective constabulary force in the latter county'.[40] In reply to this letter Barnaby stated that in his opinion a police force was not necessary and that the question would not be discussed until a 'requisition, signed by five magistrates, and presented to the Clerk of the Peace' had been handed in. He further argued that 'winter would soon be over' and he hoped 'by that time, a force would not much be required'.[41] Barnaby effectively stalled the pro-police lobby, knowing full well that even with the necessary signatures the question of a rural constabulary for the county would not, nor could not, be discussed until the following summer. If Barnaby and the majority of the county's

---

[38] HRO: Q/SO/9. *County of Hereford Orders of Sessions Relating to County Business (1839–47)*. *HJ*: 10 April 1839.
[39] Critchley, *A History of Police*. 79.
[40] *HJ*: 1 January 1840.
[41] HRO: Q/SO/9. *County of Hereford Orders of Sessions (1839–47)*.

magistrates thought the matter would then be dropped they were to be disappointed. Indeed, at the following Trinity Sessions the pro-police section of the magistracy raised the subject once more. Samuel Peploe argued on their behalf that:

> It was evident from the calendars at the Assizes and Sessions that (criminal) offences had increased in the county, although they might not be of a very serious or malicious character, there was every reason to believe that thefts would become more numerous unless an effective police were established to overawe those vagabonds who infest the county. Parish constables were employed in their daily occupations, and were consequently inadequate to the protection of cottages and other peoples property, but a rural police force, always on the watch, would be most effective for that purpose. (The Chairman read his resolution, which was) to the effect that it appearing the ordinary officers were insufficient for the preservation of the peace and due protection of property, (he) resolved that the provisions of the Acts for the establishment of county and district constables be adopted in this county.[42]

Although the pro-police section of the county's magistracy were defeated once again, they eventually got their way at the following January Sessions in 1841. On 2 January the Clerk of the Peace read out a notice of the intention of the Kington magistrates to apply to the court for permission to appoint, under the Act of 1840, constables to police their area. While the Chairman made it clear that 'at a recent Session a large majority of the justices at Quarter Sessions had resolved *not* to appoint a constabulary force for the whole county', permission was granted because it was in 'accordance with the wishes of a large body of the inhabitants of Kington'.[43]

The Kington police force, however, was to be a short-lived failure. Not only does the evidence suggest that the Kington constabulary were not particularly efficient but also that many of the local ratepayers regarded the force as an expensive luxury. These points are illustrated graphically by the 'memorial' presented to the Herefordshire magistrates at the Michaelmas Quarter Sessions in 1843, composed by the ratepayers of Stapleton, near Kington. It read:

> We the undersigned, inhabitants and ratepayers of Stapleton, respectfully beg leave to express to you our decided opinion (that) as far as this township is concerned of the utter uselessness of the Rural Police; and we earnestly beg to be relieved from the expenses of the maintenance of a force in which we have no confidence, and from which we are convinced we derive no protection.[44]

---

[42] HRO: Q/SO/9. *County of Hereford Orders of Sessions (1839–47)*. See also *HJ*: 19 July 1840.

[43] *HT*: 2 January 1841. Italics in original.

[44] *HJ*: 25 October 1843. The ratepayers of Herefordshire were not alone in complaining

It soon became clear that it was not just the township of Stapleton who were dissatisfied with the new police arrangements. Three months later the Chairman of the Epiphany Sessions received another three petitions 'against the continuance of the Kington police'.[45] Again the magistrates refused to discuss the matter without the necessary five signatures from the magistrates of the area. It eventually took the discontented ratepayers of Kington nine years to get the force disbanded and the Kington police finally ceased to exist in 1850.

While the Kington force was hardly a success it did little to dampen the enthusiasm of some other county districts. Indeed, the Kington experiment opened the way for other districts to set up their own forces. The Bromyard district set up a force that was to be relatively successful in 1844. Indeed, between its formation and March 1850, the force apprehended no less than 390 suspected criminals and secured 316 convictions, a conviction rate of 81 per cent. In 1846, two years after the establishment of the Bromyard force, the Ledbury district employed a man named Snead as superintendent of police.[46] Leominster, utilizing the Municipal Corporations Act of 1835, established a force in 1840 and, as with the Ross and Hereford forces, the officers did not confine their activities to the town. It is likely that the farmers around Leominster subscribed, in a similar manner to the Ross farmers, to pay the police officers' expenses when their duties were called upon. The Leominster force, however, faced the same problems as the Kington police and, following a letter sent by the ratepayers and addressed to the Mayor, which expressed a desire 'to materially lessen the burdens pressing so heavily on the ratepayer', the force was reduced from four men to two in 1850.[47] There is some evidence to suggest, however, that by late 1851 the county's magistrates were beginning to soften their stance on the question of rural policing. Indeed, they appointed a number of paid 'Rural Special Constables' at the following Epiphany Quarter Sessions.[48] Their success was immediate and the *Hereford Times* noted that:

> It is gratifying to find that since the appointment of rural constables, in this district, the crimes which previously, almost every night, disgraced it have ceased, at least for a time. The storm has lulled into a calm.[49]

about a rate levied for the police. Emsley notes that in Bedfordshire there were 'persistent protests' from the ratepayers and argues that two-thirds of the county's parishes 'petitioned in favour of abolition'. Emsley, 'Bedfordshire Police'. 82.

[45] *HJ: 3 January 1844.*

[46] See *HJ: 3 March 1850.* For the first mention of Ledbury's superintendent see *HJ: 30 September 1846.*

[47] *HT: 6 March 1850.*

[48] HRO: Q/SO/10. *County of Hereford Orders of Sessions Relating to County Business: 1847–56.* This implemented the Parish Constables Act of 1842 (5 & 6 Vict., Cap 109).

[49] *HT: 3 February 1852.*

The local press was eager to publicize any success the rural police gained. In its next edition the *Hereford Times* carried the story of the arrest of two wood-thieves by George Preece, 'the newly appointed constable of Burghill'. 'Proof', the editor claimed, 'that rural constables are of some efficiency'.[50] Other parishes soon followed in appointing special constables; however, it is noticeable that it was a village's landowners whoc approached the county's magistrates. For example, in 1854:

> Capt. J Harris, E J Lewis esq and J Davies made an application to the Bench for the appointment of George Paine as Special Constable for Breinton. It was stated that petty crimes prevailed in the neighbourhood to a great extent: fruit, poultry and vegetables being carried off, principally on Sundays while the owners were in church. The occupation of the parish constable was such that he could not attend to police duties, and the property of farmers was not sufficiently protected. Mr Griffiths reminded the applicants that the parish would have to pay the constable themselves. The appointment was made for a period of five months.[51]

Despite the enthusiasm and praise of the local press, these so-called 'special rural' police were too few to make a great deal of difference. Moreover, they were employed for only short periods of time, in areas that were seen by the magistrates as troubled parishes. Arguably, the employment of a handful of rural police officers was a short-term compromise and, despite letters to the *Hereford Times* in 1852 from 'respectable farmers' claiming that the plan of having a rural constabulary worked well and expressing hopes that it would be continued, it was never extended to include the whole county.[52] The same year saw further attempts to raise the question of rural policing and it was proposed, again via letters sent to the local press by farmers, that a committee be set up to 'consider the state of the county's police'. However, R. B. Phillipps esq., on behalf of his fellow magistrates, made it clear that this suggestion 'will not be brought forward', claiming that 'the appointment of a few district constables (has) proved effectual for the restoration of the tranquillity of the several parishes which were, November last, so disturbed.'[53]

It is difficult to gauge the reaction of the county's farmers, the most likely victims of crime, to the refusal of the county's magistracy to have the whole of Herefordshire policed when the opportunity presented itself in 1839. The contemporary local press tells us little, yet there was clearly a renewed interest in the forming of new associations for the prosecution of felons during that time. Between 1839 and 1841 the United Parochial, the

---

[50] *HT: 7 February 1852.*
[51] *HJ: 4 November 1854.*
[52] *HT: 28 February 1852.*
[53] *HT: 6 March 1852.*

Herefordshire, the Stoke Edith and the rural areas of St Weonards and the Walford/Bridstow district all formed associations. To what extent the birth of these associations can be attributed to the magistrates' refusal to have the county policed is open to conjecture, but it seems likely that they were formed as much as a reaction against the county's magistrate's conservatism as against the rising tide of criminal activity. Despite the existence of the police, village constables and associations, some areas of the county remained lawless. This was particularly true in parts of the Welsh border regions. Whitchurch and Doward, near the Monmouthshire border, where 'the reputation of the population of the neighbouring hills was not of the best description', was such a place.[54] The lawlessness of this area in the late 1840s prompted the editor of the Hereford Journal to write:

> Deprivations upon property have, of late, been nocturnally committed at this picturesque and retired village, and the want of police constables renders it exceedingly difficult to detect the offenders. Mr Tomiss has been robbed of wheat, Mr Collins of malt and Mr Jones of potatoes etc.[55]

Despite the calls for police constables the area remained turbulent and its reputation as a crime blackspot did not improve during the period under study. Indeed, the reputation of Whitchurch's population was such that farmers were reluctant to take out tenancies in the area and, as a result, landowners found their land to be worth less than in other parts of the county. The Hereford Journal reported in 1855:

> Whitchurch and the Doward have always been notorious localities for offences against the laws of property; sheep-stealing and minor offences being prevalent. Some will probably say, 'Ah give a dog a bad name, and Co' . . . but with respect to the neighbourhood in question, we were last week credibly informed that the land there is worth less by 5s an acre than it would otherwise be, in consequence of the thieving population which inhabits it.[56]

While, from 1856, under the County and Borough Police Act, a rural constabulary became obligatory, rather than at the discretion of the local magistrates, its existence covers only three years of the period under study. For much of the period, then, there existed a variety of forces that sought to protect private property from the deprivations of criminals. Traditional forms of policing, personified by the village constable, coexisted with more professional policemen. There were also in existence private policemen, employed by the associations and the urban police who were paid, not just by

[54] HJ: 15 November 1848.
[55] HJ: 1 March 1848.
[56] HJ: 13 June 1855.

the town rate, but by farmer's subscription to solve rural crimes and to arrest rural criminals. When all the different forms are taken into account it seems that by 1850 the county of Herefordshire was more extensively policed than ever before. Police superintendents, such as Colley from Ross, the unnamed officer from Bromyard, and Adams from Hereford, enforced the law and brought offenders to court. These officers realized that to protect their livelihoods it was necessary to make arrests, unlike the traditional village constable who, judging by contemporary evidence, did his best to keep a low profile.

Even though the police may have found favour and gained support from the county's farmers there is evidence to suggest that they found little favour with the plebeian section of the rural community. Indeed, the new uniformed police were as likely to be insulted and assaulted as the old-style village constable, especially when attempting to make an arrest. Superintendent Adams and his men were set upon by a 'mob' and forced to retreat to the city when they attempted to break up 'a pugilistic contest' at Redhill in 1836.[57] A policeman was shot and wounded near Knighton in 1840 by a convicted poacher who had just been released from serving two months in gaol because of 'the officer's industry'. The *Hereford Journal* pointed out that he was hated by 'some desperate characters' because of his 'vigilance and activity in the discharge of his duty'.[58] At Ross, in 1843, an officer was attacked and beaten by a suspected sheep-stealer's fellow harvesters. After a fearsome struggle 'the intrepid officer succeeded in carrying off his prisoner from the field in which he was employed'.[59]

Despite a number of assaults upon the police, magistrates did not always take a hard line on the offenders; in fact they were relatively lenient. The recommended maximum fine for assaulting the police was £5, yet offenders were often fined only shillings. The soft sentencing of police assailants by Herefordshire's magistrates drew complaints and prompted the editor of the *Hereford Times* to comment in 1850:

Value of Policemen's Heads – It has been remarked that policemen's heads in Hereford are of less value than in any other place . . . since any man who has spite against a policeman may thresh him to his hearts content for a two and six or five shilling fine . . . it appears a policeman's head is worth little more than a sheep's.[60]

Arguably a sheep's head was worth more. There is little evidence to suggest they were treated with reverence and respect by the labouring population but

---

[57] *HJ: 31 August 1836.*
[58] *HJ: 20 May 1840.*
[59] *HJ: 20 September 1843.*
[60] *HT: 29 June 1850.*

there is a substantial body of evidence to suggest they were treated with distrust and seen as paid bullies. Several of the Herefordshire police were often little better than criminals themselves and complaints about their behaviour were frequently being made to the courts and the press. John Parry, a member of the Hereford police, collapsed on a cell floor while on duty and died in 1847. At the inquest the coroner recorded the cause of death as due to 'excessive drinking'.[61] Similarly, at the Epiphany Sessions of 1853, a woman was charged 'with using profane and indecent language towards P C Vaughan' after he allegedly 'pushed her child'. Under examination by the magistrate Vaughan confessed that he was an unpopular figure and argued 'that persons took a dislike to him because he happened to be an Irishman'. The defendant, however, argued that Vaughan's origins had little to do with his unpopularity and she stated that 'it was well known that he was in the constant habit of getting drunk and, on the night in question, he had beaten his wife to such an extent that she was confined to the house with two black eyes'.[62] Admittedly many labouring people also got drunk and it would be naive to believe some did not beat their wives as well, but the policemen of Herefordshire hardly set a moral example. The majority of the police, however, were of working-class origin themselves and we can only assume it was difficult for them to command respect as they sought to control their social counterparts. A constable was paid 15s per week in 1848, almost twice as much as a farm labourer could earn, but his relatively high wage was often small compensation for his ostracized lifestyle. It may have been because police officers were shunned by the labouring population that some were reluctant to wear their uniforms, perhaps wishing to be less conspicuous. The Chairman of the 1856 Epiphany Quarter Sessions 'observed that several of the county police were dressed in plain clothes' and he 'begged that officers would appear in uniform' in future. He also made it clear that 'he hoped that he should not have to make this request again'.[63]

On occasion, the county's police officers broke the law and stood in the dock themselves. In 1853 William Jarvis, a constable at Walford, was charged with stealing a sovereign from a neighbour. The magistrates were extremely lenient to Jarvis and his only punishment was a week's suspension from his duties and an order to repay the money.[64] It was not only constables who felt they were above the law and benefited from the magistrate's forbearance but also their superior officers. The magistrates at Hereford were lenient to Superintendent Blossett of Ross in 1853 when he was brought up on a charge of 'using profane and abusive language', while drunk, to Mr Grey, a builder of the same town. Had a labourer committed the offence he could have

---

[61] HJ: 3 March 1847.
[62] HRO: Q/SR/141. HQS: Epiphany, 8 January 1853. HT: 15 January 1853.
[63] HRO: Q/SO/10. HQS: Epiphany, 2 January 1856.
[64] HJ: 10 September 1853.

expected to be gaoled for a week or more. Blossett, however, was merely forced to apologize to Grey.[65] Superintendent Adams was accused of a crime far more serious than rudeness or theft and was forced to face an Assize jury in 1856, charged with the rape of 17-year-old Mary Ann Roberts at Hereford. Although Adams was later acquitted it is clear from the evidence presented to the court that he was given the benefit of the doubt. That he was refused bail and relieved of his post three weeks after his committal shows the case against him was a strong one.[66] Arguably, Adams walked free because, in the nineteenth century, rape cases were notoriously difficult to prove. It was his word against that of Roberts and it is clear from the newspaper coverage that Adams was both confident and articulate in court while Roberts was timid and overawed.

Foster has argued that the police were 'at worse begrudgingly accepted by the vast majority of the population'.[67] He argues that this is shown by the decline in the number of assault cases on the Hampshire county police between their establishment in 1840 and 1850. However, just because people began to assault them less does not necessarily mean they liked them more. Foster does not mention the sentences the Hampshire magistrates normally handed out to police assailants; however, bearing in mind their enthusiasm for rural policing, it is quite possible that they were tougher than those handed out in Herefordshire. Quite simply, it may have been the harsher sentences that led to a decline in assaults on the police in Hampshire rather than a growing respect, popularity or tolerance. Moreover, as Gatrell has argued, the police often used the offence of assault 'at their discretion to achieve quick and simple arrests, and its apparent decline might reflect nothing more than a progressive shift, with experience, to the use of more appropriate charges which would withstand the scrutiny of sceptical magistrates'.[68]

Throughout the period the police of Herefordshire were subject to many attacks, as the court records and contemporary press will testify. Some were physical assaults, but they also suffered the symbolic assault of effigy burning and ridicule. The evidence from Herefordshire suggests that they were not, as Foster suggests, 'accepted by the vast majority' of the population.[69] After all the vast majority of the population in Herefordshire, and one suspects in Hampshire too, was overwhelmingly working class. It was upon this majority that the constables concentrated their efforts. It was the working class that

---

[65] HJ: 19 November 1853.
[66] Adams was committed to Hereford Gaol on 21 January 1856, dismissed on 10 February 1856 and acquitted at the Easter Assize 1856. See HRO: BG/11/8/9 and HJ: 23 January 1856, 13 February 1856 and 26 March 1856.
[67] Foster, 'Cure for Crime'. 55.
[68] Gatrell, 'Crime and Authority'. 286.
[69] Foster, 'Cure for Crime'. 55.

the police suspected, searched and bullied, not the middle class or the gentry. These two classes were, after all, both the usual victims of property theft and the police's employers. Moreover, it could be argued that the experience of being policed sharpened class conflict, stimulating the growth of class-consciousness through class experience. The nineteenth-century policeman replaced the Assize judge of the eighteenth century as an agent of social control and, seen in this context, it is little wonder that the 'new' police, both urban and rural, were viewed with such suspicion.

The rise in the crime and conviction rates must be attributed, in part, to the policing of the county. Where the parish constable had once turned a blind eye, mediated in a dispute or sent a drunk home, the new police did not, and since success for the police was measured in convictions the crime rate inevitably rose. Yet the quality of these convictions is debatable. For example, 41 per cent of prisoners, male and female, who were taken into custody between 1841 and 1852 were drunk and disorderly.[70] Admittedly being drunk and disorderly was a criminal offence; nevertheless, the 2,147 arrests for this offence over a ten-year period made the police's figures respectable, or at least respectable enough to show that they were a great improvement on the old style of policing. This is not to suggest that they were no more effective than the parish constables; they clearly were. Not only did they apprehend more criminals but they were also a visible sign that property was being actively protected. The farmers, as well as the shopkeepers and the property-owning middle class in general, were probably psycho-logically comforted by the sight of a constable doing his rounds. This was likely to be the case even if the area the constable had to cover was so great and remote that it meant the constable could pass a certain point only once a day.

The landed gentry had no need for a rural police force. Their grounds, preserves and other property were policed by their own force of bailiffs, gamekeepers and other paid staff. Moreover, they sat as JPs, as members of juries and they chaired associations. They had a long familiarity with the law and how it could be dispensed in their favour.[71] They resisted, as long as they could, the development of a police force in the Herefordshire countryside. Although they feared the rural criminal they feared centralization even more. While criminals may have relieved them of some of their property, central-ization threatened to relieve them of their authority over local affairs. The Act of 1856, which made rural constabularies obligatory, offered Treasury money to efficient forces. This allowed the Home Office a foot in the door, enabling central government to oversee the development of the provincial forces, though, even as late as 1858, the magistrates of Herefordshire still

---

[70] See 'Crime in Hereford', an article published in the *HT: 20 August 1853*. Figures based upon the returns from the county gaol.
[71] See Hay, 'Property, Authority and the Criminal Law'.

refused to comply fully. At the Epiphany Sessions of that year the assembled magistrates were informed that Sir George Grey, the Secretary of State, refused to reimburse the county a quarter of the cost of establishing the rural force because it was not up to strength. The Report of the Government Inspector argued that with only 'forty-five officers and constables I consider the force to be insufficient for the requirements of the county' and he recommended a further twelve men to be employed as constables as soon as possible.[72] Indeed, some of the attending magistrates agreed with the inspector, and one, C. T. Bodenham, pointed out that a fight at Rotherwas, 'where over 200 people were present', could not be broken up as 'no constables could be found to disperse the mob'.[73]

While the old system of policing existed the county's gentry still maintained a grip upon law and order in Herefordshire. It is possible the Home Office believed that until a uniformed system of policing existed for the whole of the county the police would continue to reflect the wishes of their main paymasters – the rural elite, as ratepayers. The resistance to professional rural policing was not confined to Herefordshire, thus suggesting that the fears of property owners were mirrored in other counties. That only twenty-one counties had set up police forces by the end of 1841 suggests this was the case.[74] Unfortunately no local studies have been carried out to examine county magistrates' reluctance to implement the Act of 1839. It is significant that the two most influential local studies concerning the establishment of a rural constabulary, following the passing of the Act, have come from counties that took the opportunity to implement it.[75] What is needed therefore are more studies from counties such as Herefordshire whose magistrates were against the imposition of a new police and fought a rearguard action by refusing to bow to the pressure of the reforming middle classes. It was the 'respectable' middle class, the county's farmers, shopkeepers, lawyers, doctors and teachers, who wrote to the local press calling for a professional police force. It was they who complained the loudest about rural crime. Paradoxically, however, it was members of this class who complained the loudest about the cost of maintaining a force.

The improvements in policing would have been ineffective had the courts been unable to support their work. The police, therefore, were pre-dated by improvements in the administration of the criminal law. Moreover, the rising tide of criminal prosecutions may be attributed as much to the changing nature of the criminal justice system as to the extension of rural policing. The period 1800 to 1860 was an era of criminal law reform and this was especially

---

[72] HRO: Q/SO/11. *County of Hereford Orders of Sessions, 1857–60.* See also HRO: Q/SR/146. *HQS: Epiphany, 1858.*
[73] *HJ: 6 January 1858.*
[74] Emsley, 'Bedfordshire Police'. 73.
[75] See Emsley, 'Bedfordshire Police' and Foster, 'Cure for Crime'.

true after the mid-1820s. Before that date the criminal law still centred around the administration of the eighteenth-century Bloody Code. As a result the period as a whole embraced two distinct types of criminal law administration: the eighteenth-century criminal law, which sought to instil deference, obedience and fear, and the reformed nineteenth-century system that sought compensation, accessibility and availability to all sections of society.[76] In short, whereas at the beginning of the century the sheep-stealer was faced with execution or transportation, he could expect a gaol sentence of nine to twelve months by the 1850s.[77] Moreover, where a poor man may have found the cost of prosecution prohibitive until the 1820s, access to the law after that date became not only possible, but widespread. Indeed, it was argued that accessibility to the law was the key to fighting crime.

It has already been noted that the greatest deterrents to victims of crime, in bringing a prosecution to the courts, was the expense to the victim in both time and money. Because victims feared losing money by bringing prosecutions, the new arrangements for refunding costs were of great importance. Before 1818 the only way in which victims could recoup any losses that were incurred through bringing a prosecution was through the parliamentary reward system.[78] Unfortunately this system, which rewarded prosecutors between £10 and £40, was paid only on the conviction of the felon. Cases had to be watertight, juries had to be sympathetic and judges had to be generous. A victim could easily lose out and it was possible that he would have to bear the costs of the court case, in addition to what he had lost, if any of the above conditions were not in place. It was also argued that the reward system was open to abuse and it was claimed that prosecutors often waited until an offender had committed a felony before it was brought to the court's attention. Police officers, where they existed, bore the brunt of this accusation and it was argued that criminals would be watched until they 'weighed forty pounds' before being brought to justice. Juries were aware of

[76] Hay, 'Property, Authority and the Criminal Law', King, 'Decision-Makers and Decision-Making', Hay and Snyder, 'Using the Criminal Law', J. H. Baker, 'Criminal Courts and Procedure at Common Law: 1550–1800', J. S. Cockburn (ed.), *Crime in England: 1550–1800*, Methuen, London (1977). Leon Radzinowicz, *A History of English Criminal Law and its Administration from 1750*, 5 Vols, Stevens and Sons (1948–86), W. R. Cornish, 'Crime and Law in Nineteenth Century Britain', in W. R. Cornish (ed.), *Crime and Law in Nineteenth Century Britain: Commentaries on British Parliamentary Papers*, Irish University Press, Dublin (1978), R. Swift, 'The English Magistracy and the Administration of Justice During the Early Nineteenth Century: Wolverhampton 1815–1860', *Midland History*, Vol. 17 (1992), Richard Williams, 'Securing Justice in Eighteenth Century England: The Example of Berkshire', *Southern History*, Vol. 18 (1996).

[77] Towards the end of the period, the length of sentence was determined by his past record. Transportation or a lengthy gaol sentence was possible if the convicted had a previous conviction for felony.

[78] 25 Geo. II, c. 36 (1751), 27 Geo. II, c. 3 (1754) and 18 Geo. III, c. 19 (1778).

this and they were often reluctant to pass a guilty verdict on the evidence of what were little better than bounty-hunters. Moreover, the reward system applied only to felonies and not to misdemeanors and, as a result, it failed to embrace many criminal acts. Generally the parliamentary reward system was open to abuse; it was selective and prosecutors were as likely to find themselves out of pocket as rewarded or reimbursed. Essentially the reward system did little to mitigate the risks of prosecution.

An Act of 1818 swept away this system and it was replaced by a much more flexible method of granting rewards.[79] Rather than fixed amounts for specified crimes the act enabled magistrates to provide expenses at their own discretion. Again, this system was far from perfect. Prosecutors were effectively at the mercy of the judge's or magistrate's personalities and prejudices. For example, a married horse-trader was allegedly robbed in his lodgings of his money by a girl of 'right character' at Ross in 1835. The trader not only saw the alleged thief, Jane Woodhouse, acquitted of the crime but the judge added to his loss by refusing to pay his expenses. Moreover he received a ticking off from the judge:

> The prosecutor was then called by his Lordship, who told him that his conduct had been extremely irreligious and improper, and that his expenses would not be allowed. His Lordship, however, added that the expenses were not refused because he disbelieved his story, for on the contrary he did believe it. Addressing the prisoner his Lordship told her she had a lucky escape and met with a most merciful jury.[80]

Despite the judge's comments the horse-trader had a right to seek justice through the lawcourts. Moreover, he was entitled to feel aggrieved that he was unfortunate enough to have his case heard before a supporter of family values. Magistrates and judges could still refuse expenses on a whim; thus the Act of 1818 was as uncertain, for victims, as the system of parliamentary rewards. The breakthrough for prosecuting victims came in 1826 when Peel scrapped the existing system and replaced it with a comprehensive method of payment covering prosecutions for felonies and misdemeanors alike.[81] Despite criminal law reform, however, magistrates, in Herefordshire at least, still refused expenses to prosecutors if they felt the case presented to them was 'trifling' or a 'waste of time'. It is also interesting to note that following the only case of poaching to reach the Quarter Sessions, between 1849 and 1860, the magistrate refused the prosecution expenses because he felt the case should have been dealt with at the Petty Sessions. His decision

---

[79] 58 Geo. III, c. 70 (1818).
[80] *Lent Assize: 11 March 1835. HJ: 18 March 1835.*
[81] The Criminal Law Act: 7 Geo. IV, c. 64 (1826).

was surprising, as the case involved an assault on two gamekeepers. [82] After 1826, and probably because the majority of the expenses could now be reclaimed, the number of prosecutions rose. Despite the near certainty of victims retrieving their expenses there is some evidence to suggest that this was not widely known. As late as 1841, in some of the more remote areas of the county, it was still widely believed that the cost of prosecution would not be covered by the courts. The *Hereford Journal* found it necessary, in the same year, to inform its readership that this was not the case:

> Prosecutors Expenses – A notion prevails in the southern part of the county that persons prosecuting felons at the Assizes or Quarter Sessions are not entitled to have their costs paid for them out of the county rate unless the Grand Jury find a True Bill. For the information of such persons we state that where prosecutors are bound by recognizance to prosecute by the committing magistrate (as they always are), they are in all cases entitled to their costs, no matter whether the Grand Jury finds the Bill a true one or ignore it – A similar rule prevails as regards witnesses, who are entitled to their expenses, if they have been bound by recognizance, or subpoenaed to give evidence. [83]

The cost of prosecution was reduced further and the process of prosecution was made simpler by the extension of summary powers granted to magistrates from 1827. After that date, and through to the end of the period, they were able to deal with an increasing number of petty crimes. Magistrates were now able to dispense summary justice on those who stole game, pets, fruit trees and so on, and for damaging trees, hedges and fences. [84] They were able to deal with common assault from 1828 and, after 1847, they were able to deal summarily with simple cases of larceny if the offender was under the age of 14. [85] The age limit for young offenders to be summarily tried was extended to 16 in 1850 and, from 1855, magistrates dispensed summary justice upon cases of theft to the value of 5s with the consent of the accused, and over 5s if the accused pleaded guilty. [86] Jurisdiction was not extended merely for summary convictions but the jurisdiction of the Quarter Sessions was likewise increased and from 1842 most cases of rural crime were tried in this court, with the Assize now only dealing with the most serious of rural crimes. [87]

---

[82] HRO: Q/SR/142. HQS: *Epiphany, 2 January 1854.*

[83] *HJ: 9 June 1841.*

[84] Larceny Act: 7 and 8 Geo. IV, c. 29 (1827) and Indemnity Act: 7 and 8 Geo. IV, c. 30 (1827). For changes relating to poaching and wood- and crop-theft see chapters 5 and 6.

[85] Offences Against the Person Act: 9 Geo. IV, c. 31 (1828) and Juvenile Offenders Act: 10 and 11 Vict, c. 82 (1847).

[86] 13 and 14 Vict, c. 37 (1850) and the Criminal Justice Act: 18 and 18 Vict, c. 126 (1855).

[87] 5 and 6 Vict, c. 38 (1842).

The net result of the changes to the administration of the criminal law and the growth of policing in the county reflects a greater willingness to prosecute offenders. This willingness to take recourse to law is illustrated graphically by the rising numbers of convictions.[88] If Peel believed that a greater access to the criminal law would lead to more convictions then he was correct. If he also believed that a greater access to the law would reduce crime, however, he was to be proved wrong. Crime continued, and it continued to rise. Undoubtedly the improvements to policing and the law pushed the conviction rates up; yet crimes had to be committed for this to be the case. In short, if there had been less crime there would have been fewer convictions. The rising tide of crime in the county was the result of economic factors that were largely out of the control of politicians, the police or the magistrates. A rising population and a shrinking job market, rapid price fluctuations and changing work practices, and alienation, bitterness and displacement caused by the change in the relationship between the rural workers and farmers, and, above all, grinding poverty ensured that criminal activity in the countryside was destined to increase.

[88] See Chapter 2.

4

Rustlers, social criminals or common thieves?

Sheep-stealing in rural Herefordshire

Mr G, do not weep
for the loss of your fat sheep:
You are rich, we are poor
when this is gone, we'll come for more.[1]

Sheep-stealing was a common crime in the English countryside but sheep-stealing, as a subject of historical research, has not received the attention given to other types of rural crime, notably poaching and arson. Although seen as 'marginal', arson was the tool employed by many rural protesters, especially, although not exclusively, during the 'Swing' years.[2] Equally poaching is seen as the classic social crime that, although illegal, was not regarded as such by rural communities.[3] Sheep-stealing, it could be argued, fits either of these categories. Moreover, the crime could be purely acquisitive, or simply committed as a defence against hunger. As a result Roger Wells argues that its 'motivational miscellany' as such 'eludes any precise categorization'.[4] Research into sheep-stealing in Herefordshire, however, suggests that the crime was overwhelmingly committed by the rural poor. There is also evidence to suggest that, in some communities and within some occupational groups, sheep-stealing was indeed a social crime, while the crime may also have been a proto-political form of protest carrying a message of discontent.

Wells' article concerning sheep-stealing was written in response to Rule's call for a regional study of the subject of sheep-stealing, which would

---

[1] Note found pinned to the entrails of a slaughtered sheep in East Glamorgan. See *HJ*: *28 March 1804*.

[2] Rudé, *Criminal and Victim*. 86. Rudé classified a great deal of rural incendiarism as 'marginal'. Wells, in 'The Development of the English Rural Proletariat', clearly shows that incendiarism, as a tool of protest, pre-dated 'Swing'. Moreover, Jones, 'Thomas Campbell Foster', P. Muskett, 'The Suffolk Incendiaries: 1843–45', *The Journal of Regional and Local Studies*, Vol. 7 (1987) and Archer, 'By A Flash And A Scare' clearly show that incendiarism continued to be a tool of the rural protester well after the 'Swing' years.

[3] Rule, 'Social Crime'.

[4] Roger Wells, 'Sheep-Rustling in Yorkshire in the Age of the Industrial and Agricultural Revolutions', *Northern History*, Vol. 20. 145.

either 'complement or redefine' his own work. Wells' study, however, complemented rather than redefined Rule's earlier work.[5] Essentially Wells agreed with Rule's suggestion that the causes of sheep-stealing in England were 'manifold'. Wells argues that sheep 'rustling' was carried out by all sections of society and included middling farmers, artisans, butchers and the socially deprived. While Wells' conclusions are convincing the study as such covers only one county, Yorkshire, a county in the throes of the industrial revolution and likely to present a very different picture from Herefordshire, a county that was still wholly agricultural and where the majority of its inhabitants depended upon the land, in one way or another, as a means of employment.

Herefordshire is a small county bordering Wales to the south and west, Gloucestershire and Worcestershire to the east and Shropshire to the north, and covered, in 1831, an area of 837 square miles.[6] The county, in 1801, had a population of only 88,436 while the city of Hereford itself, little more than a market town, accounted for 6,828 of the total.[7] When these figures are compared with the West Riding of Yorkshire, the population of which stood at 564,000, with Bradford alone containing 29,000 people, it puts the size of Herefordshire into perspective.[8] Although John Clark wrote in 1794 that 'the principle part, two thirds, of the land is under tillage', sheep were 'articles of some importance'.[9] This was especially true of the western parts of the county where, Clark argued, land of 'that part . . . can boast of no high degree of fertility'.[10] Although wool was still an important commodity in such areas it would seem that by the period under discussion it came behind crops and cattle. Despite crops, especially wheat, and cattle being prominent, sheep were common, as indeed they were throughout England and Wales and, although the county lacked the vast moors of Yorkshire, very few sizeable farms would have been without them. The opportunities, then, for potential sheep-stealers were there and in times of hardship there was no shortage of those who were prepared to take the risk of being apprehended.

While this chapter will show that the motivations for sheep-stealing and the nature of the crime remained unchanged throughout the period the criminal law relating to the offence was far from static. Indeed, the sentencing powers of the judiciary changed radically after 1832, when sheep-stealing ceased to be a capital offence. Because of this change in the criminal law it is possible to present this chapter in two parts: 1800 to 1832 and 1833 to 1860.

---

[5] J. G. Rule, 'The Manifold Causes of Rural Crime: Sheep-Stealing in England, c1740–1840', in Rule (ed.) Outside the Law. 129.

[6] Major A. E. W. Salt MA, 'The Economic Geography of Herefordshire', in Herefordshire Naturalists Field Club, Priory Press, Malvern (1954). 159.

[7] Littlebury's Directory (1867). 1.

[8] Engels, The Condition. 67.

[9] Clark, 'General View'.

[10] Duncumb, 'General View'. 9.

Presenting the chapter in this way makes it possible to examine the effect of the removal of the death penalty from the statute books for the crime of sheep-theft.

I 1800 to 1832

Between 1741 and 1832 the theft of sheep was a felony, without benefit of clergy, and a conviction for the crime was punishable by hanging.[11] Considering the possible, although not often carried out, consequences the crime was committed to 'an alarming extent'.[12] Indeed, between 1800 and 1832 there were eighty-six convictions for sheep-stealing. Moreover, it seems clear that this figure is likely to represent a mere fraction of the crime's true extent. We will never know for instance how many farmers lost the odd sheep, especially in the more remote western border area of the Black Mountains, or how many put down the disappearance of a lamb to the work of a fox or a stray dog, or guessed that an animal may simply have fallen into a nearby river to be washed away. Nor will we ever know how many thefts were not pursued, either through lack of finance or lack of evidence. In general only those with adequate resources, of both time and money, sought justice. A sheep-stealer could not, after all, repay his victim if executed or transported to Australia and, for this reason alone, there may have been many cases where the victim settled for some form of out-of-court compensation. David Jones noted that the head of the Glamorgan Constabulary, in the mid-nineteenth century, complained that 'depredators are encouraged' because injured parties, especially in the rural districts, were prepared to accept a compromise rather than incur the expenses and delay of a trial. This applied to 'quite serious crimes', as well as to 'petty offences'.[13] Jones went on to explain that in Monmouthshire, a county adjacent to Herefordshire, during a six-month period in 1867, less than one criminal case in five actually reached the courts. The rest had been 'compromised'.[14]

Local newspapers often carried stories of sheep-stealing acts that failed to bring the criminal to court. Advertisements seeking information as to the whereabouts of sheep 'strayed presumed stolen' were common and, from time

---

[11] Benefit of clergy originally meant that ordained clerks charged with a felony could only be tried at an ecclesiastical court. Over time, however, its meaning changed. Thus by the eighteenth century benefit of clergy came to mean that certain persons found guilty of certain felonies were exempt from capital punishment. Therefore to be found guilty of a felony 'Without Benefit of Clergy' the court was obliged to sentence the offender to death. See Radzinowicz, *English Criminal Law:* Vol. 1. 3.

[12] *HJ: 10 October 1825.*

[13] Jones, *Crime in Wales.* 6–7.

[14] Ibid. 7.

to time, lists of victims appeared.[15] On 21 February 1827 the *Hereford Journal* reported that:

> On Wednesday night two sheep were killed . . . from a field over Ailstone Hill. On Saturday one from Barr's Court, and on Sunday one from Hampton (Court).[16]

Or more dramatically:

> On Monday last a man was discovered in the act of stealing a sheep (At Allensmore). The thief had placed the animal on his shoulders and was making off with it, but seeing a person approaching him, threw down the sheep and escaped.[17]

Sheep-stealing in Herefordshire was common enough to alarm those who farmed flocks of sheep and, because of its frequency, tenant farmers and landowners, through the organ of the local press, occasionally called for tougher sentences. The editor of the *Hereford Journal* often felt that the mere threat of a violent death was not enough and that the ultimate sentence should be carried out more frequently in an attempt to protect farmers' livestock. He argued in 1825, for example, that 'the extremity of the law (should) be put into force and examples made . . . (or else) sheep-stealing will prevail to a very alarming extent'.[18] Despite the frequent calls for judicial examples, however, only three unfortunates forfeited their lives for the crime at Hereford between 1796 and 1832.[19]

Rustling, as Roger Wells suggests, did make up a fair percentage of the sheep stolen from the English countryside but Herefordshire, like other rural counties, lacked the necessary outlets for the sustained, organized and large-scale rustling that he attributes to Yorkshire. Sheep, in Herefordshire at least, were owned mainly by landowners and farmers. The available pasture which could support animals and which remained in the ownership of the rural poor was disappearing all the time. Wells' argument that sheep were kept by all sections of society on 'massive unenclosed moorlands' is not applicable when placed in the context of pastoral Herefordshire.[20] Although there were wholesale sheep-thefts in Herefordshire between 1800 and 1832, it is clear that 'rustling' was the exception rather than the rule. Indeed, of the

---

[15] The advertisement, as an aid to apprehending sheep-stealers and other thieves, was not particular to Herefordshire. See Styles, 'Print and Policing'.

[16] *HJ: 21 February 1827.*

[17] *HJ: 10 October 1825.*

[18] Ibid.

[19] HCL: FALC343.2. *Executions At Hereford, Commencing with the Year 1770*. Broadside, c.1832. The unfortunate men were William (alias John) Philips in 1796, Stephen Price in 1804 and James Webb in 1818.

[20] Wells, 'Sheep-Rustling'. 130.

eighty-six convictions between those years only twenty-four, 27.90 per cent, involved the theft of more than one sheep. Such figures give us an average of less than one case per year of anything resembling rustling. Moreover, this figure can be reduced still further when we consider the number of thieves who could be involved in the theft of several lambs, or even a sheep and a lamb.

A few professional sheep-stealers did operate in the county. Edward Jarman, William Sheen, Ezekiel Watkins and James Davis were committed to Hereford Gaol, on 22 December 1824, for 'having in their possession upwards of fifty sheep, supposed to be stolen'.[21] It would certainly seem that this gang were organized rustlers. Moreover, that only seven of the beasts could be formally identified by local farmers suggests that their activities were not only confined to the county of Herefordshire. In the same professional vein a field was emptied of sheep in 1829 and the *Hereford Journal* reported that:

> During the night of Sunday sen'night some villains entered a field at Maidstone Court, nr Ledbury, and stole 43 sheep and lambs of the Welsh breed. Although an active pursuit was commenced on the following day, and a handsome reward offered, no discovery has yet been made as to the means employed in the conveyance of so large a number of animals.[22]

It is not known if the sheep were ever recovered and, as there is no record of the culprits being apprehended, it is likely they evaded detection. Not all potential rustlers were as skilful though. On the night of 21 January 1832 a lone would-be rustler was driving nine ewe sheep 'through the town stile, in the village of Mordiford, towards Hereford'. He was challenged by the local constable whereupon he 'took to his heels' and fled. The man's panic was justified, since the constable, who was also a tenant farmer, 'actually owned the beasts'.[23] Presumably the constable was as taken aback as the 'felon' who seized the opportunity to make good his escape. Such cases were the exception, however, and, as the figures indicate, rustling enterprises were a rarity in Herefordshire between 1800 and 1832.

The group which most closely resemble professional rustlers were the bargees, or navigators, who worked the River Wye. These men and women had ample opportunities to plunder the unprotected riverside fields and it would seem they often did so. As Judge Baron Garrow commented in 1826, when reluctantly acquitting a crew of bargees accused of sheep-stealing:

> The property of the public on the borders of all navigable rivers and canals is continually exposed to the nightly deprivations of those who are navigating those

[21] *HJ: 13 December 1824.*
[22] *HJ: 5 August 1829.*
[23] *HJ: 21 January 1832.*

rivers and canals; and it is a matter of experience; nay a matter now of history, that every necessary for the supply of barges from one place to another – hay for the horses – mutton and poultry and everything else for the men – are but too generally procured by acts of plunder.[24]

That the men and women who worked and lived upon the barges helped themselves to sheep provoked a great deal of resentment from the landowners and tenant farmers along the banks of the river. This animosity was so great that it often sparked into open hostility and calls were frequently made for a harder line to be taken against them. The tone of the *Hereford Journal* in February 1819 was typical:

> The extensive deprivations which have been so long committed with impunity on the property of those who occupy lands on the banks of the Wye, between the City and Ross (on-Wye), particularly by sheep-stealers have at length received a check in the apprehension of five men, the crew of a barge, whose fate we hope will be a warning to others, as there is no reason to believe the above are not the only bargemen who have been concerned in the late infamous system of sheep-stealing from the grounds adjoining the Wye, whilst navigating barges down the river, and for which crime the five unfortunate individuals who's commitment we now state, are becoming the inmates of a prison and at the approaching Assizes will be tried for the offence they have committed against society and the laws, when they may answer with their lives for their deviation from the paths of rectitude.[25]

Victories for the owners of sheep, however, were few and far between against this highly mobile enemy. Thus when they did occur they were well covered by newspaper correspondents. Indeed, the arrest of the five men mentioned above warranted a blow-by-blow account:

> It appears on Sunday evening two men on the look out for poachers, at Holm Lacy saw some people take and carry off two sheep, the property of Mr Knill of Bullingham to a barge, on which they immediately gave the alarm and Mr Knill, Mr Apperley of Fownhope, Mr Smith of the Bower, Mr Stephens of Hollerton, and others with equal spirit and promptitude assembled their men and proceeded to the barge and boarded it and secured the crew, one of whom offered some resistance, but he was knocked down with a gun, and submitted with the rest . . . they are Jas Harrison, Henry Harrison, John Harley, Thos Evans and Joseph Williams.[26]

---

[24] *HJ: Assize Intelligence, 2 March 1826.*
[25] *HJ: 10 February 1819.*
[26] *HJ: 17 February 1819.*

Although, according to the authorities, they were able to 'plunder' the riverside at will, the theft of two sheep between five crew members hardly constitutes rustling. Of course, we will never know how often this particular crew did steal sheep, or in what numbers, before they were caught, but the available evidence suggests that sustenance was the motivating factor for the crime rather than profit. Bargees were generally seen as lawless characters and they often led a charmed life. When sheep-stealing was carried out with forethought these water-borne criminals were unlikely to be detected, as a report printed in the *Hereford Journal* of 23 August 1826 indicates:

> Last week, the skin of a fine wether sheep, recently and skillfully taken from the carcass, was discovered in a river near Pontrilas, where it had been sunk by means of lime stones tied up within it. The feet and ears, which were probably of mottled colours, had been carefully cut off to impede or prevent detection.[27]

The bargees who plied the coal trade from Mommouthshire and the Forest of Dean to Hereford, via the River Wye, were adept at the crime and they were reputed to hide the carcass of a stolen sheep in a barrel, which was then dragged along in the barge's wake; and to be quickly released if challenged.[28] The five arrested bargees never appeared in a Herefordshire court. Possibly they had crimes to answer elsewhere, perhaps Monmouthshire or Gloucestershire, and were sent to answer those charges. Alternatively, because the sheep had not been slaughtered, they may have been released with a warning as to their future behaviour. Whatever the reason, if they had managed to escaped the transport ship, they were very lucky. Equally fortunate were John Voice, John Harris, Paul Harrison and Joseph Hatton, bargees who committed a similar crime in 1826 when they stole a single sheep from the banks of the Wye. Although Voice and Harris admitted the crime and vividly described the slaughter of the animal they were found not guilty. This is surprising as the evidence suggests that they were in fact clearly guilty. The carcass was found in a field by their barge and the skin, which was discovered weighted down with coals in the river matched the joints found in the barge. This seemingly watertight case for the prosecution sprang a leak when Mr Horace Twiss, for the prisoners, exposed the chief witness' past. Hatton, one of the gang who had turned 'witness for the Crown', had previously been acquitted of, and served sentences for, other offences, notably 'stealing boards' at Gloucester, as well as having been previously acquitted of sheep-stealing. It would seem that the jury was loath to damn Voice and Harris on the word of a known criminal. Although the prosecution's witness effectively gave Harris and Voice their freedom Justice Park was furious, remarking that:

---

27 *HJ: 23 July 1826.*
28 HRO: AK/95. M. P. Watkins, *Stories of Sheep-Stealing.*

You have had one of the narrowest escapes that I ever remember persons charged with so high an offence as yours to have experienced, during a very long attendance in the course of my life on Courts of Justice . . . you two men are the most fortunate men I ever knew . . . but do not imagine, nor let others in your profession imagine, that such a narrow escape is at all probable to occur again.[29]

Juries, despite their social composition, were often reluctant to convict men, especially on the testimony of a known criminal. Perhaps they also understood that the punishment for sheep-stealing did not necessarily fit the crime.[30]

There is little doubt that a great many sheep-thefts during this period were directly linked to the poverty of the agricultural labourers.[31] Indeed, the evidence suggests that the overwhelming majority of sheep-stealing cases were purely and simply acts perpetrated to provide food. Abject poverty, rather than naked acquisition, was the usual motivation behind the crime. Beattie notes that unemployment, underemployment, low wages and high prices were all motivating factors behind theft in eighteenth-century England and it would seem that this link continued into the next century.[32] It is almost possible to determine the good years from the bad by merely flicking through the gaol calendars, or the Petty Session returns. Apologizing to the visiting justices in March 1817, the local magistrates complained that 'our calendar, we are sorry to state, contains the largest number of prisoners for trial we ever remember' (seventy – eleven of whom were to be tried for sheep-stealing).[33] And 1817 was a bad year. Farmers, especially those who relied heavily upon grain production, were cutting back on labour following the onset of the post-war agricultural depression. Wheat prices reached almost unaffordable levels and at their highest, on 4 June, stood at £1 per Winchester bushel.[34] At the Bread Assize on the same day (at avoirdupois weight), the weight of an 18d loaf was set at 3lb 10oz 2dr by the magistrates at Hereford. This effectively excluded many families from a subsistence diet. Using Neal's guide, that at subsistence level a family of two adults and two children require 33.5lb of wheat bread per week, such a family would have to spend well in excess of what it could bring in by honest means.[35]

---

[29] HJ: Assize Intelligence, 22 March 1826.
[30] See also Chapter 6 for the case of Jasper Eckley, a poacher, who was acquitted because the jury felt that transportation was too severe a punishment for a breach of the game laws. HJ: 17 January 1825.
[31] For a full discussion concerning the plight of Herefordshire's agricultural labour force c.1800–60, see Chapter 2.
[32] Beattie, 'The Pattern of Crime in England'.
[33] HJ: 26 March 1817.
[34] HJ: 4 June 1817.
[35] R. S. Neal, 'The Standard of Living in Britain in the Industrial Revolution', A. J.

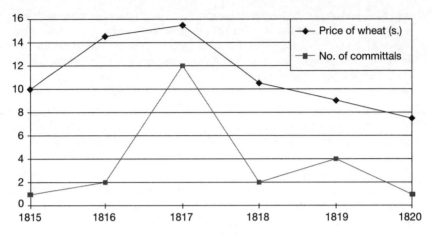

Figure 4.1 Committals for sheep-stealing and wheat prices, 1815–20[36]

As Figure 4.1 illustrates the exceptional bread prices of 1817 correspond with the exceptional year for sheep-thefts. Prices alone, however, did not dictate the extent of crime. The state of the labour market was also important. Writing in 1816 Edmund Jones noted that 'the farmers distress is such, that he cannot employ the poor, and (they) are wandering and begging their bread'.[37] In the same year a Herefordshire landowner, T. A. Knight, wrote that 'the state of the poor and labouring classes is worse than I ever remember it, and every week becoming more so, as the prosperity of the farmer decreases'.[38] Undoubtedly the areas of the county that would have been hardest hit by the depression would have been those which concentrated upon grain production, those areas that John Clarke in 1794 quaintly called the 'wheatlands' of the county which covered the central, southern and eastern lowlands. It was no mere coincidence that the majority of sheep-stealing activities occurred in these areas. Indeed, during this period the western and northern border areas were virtually free of the crime. This is surprising because not only were these districts more suited to sheep farming, but their terrain and relative remoteness suggests that the crime could have been carried out more easily than elsewhere. If large-scale rustling had been the norm it seems likely that it would have been these areas that professional

Taylor (ed.), in Roger Wells, *Wretched Faces: Famine in Wartime England, 1763–1803*. St Martin's Press, New York (1988). 404.
[36] Committals for sheep-stealing, *HJ*: 1815–20. Prices of wheat as sold in Hereford Market, taken from *HJ*: 1815–20.
[37] 'The Agricultural State of the Kingdom: Hereford' (1816), *Board of Agriculture*. Adams and Dart, London (1970). 102.
[38] *Board of Agriculture*. 102.

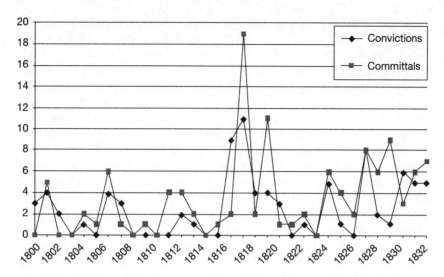

Figure 4.2 Committals and convictions for sheep-stealing, 1800–32[39]

criminals would have targeted. Sheep-stealing activity was predominantly carried out east and south of Hereford, areas that were given over largely to grain production and reflected, in part, the rural worker's reaction when faced with rising food prices and a shrinking labour market. Such evidence is far from conclusive but we have to accept that if rural crime was motivated by necessity then the economic preconditions were in place.

While sheep-stealing was a frequently committed crime, Figure 4.2 shows that it peaked during years of exceptional hardship for the agricultural labourer. From the evidence presented it is clear that sheep-stealing convictions peaked during 1817 and that this peak coincided with the onset of the post-war agricultural depression and periods of high food prices.

The majority of sheep thieves to appear at Hereford Assizes during this period were charged with stealing a single sheep. Of the eighty-six convictions between 1800 and 1832, sixty-two (72.09 per cent) concerned the theft of a lone sheep. In the peak year for Herefordshire sheep-stealing, 1817, a total of eleven out of the twelve cases (91.66 per cent) fell into this category. The prominence of thefts of single beasts suggests that personal consumption rather than profit was generally the motive and that these crimes were often attempts to stave off hunger. Wells makes the same point, arguing that the theft of one or two lambs was 'sure signs of rustling for personal consumption'.[40] This argument is reinforced when we discover that the theft of a single sheep was often carried out by up to four, or even five,

[39] HJ: 1800–32.
[40] Wells, *Wretched Faces.* 167.

individuals. Although sheep were valuable beasts (the market price in Hereford was 39s in 1822), criminals who risked a violent death at the end of a rope for the sake of less than 8s or 9s were likely to have been desperate rather than greedy. Indeed, as the stolen carcass would be unlikely to realize the full market value the prospect of actual financial gain was minimized. One hesitates to call these groups of hungry individuals 'rustlers'. The word suggests a professionalism which many clearly lacked. Animals were often crudely butchered in the field and more than one sheep-stealer left an incriminating trail of blood leading to their home. In 1830, for example, Thomas Jones and John Lewis were unprofessional enough to leave a trail of sheep's blood and footprints in the snow from the scene of their crime to their cottage where the city gaoler, armed with a warrant, found the butchered sheep.[41]

Many of the cases which came to court confirm the idea that those who broke the law often did so as a means of survival. Ann Perkins, described by the prosecution as a 'miserable old lady', single-handedly cut the throat of a ram with a penknife before butchering it on the spot and hiding the joints beneath a hedge at Aconbury in 1830. She pleaded in her defence: 'my Lord I was perishing from hunger when I caught the ram (and) I was almost ready to eat the wool off the skin.'[42] 'The hunger of the old lady,' as the *Coventry Mercury* argued, 'appears to have strengthened her arm as well as her appetite.'[43] The tendency to butcher, joint and hide the meat at the scene of the crime was commonplace. Four unemployed day labourers from the village of Dewchurch also butchered a single sheep 'on the spot' and hid the joints in a hollow tree.[44] In a similar vein Benjamin Pritchard, 'an old man of sixty years', had the sentence of death recorded against his name, his footprints having been traced to his home. Despite his daughters dutifully offering alibis in his defence, one claiming she bought the animal for him the previous week in Abergavenny, and the other claiming he was ill in bed on the night in question, the mutton found at his cottage confirmed his fate and he was sent to the hulks to await transportation.[45]

As Chapter 2 has illustrated, the Herefordshire agricultural labourer was no stranger to unemployment, and since many were reduced to day labour they were particularly vulnerable to seasonal unemployment. While employment was, if not assured, at least more available during the summer months the opposite was often the case in the winter. The county's farmers were not slow in taking advantage of the labour surplus during the harvest

41 *HJ: 20 January 1830.*
42 *HJ: Assize Intelligence, 18 August 1830.*
43 *Coventry Mercury*, cited in Clifford Morsley (ed.) *News From the English Countryside.* Harrap, London (1979). 245.
44 *HJ: 8 February 1829.*
45 *HJ: Assize Intelligence, 28 March 1832.*

months, and they were equally quick to shed workers once the task was completed. Impoverished by their unemployment, many were forced to resort to illegal means, either to supplement inadequate poor relief, or, simply, to survive the winter. The crimes of poaching and wood-theft often peaked during the winter months and the incidence of sheep-stealing followed the same pattern.

The peak months for committals to Hereford Gaol on suspicion of sheep-stealing between 1800 and 1832 were those between late autumn and spring.[46] Indeed, committals during the three-month period from July to the end of September, with nineteen cases, amounted to only 16.37 per cent of the total. But if sheep farmers could, to a certain extent, relax their guard in the summer months, this was not the case during the winter. The reduction in employment opportunities after the harvest was gathered in was mirrored by an increase in all types of rural crime, including sheep-stealing. Between 1800 and 1832 there were a total of 116 committals for sheep-stealing and seventy-one (61.20 per cent) of these were committed during the six-month period from October to March. There was, it seems, a clear link between sheep-theft and the extent of employment opportunities. When employment was more readily available, as in the harvest months, the numbers of labourers being committed for the crime dropped dramatically.

That the thefts of single sheep were the recourse of the hungry and those displaced by agricultural change is further shown in that this type of crime was often a family affair. Brother/sister, father/son, husband/wife combinations were all, at one time or another, involved. It is interesting that of the two husband-and-wife teams, William and Eleanor Griffiths, committed in 1817, and Thomas and Elizabeth Taylor, committed in 1827, the wife on each occasion was spared an appearance in the dock.[47] Whether this was because of chivalry on the part of the husband or through the prosecution's reluctance to leave a family parentless (for financial rather than sentiment reasons) remains an open question. It is more likely, however, that prosecutors felt there was less chance of securing a conviction if the criminal was a woman, and even less if she was a mother.[48] Female participation in sheep-stealing, while uncommon, did occur, although we can only imagine its extent. Indeed, while there was only one gang of female sheep-stealers committed to gaol during the period they also had a family link. Maria Tyler, Mary Walters, Ann Walters and Mary Walters the younger comprised a 'bold female gang' who stole a sheep and a lamb from a field at Fownhope.[49] Sheep-stealing, however, was a physical task and the sheer strength needed to wrestle a sheep

---

[46] Months of sheep-stealing committals to Hereford Gaol taken from *HJ: 1800–32*.

[47] *HJ: Assize Intelligence, 9 July 1817*, and *HJ: Assize Intelligence, 13 June 1827*.

[48] For a discussion of female criminality see Chapter 5.

[49] *HJ: 5 July 1819*. They were all later acquitted.

to the ground, kill it and then butcher it may help to explain why the numbers of female sheep-stealers were relatively low.

Once more, female and family involvement in sheep-stealing suggests that the theft was for domestic purposes. The ages, employment status of the perpetrators and the thefts of single sheep all indicate that the overwhelming motivation behind the acts was poverty. Couple this with the depressed state of the Herefordshire rural working class during the period and it seems likely that many had little choice but to commit crimes of this nature to survive. The evidence suggests that most sheep-stealers did not commit their crimes because they fancied a change from bacon but because they had no bacon at all.

The question remains, however: Was sheep-stealing a social crime or, because of its 'miscellaneous motivational forces', merely a theft on a par with other thefts? As we have seen, the majority of sheep-thefts in Herefordshire were carried out by the poor and involved the theft of a single beast which was then consumed by the thief, or thieves, and their families. There was rarely any attempt to sell the proceeds of the crime during this early period and the carcass carrying valuable wool and 'rough fat' was often discarded, either sunk in a river or burnt, or, perhaps significantly, left at the scene of the crime. Having established that the crime of sheep-stealing was mainly a crime of the poor, if not hungry, it is now necessary to establish if these acts were a socially sanctioned means of expressing discontent.

John Rule defines a social crime as a 'criminal action legitimized by popular opinion'.[50] The 'classic' social crimes are poaching and smuggling. Both crimes were 'openly or tacitly' supported by the community and thus were not regarded as crimes at all by the majority of the labouring population.[51] Poaching was not seen as immoral or illegal; the wild beasts of the wood and field were a gift from God and belonged to whoever could catch them, be they peasant or gentry. Similarly, wrecking, the plundering of stranded ships, was simply to take advantage of an unanticipated act of God, while smuggling, the non-payment of duty on imported goods, was a socially acceptable crime. Sheep, although not regarded as a gift from the Almighty, were as much private property as game, the contents of ships and His Majesty's taxes. The important factor is whether the criminal felt that he or she, or even a community, had a 'right' to take a hare, or to evade taxation, or to take a sheep, when legislation clearly dictated otherwise. It seems likely that the very fact that the motive for theft was desperate hunger would have been sufficient to attract widespread sympathy in the local face-to-face community. The cases of several sheep-stealers, notably those of Ann Perkins and Thomas Vaughan, excited sympathy from several sources and even the

---

[50] Rule, 'Social Crime'. 138–9.
[51] Ibid.

editor of the *Hereford Journal*, who was not notably compassionate towards the county's criminals, spoke of their fate in apologetic tones.

From contemporary comments concerning sheep-thefts by navigators, it would seem that the bargees saw riverside sheep as 'fair game', an acceptable theft, perhaps even a perk of the job. Similar attitudes were to be found in Whitchurch and the Doward where, even in the late nineteenth century, one of the hills was known locally as 'mutton tump'. It:

> had once been occupied by folk who were all concerned with sheep-stealing, actively or passively, and once sheep got into the Doward Lanes they could be regarded as irrecoverable. They said that when (men) found a sheep on the hill, or one was bought there, it was no good folk coming to look for it, it was killed at once, and the head and the rest was (taken) down a mine hole and the joints taken to ovens, in houses or out in the woods.[52]

Such activity, in that locality at least, was both well known and seemingly tolerated, although clearly not by the farmers. The sheep that were unfortunate enough to wander into the Doward Lanes were seen as a gift, in much the same way that Cornishmen saw a wreck as a gift. If such stories can be relied upon it is possible to argue that in many areas of the county, especially during periods of high rural unemployment, sheep-stealing was community sanctioned. Viewed in this light it could be seen as a social crime. Sheep were everywhere and the temptation must have been great for many a poor labourer with a family to feed. Equally, many sheep-stealers may have felt a certain justification in the act, arguing that it was not right that a few should have so much when his family went hungry. Was not compensation morally owed by the landowner, or employing tenant, in lieu of loss of land use, or employment? Indeed, such an act, and in such circumstances, would seem to satisfy a primitive sense of justice.

Evidence of community sanction is further illustrated by a community's reluctance to give up its criminals. It has already been noted that the press of the period abounded with rewards offered for information of 'sheep missing presumed stolen'. Yet, while it is difficult to judge the success rate of such advertisements, there are very few recorded cases between 1800 and 1860 where information from a peer led to the appearance of a sheep-stealer at the Hereford Quarter Sessions or the Assizes. As we have seen the usual mode of detection was either tracking, via footsteps or blood trail, or being caught in the act. The sheep-stealer, along with the poacher, often enjoyed the protection of the community; arguably he had more in common with the 'social bandit' than the common thief.[53]

---

[52] Watkins, *Stories of Sheep-Stealing.*
[53] For a full analysis of social banditry see Hobsbawm, *Primitive Rebels.*

Hopkins, when discussing poaching, has suggested that the unwillingness of communities to cooperate with the authorities constituted an act of protest. He argues that 'the almost audible silence . . . (the act of) denying all aid to the authorities . . . was the silence of protest'.[54] Sometimes, however, protest took a more active form. A community could make its feelings felt towards the 'victim', even after a sheep-stealer was tried and condemned. At the 1827 summer Assizes Thomas Taylor was found guilty of stealing a sheep from Mr Bond, a farmer at Linton, for which he received transportation for life.[55] Taylor's 'most sanctimonious manner' in court, coupled with a sense of injustice on his part (see below for trial details), probably encouraged some of his friends and neighbours to steal and kill Mr Bond's dogs, a crime that later saw two men, named Treherne and Brimmell, appear at Hereford Quarter Sessions.[56] Although such revenge attacks were rare this case does suggest a certain amount of the 'psychological terrorism' associated with animal maiming.[57] Similarly, the *modus operandi* of many sheep-stealers may be seen as a means of conveying a message to tenant farmers and landowners. As Peacock argued:

> There must have been scores of incidents, perhaps the vast majority, when animals were stolen simply to feed a labourers family. But, although the labourers stole to feed themselves and their families, this does not rule out the possibility of the act becoming one of protest as well. And this is the way the crime must be seen. The methods used make the point.[58]

The methods used by the East Anglian sheep-stealer, described by Peacock, were remarkably similar to those employed by their counterparts in Herefordshire 'as the creature was killed, skinned, and only the best cuts of meat were taken – the head, skin, fat and entrails were left as an awful reminder of the power of the labourers'.[59]

Admittedly, to steal a sheep by taking the beast home before butchering it was to invite detection. However, while some thieves chose either to dispose of or hide the evidence, others chose to leave the carcass on view, suggesting that they were inclined to give the employing classes an awful reminder of their impoverished condition. A farmer lost an animal in 1827 whose 'entrails and head' were later discovered in a ditch by his house.[60] A Mr Burrows, of Dewchurch, found he had lost a sheep when its head and

---

[54] Hopkins, *The Long Affray*. 60.
[55] *HJ: Assize Intelligence, 29 August 1827*.
[56] *HJ 26 December 1827*, convicted *HQS Epiphany 1828*. HRO: Q/SR/116.
[57] For a full discussion of animal maiming see Archer, 'A Fiendish Outrage?'.
[58] Peacock, 'Village Radicalism'. 44.
[59] Ibid.
[60] *HJ: 21 February 1827*.

liver were thrown over his garden wall in 1829.[61] And farmer William Smith, of Woolhope, discovered that he had been a victim of sheep-stealers in 1832 when he found the 'head and entrails quite fresh' of a sheep hanging in one of his fields.[62] These cases exemplify the brutal similarities between the Herefordshire sheep-stealer and his East Anglian counterpart.

While such evidence, bloody as it is, could be discounted as a means of protest, we should be aware that the conditions for a response of this kind by the rural labourers were in place. We have seen that the Herefordshire farm labourers were not only poverty-stricken but often displaced, as indeed were many throughout England and Wales. Such conditions generated bitterness, frustration and anger, and sheep-stealing was but one response. Discontent was also expressed in the county, during this period, via acts of animal-maiming and arson, while poaching and hedge-breaking offences not only became more common but were more aggressive in execution. T. A. Knight could sense this growing anger and wrote, in 1816, that 'our peasantry, who become annually more profligate and idle (are), better calculated to cut the throats of the higher orders than to till the soil'.[63] It was, however, not the throats of the higher orders that were to be cut, but those of their sheep, and the animal's remains were a grim reminder that the employing classes were almost as vulnerable as their beasts.

One of the problems of accepting sheep-stealing as a crime of protest is that the crime itself was individually, and sometimes spontaneously, carried out. As we have seen in Chapter 1, George Rudé had argued that a crime could only be recognized as an act of protest if it was a collectively sanctioned act with a preconceived goal.[64] Such a conceptual framework is adequate if the historian is attempting to explain industrial disputes, grain riots or anti-conscription riots. Such disputes and disturbances relied, to a large extent, upon a common experience of either low wages, high bread prices or a community's reluctance to give up its men to the army. These concerns could, and often did, become rallying points. For the farm labourer the very nature of his existence often meant that his dispute concerned mainly himself and his master. Wages could vary from farm to farm. The enclosure of common and waste occurred at different parts of the county, at different times; moreover, one farmer may have kept farm servants 'living in' while a neighbour employed only day labour. Experiences were fragmented. Couple this with Roger Wells' idea that the poor law was administrated with a view to identifying and excluding troublemakers, potential and real, and it seems hardly surprising that protest became, if not individual, then the work of

---

[61] HJ: 18 February 1829.
[62] HJ: 8 August 1832.
[63] Board of Agriculture (1816). 103.
[64] George Rudé, Protest and Punishment: The Story of the Social and Political Protesters Transported to Australia, Oxford University Press, Oxford (1985). 3–4.

small groups. Therefore, there can be little surprise that protest took the form it did by being primitive and covert in nature.[65]

Sheep-stealing, while undertaken mainly to solve immediate economic problems, was also capable of carrying a message of discontent. From the sheep-stealer's viewpoint it could be argued that the crime was a positive act as well as an expression of protest. Not only would a stolen beast help to feed the thief and his family but the carcass left at the scene of the crime would remind the tenant or landowner of his failure to provide employment or a living wage. Alternatively, it could remind him of the injustice of a recent enclosure. Crimes such as arson and animal-maiming were essentially negative acts, serving merely to express discontent without relieving the labourer's plight. Because such crimes provided no material benefits for the perpetrator it has given them a certain amount of legitimacy among historians; consequently they have been accepted more readily as protest acts. To paraphrase Eric Hobsbawm, however, historians are university-educated with middle-class mores, values and expectations, and are a long way removed from the semi-literate farm labourer of the early nineteenth century.[66] Criminal action was often the only course of action open to the agricultural labourer to solve economic problems. We cannot dismiss his or her actions as mere theft. It is necessary, therefore, to reappraise these criminal acts which provided a material benefit in view of the possibility, even likelihood, that they carried a message of protest.

The rural labouring population of Herefordshire during this period has left us precious little in the way of documented testimony. This silence is carried into the courts. Several sheep-stealers sought mercy through 'pleading their circumstances', which were usually impoverished and the reason they gave for the theft. Others were seemingly resigned to their fate, while a few were almost comic in an effort to regain their freedom. Thomas Taylor acted in this fashion in 1827. When asked if he had anything to say in his defence before sentence was passed, he recited a poem, or 'a species of canting pathos', probably composed during his confinement at Hereford Gaol. The first verse was devoted to the defendant swearing his undying loyalty to King George, while the second was dedicated to the judge, Baron Vaughan, who he no doubt hoped would be sufficiently impressed enough to acquit him. It ran:

> The next that we shall pray for,
> shall be for my Lord Judge,
> for he is a valiant man,
> and a valiant man is he,
> may the Heavens preserve him! He owes me no grudge,
> and I'm sure he will set me free.

[65] Wells, 'The Development'.
[66] Hobsbawm, *Primitive Rebels*. 22.

So now I pray you my Lord Judge, to grant me one favour,
for you to set me at liberty, and I'll praise you for ever.
So now I think I'd best conclude, and finish up my story,
may the Heaven above, protect my Lord Judge,
when he is the height of his glory.[67]

The court, reported the *Hereford Journal's* correspondent, was 'convulsed with laughter'. Justice Vaughan, however, was not so amused and pronounced Taylor 'Guilty', informing him that:

Not withstanding his contemplated device, he must rely that ample justice would be done him, but as it did not appear that he was an old offender his life might possibly be spared. As the offence of sheep-stealing, however, had gone to such alarming lengths now, sentence of death must be recorded, and the prisoner must make up his mind to a punishment sufficient to operate as a lesson of warning to similar offenders.[68]

Theatre, however, as we know, was not confined to the defendants. Once convicted, the sheep-stealer almost always had 'Sentence of Death' recorded against his name. The sentenced were then allowed to stew in the cells until the travelling justice left for the next town, Monmouth. At the last moment, however, he normally reprieved the condemned and sentences would be transmuted to transportation, usually fourteen years to life. The criminal justice system had to be not only terrible but also merciful.[69] It is difficult, of course, to assess the deterrent value of the threat of the rope; nevertheless, for the threat of capital punishment to be effective examples had to be made from time to time. The last unfortunate to 'suffer' at Hereford Gaol for sheep-stealing was James Webb who stole, significantly perhaps, nine ewes and lambs in 1818.[70] Webb, in a contrite gallows speech, attributed his fate to 'keeping low and vicious company (and) to idleness and drunkenness'. He was, however, somewhat unfortunate, a sacrificial victim selected to put an end to a concentrated spate of sheep-thefts that had begun in November 1816.[71] Indeed, between that date and his death no less than

---

[67] HJ: *Assize Intelligence*, 29 August 1827.

[68] HJ: 29 August 1827.

[69] For an excellent discussion of the 'theatre' of the eighteenth-century court see Hay, 'Property, Authority and the Criminal Law'.

[70] HCL: FALC343.2, *Executions at Hereford*. Broadside, c.1832. See also HJ: *Assize Intelligence*, 28 July 1818.

[71] HJ: 28 July 1818. For discussions on the theatre and rituality of eighteenth- and nineteenth-century execution see V. A. C. Gatrell, *The Hanging Tree: Execution and the English People, 1770–1868*, Oxford University Press, Oxford (1996) and Peter Linebaugh, *The London Hanged: Crime and Civil Society in the Eighteenth Century*, Allen Lane, London (1991).

sixteen cases, concerning twenty-three individuals, had been referred to an Assize judge. Judges, during this period, believed that it was necessary to administer exemplary justice. Perhaps the visiting judges saw this brutal tactic as justifiable, as only four cases of sheep-stealing appeared before the Assizes in the following year. We do not know, however, if the crime continued unabated or if farmers were dissuaded from prosecution after the fate of Webb.

Transportation for the convicted sheep-stealer was preferable to a violent death. Although the thought of leaving their parish and being taken to a foreign land was dreaded by most, the conditions in which the rural poor subsisted may have meant that transportation was not always unwelcome. A horse-thief from Cardiganshire, in 1828, explained under examination in court that he committed the crime solely to be transported to Australia.[72] A group of convicted prisoners in 1821, including three sheep-stealers leaving for Australia via the 'Hulks' from Hereford Gaol, seemed pleased that they were leaving the country.

> In our last (edition) we stated that nine transports left our Gaol, for the fulfillment of their sentences . . . a correspondent at Ross states . . . 'the convicts for transportation, in passing, per coach from the County Gaol at Hereford to Ross on Monday se'night exhibited a conduct alarming to mortality. They were decorated with ribbons and huzzaring as if in contempt of the sentence(s) incurred by their crimes.[73]

It would seem that the carnival atmosphere surrounding transportation was a regular event. Indeed, a letter-writer to the *Journal* explained in 1821 that on a recent occasion 'the local population joined in the merriment'.[74] While much of the ribbon-waving and cheering may have been bravado borne of apprehension, it is clear that their actions showed their contempt for the law and for the agrarian changes that forced them to steal to survive.

To a certain extent the expression 'motivational miscellany' may be ascribed to sheep-stealing in Herefordshire as to anywhere else.[75] Indeed, all rural crime may be attributed to a variety of motivational forces. This includes those crimes that have been portrayed as social or protest crimes. Arson, used so often as a means of expressing discontent in the English countryside, has also been used as a means of extracting personal revenge, or even as an act of desperation by a farmer seeking an insurance payout. Similarly, animal-maiming could as easily have been motivated by sadism rather than an expression of class discontent. The 'precise categorization'

---

[72] *HJ: 26 March 1828..*
[73] *HJ: 6 June 1821.*
[74] *HJ: 13 June 1831.*
[75] Roger Wells, 'Sheep Rustling'. 128.

that Wells hopes to find is essentially impossible.[76] Each case has to be judged upon its merits and, as George Rudé argued when attempting to classify protest crime, 'there is no easy blanket definition to fall back on . . . it all depends on the precise nature of the act and where and how and against whom it was committed'.[77]

All the evidence from Herefordshire between 1800 and 1832 suggests that sheep-stealing was generally carried out by those in need. The thefts of single beasts, the method of butchering and carrying away by those involved all point to this. It was, in short, 'a defence against hunger'.[78] The evidence also suggests that the crime was community sanctioned in some rural areas, such as Whitchurch and the Doward, and among some occupational groups, the bargees. Such sheep-stealers were not only protected by their communities but it would seem they were often found guilty only with great reluctance. Occasionally, they were even found not guilty by a jury when it was clear that they had committed a crime. Sheep-stealing was principally a social crime that was committed as and when the need arose by those who were most vulnerable: the rural working class. There was no wholesale theft of sheep to supply a commercial market; 'rustling' during this period was not a Herefordshire phenomenon. Although it would be naive to believe the odd stolen leg of mutton never made its way on to the butcher's slab, most of it ended up in the labourer's cottage, in much the same way as poached game did. While there is little evidence to show that the sheep-stealer was hostile towards capitalism there is little evidence to suggest he embraced it. Economic and social change was forced upon him and he merely reacted to survive.

II 1833 to 1860

The landowners and farmers of Herefordshire feared that sheep-stealing would escalate after the death penalty was repealed in 1832. In the event there appeared to be some justification for this attitude. As Figure 4.3 shows, convictions for the crime increased steadily from the 1830s and continued to do so until 1850 when the county's agricultural workforce began to benefit slightly from the improved economic climate. While the repeal of the Act of 1741 was not commented upon at the time, the rising numbers of sheep-thefts prompted newspapers, from the late 1830s, to bemoan the passing of the Bloody Code. In 1841 the *Hereford Journal* summed up the farmers' feelings by commenting that 'agriculturists require protection (from

---

[76] Ibid. 145.
[77] George Rudé, *Protest and Punishment*. 4.
[78] Hobsbawm and Rudé, *Captain Swing*. 77.

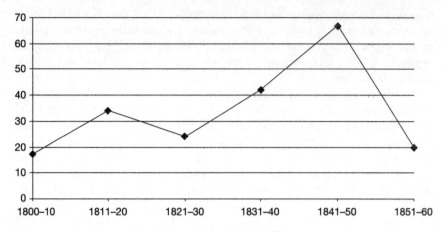

Figure 4.3 Convictions for sheep-stealing, 1800–60[79]

sheep-stealers), more effective than the present law affords'.[80] Later in the same year, the same newspaper noted that 'the frequency of the crime of sheep-stealing . . . renders some strong preventative measures necessary'.[81] The crime was so commonplace in this period that it was unusual for an Assize or Quarter Session not to have at least one case of sheep-stealing and, when this did happen, it was usually a matter for comment. They were conspicuous by their absence during the 1848 Epiphany Session and 'the Chairman showed surprise' when he found that there were no cases of sheep-stealing on the calendar.[82]

It is difficult to ascertain the influence the threat of the rope had prior to 1832, yet we must deduce that the threat of capital punishment did have some effect. Admittedly the statistical likelihood of being hanged for sheep-stealing between 1800 and 1832, at just over 3 per cent, was slim.[83] There was always the possibility, however, of being hanged as an example: the fate that befell James Webb in 1817. Convicted sheep-stealers after 1832 still ran the risk of transportation, but, as the century wore on, and as Australia became less of an option for judges and magistrates, sentences became less severe.[84] Judges, magistrates and the local press, however, in a vain attempt to curb sheep-stealing in the county, attempted to foster the belief that such criminals would inevitably be dealt with harshly. As late as 1849, nearly ten

[79] HJ: c.1800–60, HT: c.1832–60 and HRO: Q/Smc/1: *Calendar of Prisoners, c.1848–60.*
[80] HJ: 21 February 1841.
[81] HJ: 22 December 1841.
[82] HRO: Q/SR/136. HQS: Epiphany, 2 January 1848. HJ: 5 January 1848.
[83] Between 1800 and 1832 there were sixty-six convictions for sheep-stealing and only two of these were left for execution.
[84] Transportation to Australia ceased in 1853. See Cornish, 'Criminal Justice', in *Crime and Law.* 26.

years after New South Wales had stopped taking convicts, the *Hereford Times* pointed out that 'not withstanding that the almost inevitable consequence of sheep-stealing is transportation for the offender, if detected, the crime, we are sorry to say continues in this county'.[85]

The reality, however, was often very different. Magistrates and judges, their sentencing options restricted and perhaps motivated by a degree of compassion, no longer transported every sheep-stealer they convicted. Whereas a sheep-stealer at the turn of the nineteenth century faced inevitable transportation if found guilty, or execution if he was extremely unlucky, by the 1850s he could expect, for a first offence, a relatively light sentence. James Morgan, for example, a 32-year-old labourer from Welsh Bicknor, was sentenced to twelve months' hard labour for stealing a sheep in 1854, while Frederick Barnes, a 19-year-old butcher, received only nine months' hard labour for stealing a sheep at Allensmore in the same year.[86] Even members of gangs, a greater feature of sheep-stealing after 1832, did not necessarily feel the full weight of the law. Members of a 'notorious' sheep-stealing gang, operating out of Whitchurch and the Doward, when apprehended and convicted in 1849, 'seemed pleased' with their sentences of seven years' transportation. At least 'one of them had expected transportation for life'.[87]

While a relatively light sentence could not be guaranteed, a convicted sheep-stealer's chances were greatly enhanced in the 1840s and 1850s if he could secure several character references. At the county's 1838 Epiphany Sessions Henry Symmonds received only a year's imprisonment, with hard labour, for stealing six sheep at Ocle Pritchard. Such a large-scale theft was usually met with a heavy sentence but Symmonds, a farm labourer, was able to show that his transgression was out of character by producing references 'from several farmers'. These references indicated that Symmonds was both reliable and hardworking and suggested that his unlawful actions were dictated by his 'situation', namely his temporary unemployment, rather than a vicious nature.[88] The convicted sheep-stealer may also have been fortunate if the prosecutor, usually the victim of the crime, recommended that the judge or magistrate showed mercy. James Lewis, convicted in 1838 of stealing two sheep and two lambs at Weston Beggard, benefited from his victim's generosity when 'he kindly recommended him to mercy'. The judge responded to this plea and sentenced Lewis to only nine months in prison.[89]

Recidivists, conversely, were not shown much mercy and a previous conviction almost certainly led to a passage to Australia when transportation

---

[85] HT: 24 March 1849.
[86] HRO: Q/SR/142. HQS: Trinity, 26 June 1854 and HQS: Michaelmas, 16 October 1854.
[87] HRO: Q/SR/137. HQS: Michaelmas, 15 October 1849. HT: 20 October 1849.
[88] HRO: Q/SR/126. HQS: Epiphany 1838. HJ: 2 January 1839.
[89] HRO: Q/SR/127. HQS: Trinity, 1838. HJ: 11 July 1838.

was still an option, or to a lengthy gaol sentence when it was not. Two labourers named Beavan and Philips were convicted of stealing a wether sheep from out of a field at Llanrouthal in 1850. Although they were equal partners in the crime they received very different sentences. While Philips was ordered to serve a year's imprisonment, Beavan, who had a previous conviction for felony, was transported for a period of ten years.[90] Similarly, in 1849, Richard Morris, a 37-year-old labourer with a criminal past, was sentenced to seven years' transportation for stealing a ewe at Llangarren while his partner-in-crime, Samuel Saunders, was sentenced to twelve months' hard labour, 'it being his first offence'.[91] The mention of a previous conviction when the judge or magistrate was sentencing was usually followed by a transportation order for the offender.

Sentencing could also be uncompromising during periods when sheep-stealing was endemic. The *Hereford Journal* reported that sheep-stealing was 'very prevalent' in the Kington area in 1840, around Whitney in 1841 and at Eaton Bishop in 1847.[92] In addition, in 1847, 'upwards of fifty sheep and lambs' were stolen from around the Huntington area within a ten-month period and, in 1848, the farmers around Bromyard had 'half a dozen sheep . . . slaughtered within the last five months'.[93] It seems likely that outbreaks of sustained sheep-stealing reflected depressed local conditions and were short-lived. Yet in other areas sheep-stealing was a persistent problem for the authorities and farmers alike. The most prominent of these troubled areas was the countryside around Ross, particularly the area towards Whitchurch and the Doward. Between 1840 and 1850 the pages of the local press were littered liberally with reports of sheep-stealing from this area. In March 1840 the *Hereford Journal* pointed out that sheep-stealing 'was on the increase in the neighbourhood of Ross' and reported in April and October that the crime still 'continues unabated' around Whitchurch. In November of the same year the *Journal* 'regret(ed) to announce the frequent occurrence of this crime in that area'.[94]

To be apprehended and convicted during an epidemic of sheep-stealing was to invite a maximum sentence. In 1838, John Stringer, a shoemaker, and Thomas Jones, a flax-dresser, following their convictions for stealing a ram at Little Dewchurch, were told by the judge that 'severe examples must be made'. They were both transported for ten and fourteen years respectively.[95] Similarly, the magistrate at the 1841 Epiphany Sessions told a convicted sheep-stealer, William Page from Moreton on Lugg, that:

90 HRO: Q/SR/138. HQS: *Trinity, 1 July 1850.*
91 HRO: Q/SR/137. HQS: *15 October 1849.*
92 *HJ: 28 October 1840, 8 September 1841 and 27 December 1843.*
93 *HJ: 5 May 1847 and 20 October 1848.*
94 *HJ: 18 March 1840, 15 April 1840, 21 October 1840 and 11 November 1840.*
95 HRO: Q/SR/125. HQS: *Trinity 1838. Hereford Journal, 11 July 1838.*

The crime of sheep-stealing (is) so much on the increase . . . that it was necessary offences of that nature should be visited with very heavy punishments; he therefore felt it his duty to sentence him to 15 years transportation.[96]

While Page, Stringer and Jones may have felt themselves unlucky they should have been consoled by remembering that, ten years earlier, judges who wanted to make an example of sheep-stealers left them for the hangman.

As Figure 4.4 shows, between 1833 and 1860 the peak years for sheep-stealing were undoubtedly 1849 and 1850. It is clear that sheep-stealing continued to be a way of keeping off the overseer's books. Indeed, the crime only began to wane as the agricultural labourer's position improved during the 1850s.

Moreover, sheep-stealing during the period 1833 to 1860, similar to the earlier period, was still carried out predominately in the winter and spring months, when agricultural employment was hardest to find and sheep-stealing activity corresponded with the lack of employment opportunities. As Figure 4.5 shows, the farmer's sheep were most at risk between January and June, and safest during the harvest summer months when employment was more plentiful. Many of the county's farmers were aware that their sheep were more vulnerable during the winter and spring months. David

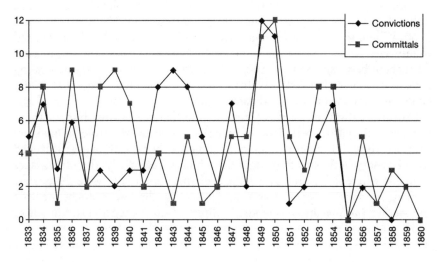

Figure 4.4 Committals and convictions for sheep-stealing, 1833–60[97]

[96] HRO: Q/SR/130. HQS: *Epiphany 1841*. HJ: *5 January 1842*.
[97] Details of convictions taken from HJ: *c.1833–49*, HT: *c.1839–49* and HRO: Q/SMc/1. *Calendar of Prisoners, c.1849–60*.

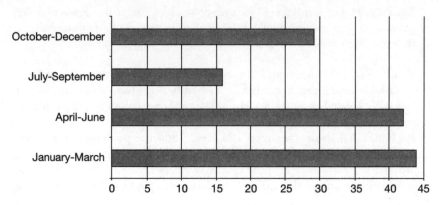

Figure 4.5 Committals to Hereford Gaol on suspicion of sheep-stealing, by season, 1833–60[98]

Bridgewater, a farmer of the Boatside, near Hay, had two fat wether sheep slaughtered and stolen in 1841, causing the *Hereford Journal* to comment that 'it is remarkable that for two or three years past, the month of February has been selected for deprivations of the above kind'.[99] The theft of single sheep, as already discussed in the section above, also suggests that sheep-stealers continued to resort to theft to solve their immediate problems of subsistence rather than in an attempt to get rich. This trend continued between 1833 and 1860. Where the theft of a single sheep between 1800 and 1832 amounted to just over 70 per cent of the total convictions, this figure rose to just over 78 per cent between 1833 and 1860. The motivation, then, for sheep-stealing appears to have changed very little and the evidence suggests that the economic motivation remained paramount.

Although the theft of sheep remained a defence against hunger there were, as in the earlier period, occasional sheep-stealers who stole for financial gain. Rustling did go on throughout the period but the thieves still lacked the necessary outlets to dispose of their booty. Essentially, the only places available where stolen sheep could be exchanged for money were the nearest market, the local butcher or another farmer. To dispose of stolen sheep at the market was precarious. George Philips attracted attention to himself in 1838, and was later arrested, for attempting to sell six sheep at Leominster market 'for less than they were worth'.[100] A similar fate befell Charles Higley

[98] Lists of committals to Hereford Gaol, c.1833–60, compiled from *HJ* and *HT*, c.1833–60 and HRO: C/SMc/1. *Calendar of Prisoners*, c.1849–60.

[99] *HJ: 24 February 1841*.

[100] *HJ: 19 December 1838*.

'after he tried to sell eleven sheep' for £3 2s at Hereford market in 1849.[101] Sheep were often marked by their owners and to attempt to sell a stolen sheep within the county was to invite detection. Victims, usually farmers, were often present at the very market where the illegal transaction was to take place.[102]

Rustling, as in the earlier period, was still the exception rather than the rule. Labourers occasionally did steal sheep to sell but it seems unlikely that the majority of the county's agricultural labour force had the resources to undertake such an enterprise. First, it would have been necessary to have access to some pasture, or at least an available piece of land, on which to keep the sheep until they could be sold. By the 1830s the amount of land available to the agricultural labourer, apart from his cottage garden, was minimal and diminished still further as the century wore on. The problem for a rustler was not so much how to steal the sheep but where to keep them until he could dispose of them. A farmer who turned his hand to sheep-stealing would have had the necessary land. The evidence, however, suggests that farmers in Herefordshire rarely stole sheep. Between 1849 and 1860 only four farmers were charged with sheep-stealing and, significantly, they were all either acquitted by juries or had the charges against them dropped.[103] They all simply argued that they had taken in strays.

Butchers would also have a piece of land at the back of their premises but few appeared in court charged with sheep-stealing. Between 1833 and 1860 there were only seven committals and four convictions of butchers dishonestly handling stolen sheep.[104] Butchers could have been the sheep-stealers' natural 'fence'. Not only did they have the means of keeping stolen sheep but they were also a legitimate outlet to dispose of the meat, carcass, wool and fat. Their omission from the court records is surprising. Far from being the 'receivers of stolen goods' they occasionally informed the authorities when they were being offered stolen sheep. For example, in 1834, a Hereford butcher informed on a 'a man from Clun' (Shropshire) after he was invited to buy some sheep 'at a price under their value'.[105] Moreover, butchers themselves were occasionally victims of sheep-stealers. In 1840 Charles Williams, a butcher near Tenbury, had a 'fat sheep' stolen, while in 1845 'a Welsh sheep' was stolen from Mr Brown, a butcher from Bromyard.[106]

---

[101] HT: 2 June 1849.

[102] Even sheep stolen in Herefordshire were recognized in another county. In 1840 Miss Powell of Focle Farm, Upton Bishop, had nine sheep stolen. They turned up a week later at Gloucester Market 'where they were being offered for sale'. The thief, however, had absconded. See HJ: 25 March 1840.

[103] HRO: Q/SMc/1. Calendar of Prisoners, c.1849–60.

[104] HJ and HT, c.1833–48. See also the case of Frederick Barnes above.

[105] HJ: 9 July 1834.

[106] HJ: 18 November 1840 and 12 November 1845.

The motivation for sheep-stealing, and the situation of the thief, changed very little throughout this later period. In short, the motivation continued to be hunger, and the thief was usually a labourer. Indeed, between 1849 and 1860 of the forty-one convictions for sheep-stealing, thirty-five (85.36 per cent) of the offenders were listed as labourers and the remaining six were made up of two butchers, two shoemakers, a mason and a wheelwright.[107] Although the term 'labourer' covered an abundance of lowly paid work in Herefordshire it was generally used in relation to the agricultural labourer. Agriculture, even at the end of the period, was still the major employer in the county and remained so until the mid-twentieth century.[108]

Although underemployed and unemployed labourers were the most likely to resort to sheep-stealing there is evidence to suggest that, after the mid-1830s, the crime was more likely than before to be dominated by organized gangs. The local press, when reporting sheep-stealing by the mid-1830s, referred to gangs stealing for resale, rather than hard-pressed individuals looking to put a meal on the table. The *Hereford Journal* reported in 1838 that 'vast numbers of sheep' were being stolen around the Tarrington and Dormington area of the county, and that it was the work of a gang of 'thirty to forty individuals (who) were regularly engaged in these deprivations'.[109] In December 1844 the same newspaper reported that 'a gang of sheep-stealers' stole a yearling ewe at Livers Ocle Farm, and went on to claim that 'upwards of forty sheep (have been) lost in this, and the surrounding parishes, within the last twelve months', suggesting the existence of a large-scale organized network of sheep-thieves in the area.[110] In 1849, the *Hereford Times* reported that a 'gang of sheep-stealers' operating out of the Doward and Whitchurch area, south of Ross, were taking 'one or more sheep' a week within a three-mile radius of Whitchurch.[111]

The local newspapers, and perhaps the sheep-owners themselves, saw the county's sheep-stealers as professional thieves supplying dishonest butchers with black-market mutton. The reality, however, as we have seen above, was very different. Wholesale sheep-theft, or rustling, was relatively rare, not least because the opportunities for resale were so limited. While the courtroom revelations of gang members apprehended over the period suggests that their activities showed a degree of organization, their actions suggest that consumption rather than profit remained the priority. The Whitchurch

---

[107] Figures taken from HRO: Q/SMc/1. *Calendar of Prisoners, c.1849–60.*
[108] Even as recently as 1951 the Census revealed that 22.9 per cent of Herefordshire's population were engaged in agriculture. See Salt, *The Economic Geography of Herefordshire.* 164.
[109] *HJ: 28 March 1838.*
[110] *HJ: 18 December 1844.*
[111] *HT: 4 August 1849.*

and Dormington gangs, for example, stole single sheep rather than several at a time. Moreover, the sheep were usually slaughtered and butchered *in situ*, again suggesting immediate consumption. At no point did either of the gangs attempt to drive the sheep away. The men who were arrested, either for stealing or for receiving sheep, from the 'thirty to forty' strong Dormington gang were acquitted for lack of evidence. The court case suggested that the men – three labourers, William and Robert Jones, and James Downes – were merely victims of a rare informer who wished to capitalize upon the offer of a £20 reward.[112] Admittedly the Jones brothers had, at some point, taken part in sheep-stealing; nevertheless, the sheepskin found at the bottom of a well near their cottage could not be identified and the joints of mutton hung up in their kitchen merely endorsed the view that they stole for food.

The Whitchurch gang, made up of six members, two of whom were released for lack of evidence, were also labourers who took to sheep-stealing as, and when, needed. George Davies, Edward Hargest and Charles James were found guilty of stealing a sheep from Mr Thomas Addis of Old Court Farm and were each transported for seven years, and John Watson was sentenced to twelve months' hard labour for receiving the same.[113] Again, single sheep were slain and butchered on the spot for food rather than being driven away to sell at a local market.

Sheep-stealing gangs were marginally more prominent in this later period, but there is still not much evidence to suggest that gang members stole other than to provide food. Arguably, gangs of professional sheep-stealers were not as common as the local press led people to believe. Indeed, when we examine the available details of these reported gangs we can see that the editors of the contemporary local press were in the grip of their own 'moral panic', or, perhaps, they were in the process of manufacturing one. Victorian commentators saw crime, perhaps somewhat conveniently, as the domain of organized gangs whose members were made up of a distinct criminal class.[114] During periods of sustained sheep-thefts, or indeed other types of crime, it was easier to write in these terms as a way of explaining away the rise in rural crime.[115] Although some journalists did see a link between crime and the availability of rural employment they were the exceptions to the rule.[116] To blame the rise of rural crime in Herefordshire on organized gangs served two purposes. First, editors could not put sustained sheep-stealing activity down to low wages, unemployment or inadequate poor relief. While these

---

[112] HRO: BG/11/8/9. *Lent Assize 1838. HJ: 28 March 1838.*
[113] HRO: Q/SR/137. *HQS: Michaelmas, 15 October 1849. HJ: 20 October 1849.*
[114] See e.g. Davis, 'The Garotting Panic of 1862' in Gatrell, *Crime and the Law.*
[115] See also Chapter 5 concerning crop- and wood-theft.
[116] See Chapter 3 for the comments of magistrates and contemporary commentators.

may have been the reasons for the growing incidence of sheep-stealing the editors of local newspapers would have alienated the greater part of their readership to state as much. In short, to point to low wages and unemployment as the cause of crime was to lay the blame at the farmers' feet and to point to inadequate poor relief was to blame the ratepayers. As farmers and ratepayers probably made up a substantial proportion of the county's newspaper readers, to offer such an explanation would have been economic folly.

Second, using the growing incidence of sheep-stealing to create a moral panic had political advantages for the pro-police section of the community. By hinting that criminal gangs existed in some parts of the county the newspapers were able to suggest that certain areas were lawless, and thus in need of policing. As we have seen in Chapter 3, a growing section of Herefordshire's 'respectable' society in the 1830s and 1840s favoured a professional police force. The local newspapers generally endorsed this view. Reports of sheep-thefts in the *Hereford Times* were often followed by the editorial comment on the need for 'protection'.[117] While it is difficult to sustain an argument that the local press was in league with Herefordshire's Whig politicians it is possible to contend that they endorsed the sentiments of the pro-police lobby.

By the 1840s, policing, in one form or another, did cover much of the county. Superintendents Colley and Adams from Ross and Hereford actively pursued sheep-stealers and brought them to justice. The Bromyard force alone, between 1844 and 1850, apprehended twenty-three sheep-stealers which in turn led to twenty-one convictions, fourteen of which resulted in transportation orders.[118] It is not surprising, therefore, that increasing police activity in the Herefordshire countryside pushed up the arrest and conviction rates for this particular crime. Moreover, the renewed interest between 1839 and 1842 in forming associations for the prosecution of felons (one of which was specifically formed to combat sheep-stealing) may have added to the conviction rates.[119]

Prosecution, however, was not left simply to the police and the associations. Many victims of sheep-stealing still attempted to discover the miscreants themselves. As in the period 1800 to 1832, the most frequent method employed for this purpose was an advertisement placed in the local press offering a reward for information as to the sheep's whereabouts, if missing, and the identity of the thief. Joseph Scudamore, a farmer from Pengethly, offered a reward of £10 in 1840 for information that might lead

---

[117] See e.g. HT: *24 February 1841*.

[118] 'Persons Apprehended Since the Appointment of the Superintendent Constable in the Bromyard District'. HJ: *5 March 1850*.

[119] For a full discussion of associations for the prosecution of felons see Chapter 3.

to the detection of a sheep-stealer who had taken one of his wether lambs.[120] In 1845 William Elliot, of the Brick House estate, Burghill, was also a victim of sheep-stealers and offered a £20 reward following a similar theft.[121] While James Gregg, of Ledbury, offered a mere £5 in 1847 for the recovery of 'a yearling sheep' that was 'stolen out of a meadow near the town.'[122] The size of the reward was often not stated, but in such cases it was always reported as being 'handsome' or 'generous'. Associations also offered financial rewards, although they were often well below the sums offered by individuals. The Herefordshire Association for the Prosecution of Felons, for example, paid only £2 to informants following the conviction of a sheep-stealer, though members were permitted to hire two men, 'proper persons at reasonable expense' to pursue stolen beasts.[123]

As in the earlier period, it is difficult to ascertain the effect of financial inducements to informers between 1833 and 1860. The frequent appearance of such advertisements suggests that victims did believe that the offer of rewards brought sheep-stealers to the courts. Research, however, has failed to discover many instances where sheep-stealers were turned in for a reward. Indeed, the reverse was very often true. In 1839 five sovereigns were offered, via the pages of the *Hereford Journal*, for information leading to the discovery of the 'whereabouts of James Beavan' who was suspected of stealing sheep.[124] Beavan, however, was still 'at large' five months later, although it was 'known' he was still in the county.[125] In 1845 Mr Gibbs, a farmer from Munsley, was reported to be disappointed that the offer of a 'handsome reward' for the apprehension of the thieves who stole 'a fat wether' was not taken up.[126] There is also some evidence to suggest that the police themselves thought that reward advertisements were not only futile but also that they alerted the thieves, making them aware that the farmer had discovered a sheep was missing. In 1839 the *Hereford Journal* informed the victims of sheep-stealers that:

> We suggest it would be better for the farmers to give information to Colley, (the Ross) police officer, in the first instance of any loss, before bills are issued offering rewards, which only give the offenders an opportunity of removing the property.[127]

---

[120] *HJ: 11 November 1840.*
[121] *HJ: 18 June 1845.*
[122] *HJ: 20 January 1847.*
[123] HCL: Pamphlets Vol. 21. *Articles of the County of Herefordshire Association for the Discovery and Prosecution of Felons and Other Offenders (1825).*
[124] *HJ: 20 February 1839.*
[125] *HJ: 10 July 1839.*
[126] *HJ: 2 April 1845.*
[127] *HJ: 9 October 1839.*

The conviction rate for sheep-stealing between 1833 and 1860 rose after the repeal of the death penalty in 1832. That offenders no longer ran the risk of execution probably encouraged more prosecutions and also made juries less reluctant to convict. It is clear from the earlier period (1800 to 1832) that juries were often loath to find sheep-stealers guilty, especially if they could sense that the judge was in a hanging mood. Indeed, it was not unknown for juries to acquit a guilty man rather than see him hang for a crime motivated by hunger. Apart from the abhorrence many felt towards a law that hanged a man for stealing a sheep, farmers may also have believed that prosecution, under the statute of 1741, was precarious, not only for the defendant but also for the victim who could, before the reform of the criminal law, lose out financially. Although compassion may have played a part in the acquittal of a sheep-stealer at the expense of the victim, other factors contributed to a victim's willingness to prosecute. To prosecute with the possibility of a death sentence upon a man driven to steal because he was hungry might prejudice relations of the community in general. Bitterness and recrimination could follow a conviction and many may have chosen not to prosecute for this reason.

With the threat of the rope removed after 1832, and with the diminishing incidence of transportation by the mid- to late 1840s, victims may have been more inclined to prosecute. There was also an important change in procedure. Prior to 1842 sheep-stealing offences were tried at the Assize; after that date they were examined at Quarter Sessions. Prosecution became cheaper and sentences were less severe. Although transportation orders could still be handed out to those convicted of the crime, such punishments tended to be reserved for the more serious cases of rustling, for recidivists and for those of whom it was necessary to make examples. The change from the Assize to the Quarter Sessions meant that justice was placed upon a more domestic footing. This is not to suggest that the Quarter Sessions did not dispense the law in a solemn manner. What is noticeable, however, is that when sheep-stealing cases began to appear at the Quarter Sessions chairmen began to take mitigating circumstances and previous character into account. This could not be done prior to 1832, and if a prisoner was found guilty the judge was restricted to a sentence of death or transportation. The net result was that sheep-stealers, after 1832, and more so after 1842, often received lighter sentences than the law made provision for. Furthermore, as a more efficient system for prosecutors to claim expenses evolved, enabling victims to be reimbursed regardless of the outcome of the trial, more and more sheep-stealers found themselves in the dock. The upshot of the changes in the criminal law, and its administration, was that victims of steep-stealing were more inclined to prosecute.[128]

---

[128] For a full discussion of the changes in the criminal law and its administration c.1800–60, see Chapter 3.

Despite an increase in policing, sheep-stealing continued unabated and there is evidence to suggest that as the detection techniques improved thieves became more artful. It was suggested by the *Hereford Journal* in 1839 that 'the increased cunning of sheep-stealers now renders the crime very difficult of detection'.[129] In 1840 the same newspaper noted that the cunning methods employed by sheep-stealers meant that 'in a great number of instances the thief is never detected',[130] while a year later the editor was astonished at the 'ingenuity of the robbers'.[131] In the majority of cases the vital piece of evidence that linked the thieves to the crime was the animal's skin. If a law-enforcement officer could match the skin to the butchered meat in the thief's possession a conviction was almost always assured. The skins of slaughtered and butchered sheep, therefore, were disposed of as a matter of urgency and often with imagination. Sheepskins were cut up into 'small pieces'.[132] They were also buried in coppices or under leaves, thrown into rivers and down wells or, indeed, anywhere they might not be immediately discovered.[133] As in the earlier period sheep-stealers could evade detection with a little aforethought. Not all sheep-stealers, however, were as cunning as the contemporary press suggested and some sheep-thefts were almost comic. It transpired at the 1835 Lent Assizes that one-legged Joseph Denton, who was charged with stealing a ewe sheep near Ross, left the trail of his wooden leg all the way to his cottage from the scene of the crime. He was transported for life.[134] In 1840 at Upper Sapey, a police officer arrested a labourer named Hartland after he tried to walk past him with the best part of a stolen sheep 'under his coat'. Hartland was also wanted in connection with another offence at Tenbury and was thus removed to Worcester Gaol.[135]

As in the earlier period the usual method employed by sheep-stealers was to slaughter the animal, butcher the best joints and leave the head, skin and entrails at the scene of the crime. The remains of sheep left scattered around the Herefordshire countryside continued to be an 'awful reminder of the power of the labourers'.[136] Carcasses of sheep continued to be left in

[129] *HJ: 22 May 1839*.

[130] *HJ: 5 August 1840*.

[131] *HJ: 24 February 1841*.

[132] *HJ: 11 December 1839*.

[133] As we have seen, William and Robert Jones were discovered to have had a sheepskin down their well, *HJ 28 March 1838*. The *HJ* reported, on 22 May 1839, that the skin from a stolen lamb, at Lugwardine, was found 'buried in a coppice' and the same newspaper reported on 11 November 1840, that the carcass of a sheep was discovered 'under a pile of leaves', while the *HJ of 8 September 1841* reported that the skin of a stolen sheep was discovered in the River Wye at Whitney.

[134] *HJ: Assize Intelligence, 18 March 1835*.

[135] *HJ: 18 November 1840*.

[136] Peacock, 'Village Radicalism'. 44.

prominent positions or hung up in trees for all to see. The Whitchurch gang of 1849, for example, slaughtered a sheep belonging to Mr Bright, a farmer of Bill Mill, and, after they had removed what they needed, they left 'the useless portions . . . hanging in a tree'.[137] The same gang, in the same year, were allegedly responsible for slaughtering a number of sheep apparently out of spite when it was reported that the shepherd of Mr Addis of Old Court had discovered 'a sheep with its throat cut, and nearly dead'.[138] Other sheep-stealers were even more brutal and it was not unknown for whole flocks of sheep to have had their throats cut, and there were even cases where sheep were butchered while still alive. Instances such as these cross over from sheep-stealing to animal-maiming however, and are dealt with elsewhere in this study.[139]

Sheep-stealing, even in this later period, continued to bear the hallmarks of protest and social criminality. The number of rural people who indulged in the crime during periods of economic and social hardship suggests that sheep-stealing was also seen as less than criminal. In addition, as in the earlier period, in certain remote areas of the county sheep-stealing was common-place and almost a way of life. The Doward/Whitchurch district south of Ross is the obvious example, and throughout this chapter the evidence has suggested that sheep in this area were taken as and when they were needed, regardless of the efforts made to halt the practice by the authorities. More-over, certain occupational groups still saw sheep-theft as a legitimate means of supplementing an income. Again, as in the earlier period, the bargees are the obvious example of an occupational group who did not necessarily see sheep-stealing as a particularly illegal act. Following the theft of a ram lamb at Whitney in 1841 the *Hereford Journal* observed:

> It is supposed some of the watermen who take their boats up as far as Whitney Bridge, for timber, are fond of mutton and lamb; for Mr M(onkhouse) receives a visit almost annually amongst his flocks generally being one or two minus after they have been 'kenned' by these midnight deprivators.[140]

The watermen who worked the River Wye and the canals in the county remained highly mobile and were still difficult to apprehend. Indeed, a year later Sir John Cotterell had 'a fine fat wether' slaughtered and butchered and although 'suspicion rested upon several bargemen . . . no positive proof (could be) obtained against any individual'.[141] They were notoriously difficult

---

[137] HT: 24 February 1849.

[138] HT: 5 May 1849.

[139] See Chapter 7 which discusses arson and animal-maiming.

[140] HJ: 8 September 1841.

[141] HJ: 23 March 1842.

to catch, and, perhaps because of the nature of their employment and their unregulated lives, they felt they were not bound by the same laws as other men. They were not prepared to give up this freedom lightly, as the following piece taken from the *Hereford Journal* shows.

> CAUTION – Three men with the appearance of navigators were seen . . . attempting to catch a sheep from a flock, at the Knapp Farm, Pixley, and on a man attempting to pursue the deprivators, he was attacked by a large dog, and compelled to give up the chase.[142]

Conclusion

Sheep-stealing in Herefordshire throughout the period was predominantly carried out as a defence against hunger. The motivation behind the thefts, the methods used to steal the sheep and the class of the criminal changed very little. The theft of single sheep continued to be a feature of the crime and this suggests that thefts of sheep were carried out for immediate consumption rather than for resale. Large-scale rustling, or the theft of sheep for resale, remained comparatively rare. Moreover, sheep-stealing increased during periods of economic hardship when unemployment was difficult to find, as in winter, during periods of agricultural depression, or when food prices were high. The crime and the committal rate increased and decreased correspondingly in relation to these factors. This view is endorsed further by the occupational class of the majority of those convicted. Where the court records exist, they show the sheep-stealer to be predominantly of the labouring class, the most vulnerable to changes in the rural economy.

From the early 1830s to 1850 convictions for sheep-stealing increased significantly. Again, the extent of the crime can be linked to economic factors; however, after 1832 prosecutions may have increased with the repeal of the death penalty for the crime and the guarantee that prosecutors would be reimbursed for the time spent pursuing a case through the courts. Moreover, after the mid-1830s the county's rural areas began to be policed, and while it took until the late 1850s before the whole county was protected by a constabulary force there can be little doubt that the new force contributed to the rising numbers of sheep-stealers apprehended and later convicted in the Herefordshire courts.

There is also some evidence to suggest that the crime was, between 1800 and 1860, a social crime; especially under certain economic. conditions,

---

[142] *HJ: 2 September 1840.* It has to be admitted that these particular 'navigators' may not have been bargees but railway workers. Nevertheless, railway navvies were seen as equally lawless. See David Brooke, 'The 'Lawless' Navvy: A Study of Crime Associated with Railway Building', *The Journal of Transport History*, Vol. 10 (1989).

within certain occupational groups and in certain areas of the county. The bargees and the Doward and Whitchurch communities, for example, seemed to have had little compunction about sheep-stealing and they slaughtered sheep as and when they needed to. In addition, the fact that the labouring poor stole sheep during times of economic hardship suggests that, similar to poaching, the criminal sought to convey a message of discontent. The heads and entrails of slaughtered sheep were more than a 'grim reminder' of the labourer's plight; they were also a symbol of social justice.

5

Criminal women, crop deprivators and crop-thieves

None of the rural crimes dealt with in this thesis are glamorous. Nevertheless, they may all be seen as assertive actions carried out as a defence against hunger or as an expression of discontent. The crimes of wood- and crop-theft, on the other hand, are often portrayed differently. Because of their petty nature these crimes are often seen as the acts of the very lowest economic stratum in rural society. Moreover, because of the frequency of female involvement in the crimes of wood- and crop-theft they have often been dismissed as acts that merely contributed to the domestic economy. This chapter, quite simply, seeks to reconsider the actions of the wood- and crop-thief. It argues that the perpetrators of these crimes, similar to the other rural crimes dealt with in this thesis, were as assertive as the sheep-stealer or the poacher.

Very little serious historical research has been carried out into the motivation, extent and nature of crop- and wood-theft. These two crimes, when compared to incendiarism or animal maiming, were trivial offences yet they are important if an attempt is to be made to reconstruct the 'experiences of the dispossessed and inarticulate' in Herefordshire during the first half of the nineteenth century.[1] Moreover, that these crimes were committed frequently by women gives this chapter the opportunity to discuss three underresearched areas of rural history: wood-theft, crop-theft and female criminality.

A historiography of these crimes is virtually non-existent. This is, in part, because of the petty nature of the crimes or, perhaps to quote Innes and Styles, it is because they 'lack the historiographically attractive, pro-topolitical associations of the social crimes'. They have argued further that research into such crimes is necessary, if only to discount them as social crimes, concluding that 'there exist no detailed studies of (the) petty larcenists . . . who made up the bulk of the business of the courts of Quarter Sessions and Assizes'.[2]

Wood-theft has attracted some attention, principally in the work of Bob Bushaway, who has focused on the 'customary use' rights of wood-gathering

---

[1] Innes and Styles, 'Crime Wave'. 382.
[2] Ibid. 397.

and the conflicts that ensued when they disappeared during the eighteenth and early nineteenth centuries.[3] Unfortunately, research had failed to uncover the existence of any such rights in Herefordshire during the late eighteenth century or in the period covered by this study. The taking of wood without the owner's permission was essentially illegal and any customary rights that may have existed were extinct, if not forgotten. Moreover, the gathering of wood was often regarded as a criminal act by landowners and farmers, and they frequently seemed only too eager to prosecute those who took wood, either from their hedges, woods or trees.

Similarly, crop-theft has attracted little attention from historians. Again, what studies do exist have centred on the death of customary rights and the continuation of a practice after it had been made illegal. The seminal piece of work in this area has come from Peter King.[4] King focused on the practice of 'gleaning' or 'leasing' which continued despite a late eighteenth-century court judgment clarifying the legal position in favour of the farmers.[5] In Herefordshire leasing continued well into the nineteenth century but by then it was clear what the legal position was. Presumably by this time the ability of the poor of a particular parish to lease depended upon the charity of the local farmers rather than on any right. Nevertheless, at the time of the 1834 Poor Law Report, leasing was still being practised at Credenhill, Llangarren, Lyonshall, Weobley and Whitchurch.[6] Although the last reference made to leasing by the Herefordshire local press was in 1836, where the inhabitants of St Martin's 'took the liberty of gleaning', it seems likely that it would have continued beyond that date. Essentially the availability of leasing for the poor of any particular parish depended upon a farmer's charitable disposition.[7]

As with other crimes, it is impossible to discover the true extent of wood- and crop-theft or wilful and malicious damage to hedges, fences, trees and farm produce. Those convicted were probably a fraction of the real figure. The fragmentary nature of the court records for Herefordshire also makes it difficult to discover the total convictions for these crimes between 1800 and 1860. For example, it was not until 1822 that petty convictions for wood-theft were returned to the Quarter Sessions. Convictions for crop-theft

---

[3] See Bushaway, 'Grovely, Grovely', and 'Custom to Crime', in Rule, *Outside the Law*.

[4] The relevant court case was *Steel vs Houghton* (1788). King, 'Gleaners and Farmers'. 117. See also Peter King, 'Customary Rights and Women's Earnings: The Importance of Gleaning to the Rural Labouring Poor, 1750–1850', *Economic History Review*, Vol. 44 (1991).

[5] Gleaning, more commonly known as leasing in Herefordshire, was the practice of picking up the fallen grain left in the fields after the harvest. The act of leasing was usually carried out by the local poor women and children and, particularly in times of economic hardship, was an often crucial aid to the well-being of the family over the winter months. See King, 'Rights and Women's Earnings'.

[6] BPP: *Poor Law Report 1834*: Part 1, Appendix B1, Irish University Press. 207–16.

[7] *HJ: 2 November 1836.*

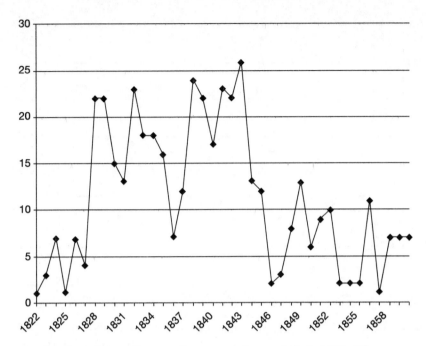

Figure 5.1 Petty Session Returns: Convictions for wood-theft, 1822–60[8]

only began to be returned after 1826 and conviction for wilful or malicious damage only appeared after 1836 (see Figures 5.1, 5.2 and 5.3).

The omission from the magistrate's returns for convictions of crop-theft prior to 1826 suggests that offenders had either been charged under another heading or that the convictions had not been returned. Prior to 1826 wood- and crop-thieves were tried before JPs but justices were not duty-bound to retain their records.[9] Despite this, some evidence of wood- and crop-thieves appearing before local justices has survived prior to 1822. In 1809 the *Hereford Journal* recorded that Elizabeth Bishop had been sent to the House of Correction for one month for stealing turnips and, a year later, the sisters Silvia and Ann Jones, in company with Hester Adams, received a similar sentence for a similar crime committed at Walford.[10] A surviving magistrate's notebook, c.1810–11, shows that Jane Ashley and Mary Wilcox were fined 2s 6d each by the local magistrate for stealing kindling 'out of Riggs Wood' in 1811.[11] These crimes were unremarkable but the fact that they do not appear

[8] HRO: Q/CM/4. *Petty Session Returns: Convictions, 1822–51* and HRO: Q/CE/1. *Petty Session Returns, c1852–60*.
[9] See Chapter 6.
[10] *HJ: 29 November 1809* and *12 December 1810*.
[11] HRO: AF/67. *Minute Book of Magistrates Meetings: Wormlow Hundred, c.1810–1811*.

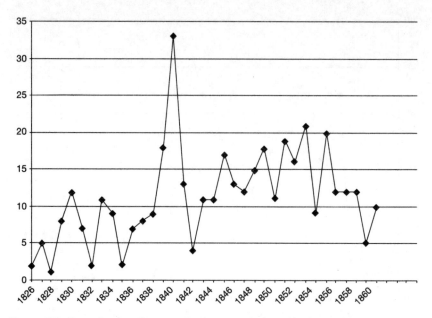

Figure 5.2 Petty Session Returns: Convictions for crop-theft, 1826–60

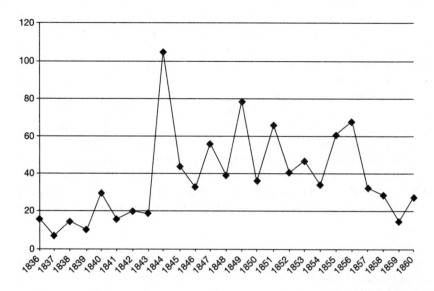

Figure 5.3 Petty Session Returns: Convictions for wilful or malicious damage, 1836–60

upon the available lists of Quarter Session convictions with any frequency suggests that they were tried and sentenced by a magistrate dispensing 'drawing-room justice'. While it may have been common for crop-plunderers and wood-thieves to be convicted by a JP, there is also evidence to suggest that prosecutions were brought under the charge of trespass. This charge, however, was utilized by prosecutors to punish several rural crimes. As the chapter concerning the Game Laws will illustrate, a charge of trespass was often brought against poachers, or, more specifically, poachers who were apprehended without any game in their possession. Wood- and crop-thieves were also prosecuted under the laws of trespass, presumably because they were apprehended before they had committed any theft.

Although the law concerning the prosecution for wood-theft was confusing, it was clarified for both criminal and victim in 1820. The object of the Malicious Trespass Act was the 'summary Punishment, in certain Cases, of Persons wilfully or maliciously damaging or committing Trespasses on public or private Property'.[12] Under this law those caught causing 'malicious injury' to any 'building, hedge, fence, tree, wood, or underwood' were liable to be convicted before a single JP. The penalty was to be, in the first instance, a fine not exceeding £5 or, if the offender could not pay, a gaol sentence not exceeding three months. There were exceptions to this summary justice. The suspected wood-thief could elect to go to trial at the Quarter Sessions and try for an acquittal. Moreover, if the prisoner had a previous conviction the case was treated as a felony, which was punishable by transportation. In these circumstances the offender was forced to face trial at the Quarter Sessions or Assizes. The *Hereford Journal* was convinced that the farmers of Herefordshire would find it 'a most useful Act'.[13] To evaluate its usefulness is difficult however, since we only have the figures from the returns presented to the Quarter Sessions to work from.

The victims of crop-theft also benefited from changes to the criminal law during this period. In 1825 an Act was passed stating that persons caught 'entering into any orchard, garden etc, and carrying away any trees, plants, shrubs fruit or vegetables' would be committing a felony, a crime punishable by transportation.[14] This piece of legislation, however, was seen by Peel as far too severe a punishment on garden thieves and remained in force for only a year. It was replaced by a modified Act which 'distinguished' between the damage and theft from gardens and orchards and that from 'open and inclosed ground *not* being a garden'; the offender was to be more harshly dealt

[12] Malicious Trespass Act. 1 Geo. 4, c. 56 (1820).

[13] *HJ: 23 August 1820.* Whereas the Hammonds felt this law was passed primarily to combat poaching, arguably more wood-thieves than poachers were prosecuted, in Herefordshire at least, under this Act. The Hammonds, *The Village Labourer.* 199.

[14] Protection of Property in Orchards, etc. Act. 6 Geo. 4, c. 127 (1825). See Radzinowicz, *English Criminal Law*, Vol. 1. 585.

with if the offence occurred in the former.[15] The editor of the *Hereford Journal* clearly felt that this Act was as important as the 1820 Malicious Trespass Act was to wood-thieves and printed the details of the legislation as a warning to would-be crop thieves:

> Caution – By an Act of Parliament in the Forty Second year of his late Majesty it is enacted that 'if any person shall steal, take away, willfully or maliciously pull up, injure or destroy any turnip, potatoes, cabbages, parsnips, beans, peas or carrots growing in any garden, orchard or lands or grounds, open or inclosed, he or they (will) forfeit twenty shillings over the value of the property, or be committed to hard labour not exceeding two months'.[16]

The revised legislation of 1826 also distinguished between first offenders and those with a previous conviction. While first offenders could expect a hefty fine or a period in gaol, second offenders could expect more draconian treatment. A second offence was to be treated as felony and the convicted crop-thief could expect a transportation order of up to seven years, or two years in gaol, with or without hard labour and to be whipped up to three times, either privately or publicly. The Act, however, did have several clauses which dictated how it was to be administered. Section 68, for example, empowered a JP to discharge offenders summarily convicted after paying compensation for damages and costs and section 72 enabled the offender to appeal to the court of Quarter Sessions if they were not 'amenable to justice'.[17]

Legislation to protect farmers did not end with these two Acts. Presumably, to be sure of a conviction under the Acts of 1820 and 1826, proof was needed that the offender intended to steal the crops or wood. To witness the offender dig up or pick the crops, or break the fence, hedge or whatever was not enough. It was necessary to catch the miscreant actually taking the proceeds of the theft off the victim's property. This was seen as a loophole that needed to be closed and led to the passing of the 'Lord Lansdowne Act' of 1827.[18] Section 24 of this Act, as the *Hereford Journal* indicated, was especially important. It made provision that:

> If any person shall wilfully or maliciously commit any damage, injury, or spoil to, or upon any real or personal property whatever, either of a public or private nature, for which no remedy or punishment is herein before provided, every such person

---

[15] Ibid.

[16] *HJ: 26 July 1826.*

[17] Section 68 was, according to Radzinowicz, intended to deal with young offenders. However, it is clear that this clause was adopted by the local magistracy to deal with a wider range of offenders, primarily the poor. Radzinowicz, *English Criminal Law, Vol. 1.* 586.

[18] Indemnity Act. 7 & 8 Geo. 4, c. 30 (1827).

being convicted thereof before a Justice of the Peace, shall forfeit and pay such sum of money as shall appear to the Justice to be a reasonable compensation for the damage, injury, or spoil so committed, not exceeding the sum of twenty pounds.[19]

Effectively, after 1827, all the loopholes were closed and the crop- or wood-thief could be prosecuted for theft, wilful and malicious damage, or trespass. Indeed, from the figures given above, it is possible to see the changes in legislation reflected by the different charges brought by the prosecution. Although the purpose of these changes was to empower local JPs to hand out summary convictions it is possible that they had the opposite effect. Some offenders were unwilling to accept 'summary justice', as Peel had hoped, and, as a result, they found themselves at the Quarter Sessions. Susan Williams in 1840, for example, claimed that she was innocent of 'breaking a fence' and stealing a 'stick' when she appeared before a magistrate at Hereford's Guildhall.[20] As a result she appeared at the next Quarter Sessions.[21] While the court records do not reveal how many offenders refused summary justice, either because they believed that they were innocent or because they felt that a higher court was more likely to acquit, we have to accept that some did. Moreover, it is impossible to discover how many wood- and crop-thieves appeared at the Quarter Sessions because they had previous convictions. Possibly, the very legislation that was passed to free the higher courts of petty offenders, by giving justices more summary powers, led to more cases appearing at the Quarter Sessions than had previously been the case.

The Criminal Justice Act of 1855 attempted to simplify the process of prosecution further.[22] Again it was an Act which attempted to give summary powers to JPs. Giving them the opportunity to pass sentence on those who stole property, under the value of 5s and over 5s if the accused pleaded guilty, the Act was a further attempt to encourage victims to prosecute. Despite this attempt at rationalization the accused could still face the Quarter Sessions if they pleaded 'Not guilty' or refused summary judgment. These changes to the way the criminal law was administered were designed to aid all victims of petty crime and not only the victims of wood- and crop-theft. Summary justice dispensed by a local magistrate was, after all, far less expensive for victims than an appearance at a higher court. Indeed, it may well have been the very cost of court appearances that encouraged offenders to plead 'Not guilty' or to refuse a summary judgment and discouraged victims from pursuing a case. It could be argued that victims of crime, even as late as the 1850s, still found prosecution at a higher court to be a major financial risk.

---

[19] HJ: 3 February 1841.
[20] HJ: 23 December 1840.
[21] HRO: Q/SR/129. HQS: Epiphany, 6 January 1841.
[22] 18 & 19 Vict, cc. 126 (1855).

Moreover, a prosecuting farmer may have made himself vulnerable to revenge attacks. Following an incendiary attack on a farm at Whitchurch in 1855, the *Hereford Journal* observed that the farmer:

> has been subject to a series of petty robberies for the last two years, but though individually small collectively amounted to a good round sum, and it is supposed that because he has put the law in force against some of the offenders on several occasions, he is persecuted in the most ruthless and vindictive manner.[23]

It may also be pertinent to note that, in many cases, prosecutions merely served to add to the burden of the county's ratepayers by forcing whole families into the workhouse by sentencing the mother or father to gaol. Prosecutions were usually brought by farmers and landowners driven to exasperation by continual plundering. Even so, they had to weigh the broader financial consequences against the benefits that might be gained from making the occasional example.

Wood- and crop-theft were probably the most extensively committed crimes of all in the English countryside and were not confined to Herefordshire alone. The Rector of a Dorsetshire village, writing to a Poor Law Commissioner in 1843, commented that:

> As to the crimes most common amongst the class we have been considering (the agricultural labourer and his family), wood-stealing is the most common overt act of crime they commit: it is practiced in some districts to an immense extent by women and young children. The boys at an early age but too often take to turnip-stealing and poaching.[24]

In Herefordshire wood of all descriptions was stolen. From hedges, coppices, fences, woods and hop yards 'wood plunderers' gathered the materials necessary for kindling, fires and repairs. Fences and hedges were particularly prone to attack probably because they bordered lanes, roads and fields. Hop yards were also highly vulnerable; hop poles made ideal logs and, once transported home, could soon be sawn off to the appropriate size. Another source were the local coppices and woods, especially after a period of windy weather when dead wood was often blown to the ground. Quite often wood thieves did not confine their activities to the gathering of dead wood but cut down living branches. Occasionally whole trees were sawn down. For example, in 1847, Wigmore Petty Sessions fined William Pugh,

---

[23] *HJ: 13 June 1855.* See also Chapter 7.

[24] Letter from the Hon. and Rev S. Godolphin Osborne, Rector of Bryanston-Cum-Durweston, Dorsetshire, to Alfred Austin Esq., Assistant Poor Law Commissioner, *Reports of Special Assistant Poor Law Commissioners on the Employment of Women and Children in Agriculture (1843)*, Cass Library of British Parliamentary Papers, Frank Cass, London (1968). 75.

a labourer of Lingen, a total of £1 7s 6d for 'cutting and carrying away two young ash trees',[25] while Thomas Cole was 'charged with wilful and malicious damage by cutting down a growing tree' and fined a total of 15s 6d in 1849.[26]

Although coal, as an alternative fuel, was widely available, it was often too expensive for many of the rural poor. Duncumb, writing in 1813, argued that the price of coal in Herefordshire was 'very high' due to the distance it had to be shipped down the River Wye from Wales and the Forest of Dean. He noted that the price had risen by 7s per ton between 1806 and 1813, to £1 11s per ton, and that a further 3s or 4s per ton could be added if it was transported into the county's hinterland.[27] Wood was used by all sections of the community and not just by the rural poor. The Berringtons of Bishopstone, for example, reportedly burnt a whole mature tree each week in their hall fireplace.[28] While the majority of the rural population were probably a great deal more economical than the Berringtons they still needed fuel. Although firewood could be bought, and bought relatively cheaply, buying faggots was yet another drain on a labouring family's already stretched resources. A gardener, in giving evidence to the Poor Law Commission in 1843, claimed that 'wood is the common fuel among the poor; the best faggots cost 32s per hundred; my fuel has cost me nearly £3 this year'.[29] As more and more areas of the Herefordshire countryside became closed to the rural poor more and more people fell foul of the law in gathering this basic material. Although coal was expensive, a free alternative lay all around them and to search the lanes and roads for 'windfalls' was a legitimate occupation. Lawbreakers were essentially those who left the public highways and trespassed or ripped wood from the roadside hedges. However, the frequency with which this crime was committed suggests that it was not generally viewed by the rural labouring community as a particularly criminal act.

That stolen wood was predominantly used for warmth is clear. Indeed, the peak months for wood-theft were also the coldest, namely the period October to April, and 68.72 per cent of all petty session convictions for wood-theft between 1822 and 1860 were recorded at the Epiphany and Easter sittings (see Figure 5.4).

Undoubtedly the extent of available employment, wage rates and food prices were factors; however, the winter weather played a prominent role in determining the extent of wood-theft. This argument is based upon the evidence of the court records which illustrate that the peak years for wood-

---

[25] HJ: 21 April 1847.
[26] HT: 10 November 1849.
[27] Duncumb, 'General View' (1813). 140–1. Moreover, the Wye was a very unreliable river for such traffic. Prone, as it was, to low levels in the summer and floods in the winter, transported coal from Wales and the Forest of Dean was both costly and unreliable.
[28] Salt, Economic Geography of Herefordshire. 171.
[29] Dispositions: Edward Norris, gardener. The Employment of Women and Children. 204.

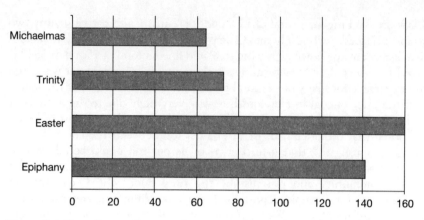

Figure 5.4 Petty Session Returns: Convictions for wood-theft, by session, 1822– 60[30]

theft did not correspond with the peak years of agricultural distress. Thus if wood-theft was linked to economic factors alone we would expect to see a significant rise in the numbers of cases reaching the courts in 1830 to 1831, 1844 and 1849 to 1850. This, however, was not the case. 1830 and 1844, for example, saw only fifteen and thirteen convictions, respectively. The peak years for wood-theft were 1843 with twenty-six convictions, 1838 with twenty-four and 1832 and 1841 each with twenty-three convictions. Although idleness was an ever-present threat throughout the period, these years were not especially notable for unemployment. It has been impossible to establish if the winters of these years were particularly harsh, but the fact that they do not peak along with other property crimes suggests that the winter weather may have been an important factor.

Similarly the crime of crop-theft peaked at certain times of the year. Whereas the theft of wood was linked to the severity of the weather the theft of crops was linked to the months in which they were ready to be harvested. The yearly convictions and committals to the County Gaol for this crime began in July with the apprehension of pea- and bean-thieves. The next two months saw grain- and potato-thefts, then in September, as the orchard fruit began to ripen, apple- and pear-thefts began to be committed. Nut-thieves, often boys and girls, followed, and finally the turnip- and swede-thieves took their place to grace the petty sessions. It is almost possible to chart the various harvests with the types of theft taking place. As Figure 5.5 shows, the majority of crop-thefts were carried out between July and the autumn months; thus the bulk of crop-theft convictions were recorded at the Michaelmas and Epiphany Sessions.

[30] HRO: Q/CM/4. *Petty Session Returns: Convictions, c1822–51* and HRO: Q/CE/1. *Petty Session Returns: Convictions, c1852–60.*

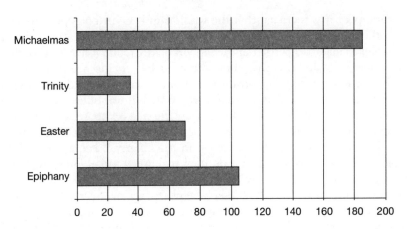

Figure 5.5 Petty Session Returns: Convictions for crop-theft, by session, 1826–60[31]

Of all the rural crimes dealt with in this thesis female participation was at its highest in the theft of wood and crops. The reasons for women's involvement in these particular crimes, above any other, are clear. Women, employed during the harvest months, had more opportunity to steal the farmers' crops and, when out collecting firewood for the home, may have been tempted by the farmers' hedges, rather than legitimately collecting windfalls. During the period 1822 to 1850 women made up over 44 per cent of all convicted wood-thieves and nearly 49 per cent of all crop-thieves. Moreover, women also accounted for over 31 per cent of those convicted of wilful and malicious damage and nearly 20 per cent of all trespass convictions. Women, then, in certain crimes and under certain conditions, were especially active.

The proceeds from this type of crime were almost certainly destined for the family table or fireplace and they were a contribution to the domestic economy. The paltry amounts of crops and hedge wood taken indicate that what had been stolen was destined for immediate consumption rather than for resale. Indeed, the only person uncovered by research who made a living out of stealing wood was a woman named Ann Green who, the *Hereford Journal* claimed, 'sells wood about Ross for her living, and destroys farmers property for that purpose'.[32]

The current historiography concerning rural women and work shows clearly that they were not unused to contributing to the domestic economy by exploiting any available seasonal and part-time employment.[33] Indeed, for

---

[31] HRO: Q/CM/4. *Petty Session Returns: Convictions, c1822–51* and HRO: Q/CE/1. *Petty Session Returns, c1852–60.*

[32] *HJ: 14 August 1839.*

[33] The historiography of rural women and work is now quite extensive. See e.g. Ivy

the rural poor it was crucial that the whole family contributed, in one way or another, to its survival. Moreover, spinsters and widows, who were without an employed male as a partner or the support of kin, found it necessary to find employment. Again this was often achieved by seeking a miscellaneous number of employment opportunities. Women, both married and single, found it necessary to undertake paid work; indeed, it was often crucial to do so if they were to avoid the clutches of the Union Workhouse. Both women and children were 'employed at the expense of the farmer, to collect, bind and stack the sheaves' at harvest time in the county.[34] Female and child employment was not, however, confined to harvest time and they could be employed in stone-picking and weeding while boys could earn a few pennies scaring crows.[35] In 1834 Joseph Stephens, the overseer of Credenhill, responded to a poor law questionnaire by claiming that women 'weeding corn, hay-making, picking stones, drawing turnips dressing meadows and Co' could earn 3s or 4s per week.[36] The anonymous respondent from Saint Weonards claimed that a child aged between 12 and 16 could earn between 2s 6d and 3s per week for the same work.[37] For a large section of the county's rural population life was maintained by adopting a scratch-as-scratch-can mentality. Indeed, Stephens argued that if a labourer's wife and two children, aged 11 and 14, could find employment throughout the year they could contribute an extra £20 to the family purse.[38] It is likely, however, that Stephens was being over-optimistic in suggesting that women and children could find enough casual work to see them through a twelve-month period without a break.

Pinchbeck, *Women Workers and the Industrial Revolution: 1750–1850*, Virago, London (1981 edn), Bridget Hill, *Women, Work and Sexual Politics in Eighteenth Century England*, University College London Press (1994), and K. Sayer, *Women of the Fields: Representations of Rural Women in the Nineteenth Century*, Manchester University Press, Manchester (1995). For women as contributors to the domestic economy see 'Agricultural Seasonal Unemployment, the Standard of Living, and Women's Work: 1690–1860', in K. D. M. Snell, *Annals of the Labouring Poor: Social Change and Agrarian England, c1660–1900*, Cambridge University Press, Cambridge (1987), Susan Wright, 'Holding up Half the Sky': Women and their Occupations in Eighteenth Century Ludlow', *Midland History*, Vol. 14 (1989), Sydna Ann Williams, 'Women's Employment in Nineteenth Century Anglesey', *Llafur*, Vol. 6 (1993) and Penelope Lane, 'Work on the Margins: Poor Women and the Informal Economy of Eighteenth and Early Nineteenth Century Leicestershire', *Midland History*, Vol. 22 (1997). For women and criminality see Lucia Zedner, *Women, Crime and Custody in Victorian England*, Clarendon Press, Oxford (1991).

[34] John Duncumb, 'General View'. 64.

[35] See Pamela Horn, 'The Employment of Children in Victorian Oxfordshire', *Midland History*, Vol. 4 (1977).

[36] *BPP*: 'Poor Law Report' (1834). 208.

[37] Ibid. 210.

[38] Ibid. 216.

The females of poor families were equals in many ways to the males in contributing to the economy of the household. They were certainly their equals when it came to the crimes of wood- and crop-theft. As Lane argues, for the poor rural woman the formal economy of legitimate employment often coexisted with the 'informal' economy of crime. We can only agree with Lane's argument that women were 'proactive' and perhaps as assertive as their male counterparts when faced with the harsh realities of poverty.[39] Although female participation was not commonplace in all rural crimes they were occasionally involved in criminal acts usually associated with males. Thus the occasional female sheep-stealer, incendiary or poacher appears in the court records and the contemporary newspapers. Women committed other crimes which were undoubtedly part of the informal economy. Herefordshire's criminal women bought and sold stolen goods. They stole from shops, from houses and from washing lines. Moreover, they passed 'base coin' and acted as decoys for their criminal partners. The list of convictions at the 1853 Michaelmas Quarter Sessions illustrates the crimes most typically committed by women. Ann Gwillim received three months' hard labour for housebreaking, Elizabeth Jenkins received six months for 'stealing wearing apparel' that was left to dry upon a hedge, Maria Derry got seven days for assaulting a neighbour and Ann Oliver was given a month's hard labour for stealing a pillow.[40] Women also specialized in certain crimes; for example, they stole milk from cows. In 1801 the sisters Margaret and Ann Bird were sentenced to a week's imprisonment and to be privately whipped for this crime.[41] Similarly in 1809 Ann Lambert was charged, and later convicted, of stealing milk from three cows at Kivernoll. This crime prompted the *Hereford Journal* to report that the crime 'has been a practice of late so frequent . . . that several proclamations have been made offering rewards'.[42] In 1832 Jane Poulton was sentenced to three months in gaol for 'milking the cows of Mr Ferrer' of Dilwyn.[43] In 1843 'Mary Pugh pleaded guilty to the charge of unlawfully milking a cow, belonging to Mr Sherwood, a farmer of Bodenham, and stealing five pints of milk'. Pugh received one month's hard labour.[44]

Women were also particularly prominent, throughout the period, in the theft, receipt and redistribution of stolen poultry in Herefordshire. Elizabeth Davis, a 47-year-old widow from Bridge Sollers, was found guilty of receiving 'six stolen geese, two cocks and one hen fowl', the property of

---

[39] Lane, 'Work on the Margins'. 87.
[40] HRO: Q/SR/141. *HQS: Michaelmas, 22 October 1853*.
[41] *HJ: 21 January 1801*.
[42] *HJ: 20 September 1809*. Lambert was sentenced at *HQS: Michaelmas, 1809* to seven days' imprisonment only, 'she being far advanced in pregnancy'.
[43] *HJ: 13 June 1832*.
[44] HRO: BG11/5/256. *Summer Assize: 31 July 1843*. See also *HJ: 2 August 1843*.

farmer James Evans, in 1850. Although she was sentenced to two months' imprisonment her sentence could not begin immediately. At the time of her trial she was already serving a sentence of one week for a summary conviction for damaging a fence.[45] Women did not only receive stolen fowl but also took them themselves. In 1853 Jane Evans and her daughter Charlotte, aged 15, stood trial for the theft of 'five fowls, the property of Joseph Wadley, of Much Marcle'. Although Charlotte was acquitted the mother, who pleaded guilty, was sentenced to nine months' gaol.[46] While the theft of fowls was relatively commonplace throughout the period the crime did peak in certain years. One such year was 1840 and the evidence suggests that fowl theft was quite organized and that women were actively involved in the crime. When Jane Vaughan was sentenced to two years' 'confinement and hard labour' for 'feloniously receiving eleven stolen fowls' the Chairman remarked:

> It is hoped that the offence of fowl stealing, which has been very common of late, and which, there is no doubt, has been much encouraged by the facilities afforded for the disposal of the stolen property, will be effectively checked by this conviction.[47]

At that time, Vaughan was seen as instrumental in the disposal of stolen poultry and it is clear that the county's magistrates saw her arrest, and subsequent prison sentence, as a triumph in the fight against this particular crime. If the gaoling of Vaughan was intended to act as a warning to other poultry-thieves, however, it had little effect. The theft of poultry continued unabated and between 1849 and 1860 some seventy-eight individuals faced the magistrates at the Hereford Quarter Session accused of the crime.[48]

It is little wonder that women made up a substantial proportion of the local prison population; they were subject to the same depressions in agriculture as their male counterparts. They too, as we have seen, were dependent on the farmer's prosperity as a means to improve the family purse. Indeed, they were more vulnerable, because their employment was almost always casual and more reliant upon seasonal work. Admittedly Table 5.1 embraces all crimes; from drunkenness to theft to infanticide. However, that women made up 24.27 per cent of prison inmates during the period shows that women were more than capable of committing criminal acts. Moreover, it is likely that many of the women were committed to gaol because they responded to depressed economic conditions, albeit in an illegal way.

[45] HRO: Q/SR/138. HQS: Easter, 18 March 1850.
[46] HRO: Q/SR/141. HQS: Easter, 18 March 1853.
[47] HRO: Q/SR/128. HQS: Easter, 2 April 1840. HJ: 8 April 1840.
[48] HRO: Q/SMc/1. Calendar of Prisoners, c1848–60.

Table 5.1 Sex of prisoners taken into custody at Hereford Gaol, 1841–52.[49]

Year	Male	Female	Female %
1841	325	138	29.80
1842	379	138	26.69
1843	419	138	24.77
1844	302	96	24.12
1845	274	94	25.54
1846	334	76	18.53
1847	341	98	22.32
1848	353	108	23.42
1849	289	113	28.10
1850	270	74	21.51
1851	273	97	26.21
1852	360	86	19.28

While men often aided women in crime, and vice versa, this does not necessarily mean that women played a subordinate role in criminal activity. Admittedly if a man and woman appeared in court together charged with the same offence it was he, rather than she, who received a custodial sentence. This was especially true if they were related by marriage. In such circumstances the prosecution quite often dismissed the wife, claiming that she was 'acting on her husband's orders'.[50] This seemingly generous gesture by the prosecution had a certain logic. First, prosecutions were more likely to receive a guilty verdict if the defendant was a male.[51] Admittedly women were found guilty and sent to gaol but there seemed to be a general reluctance to impose heavy sentences upon women. It is clear that female criminals were seen as different from their male counterparts. Using the contemporary press as an indicator of middle-class attitudes it is possible to see that criminal women were often assigned the role of 'fallen angel'. In short, women who broke the law often received more sympathy from both the press and the courts. The press, for example, used different adjectives to describe the women and men who found themselves in court. Women were often described as 'pitiful', 'wretched' or 'miserable' by both the *Hereford Journal* and the *Hereford Times*. Men, on the other hand, were usually described as 'evil disposed', 'malicious'

---

[49] 'Crime in Herefordshire': *HT 20: August 1853.*

[50] For an example of this see *HJ: 12 May 1847* when George and Margaret Preece were charged with stealing four ewes and three lambs. Margaret, who appeared in court 'pregnant with (a) child in arms', was dismissed. George was later sentenced to ten years' transportation. See HRO: Q/SR/135. *HQS: Trinity, 7 July 1847.*

[51] This was especially true if the crime was a capital offence. J. M. Beattie, *Crime and the Courts in England: 1669–1800*, Clarendon Press, Oxford (1986). 436.

and 'wanton'. Prostitutes were either tolerantly or sarcastically referred to by the press as 'fair damsels' or *'nymphs of the pave'*. This lack of malice towards prostitutes shows a certain degree of tolerance. Even Mary Gough who had, between 1833 and 1839, amassed thirty convictions for being 'drunk and disorderly' and for being a 'disorderly vagabond' in the streets of Hereford was not seen as a threat but as a figure of gossip and amusement.[52] Arguably, a man with the same reputation, and with previous convictions, would have received harsher treatment from both the courts and the press. He would have certainly been seen as 'incorrigible'. Moreover, he would have been subjected to lengthy spells in prison, whippings and perhaps, ultimately, transportation.

Second, it made economic sense to fine or gaol a man rather than a woman, especially if the partners in crime were married. To gaol a married woman with children may have forced the husband to put the children in the workhouse and the price of justice was to be paid by the ratepayer. Gaol the husband and the wife could, essentially, carry on as before; that is, taking casual, part-time work and looking after the home. It may still have been necessary for a woman to apply for aid while her husband was imprisoned but the cost to the authorities would be substantially less. Moreover, there was little logic in imposing relatively heavy fines upon women. They earned less and if they had small children they worked less and their employment opportunities were mostly of a temporary and seasonal nature. Large fines meant that offenders defaulted, and an inability to pay meant gaol. It seems likely that magistrates had little wish to fill the County Gaol with petty female criminals.

Contemporary 'respectable' society saw prostitutes as immoral and historians, with their twentieth-century sensibilities, see them as victims, or as 'a silent victim of social injustice'.[53] However, such women, especially if prostitution was resorted to as a means of survival, may have seen themselves as neither victims nor immoral but as women, assertively surviving in a hostile world. 'These women were not "dehumanized or defenseless vagabonds", but poor working women trying to survive.'[54] Prostitution was certainly commonplace in the county's market towns and there is some evidence to suggest that prostitutes and prostitution, as part of an informal economy, was an acceptable occupation to the labouring population. In 1849, for example, the villagers of Upton Bishop rioted to defend the 'honour' of Hannah Goode, a woman of 'indifferent character' who claimed she was sexually assaulted by two men.[55] Despite Goode's character, or perhaps her

---

[52] *HJ*: 6 March 1839.
[53] Linda Mahood, *The Magdalenes: Prostitution in the Nineteenth Century*, Routledge, London (1990). 42.
[54] Ibid.
[55] John Hammond and Peter Davis were summoned to answer the charges of Hannah

'trade', it is clear she was not treated as a criminal. Indeed, she drew support from all sections of her community. From the court records we can see that the rioters, twenty-seven in all, were charged, found guilty and each fined 2s 6d, and covered a cross-section of rural society from shopkeepers to tradesmen to labourers.[56] To what extent the rioters can be seen as merely exercising their own sort of rough justice or in defence of Goode's honour, despite her 'indifferent character', is open to conjecture. What is certain, however, is that Goode was not ostracized by the labouring population because she was a prostitute.

Criminals, motivated by circumstance, were responding positively to a negative situation. Lawbreakers were undoubtedly created through economic circumstances and as such they were the victims of trade depressions, changes in work practices, lowered wages or high prices. However, to use the term 'victim' is to suggest a certain fatalism or passivity on the part of the rural poor. Criminals were clearly not passive, neither were they fatalistic. They rose to the challenge of poverty by ensuring that life continued, even if this meant they had to resort to illegal means to do so. The unnamed man found in 1840 by the Leominster police dying 'apparently from want' was a passive victim to his circumstances.[57] The hundreds of men and women who appeared in the courts may have been victims but they were not passive victims because they were assertively trying to change their immediate circumstances. It could be argued that for every man or woman who curled up in their rural hovels and died from the cold or from hunger many more chose not to. Equally, for each person who turned up at the steps of the Union Workhouse seeking assistance more turned to theft in an effort not to.

Even in the workhouse men and women were not entirely demoralized and protests over conditions and food were not unusual. In the winter of 1844 to 1845 the harsh regime at Weobley Workhouse brought a refusal to work by some of its inmates. On 4 December twelve of Weobley's inmates were convicted of 'vagrancy for refusing to work as casual paupers' until conditions improved.[58] The prosecutions, however, did little to break the spirit of the protesters and by the following February a further fifteen men had been gaoled under the same charge.[59] Women were equally unafraid to give vent to their feelings. Mary Boulter, Ann Preece, Esther Smith, Tryphena Hope and Caroline Saunders were each sentenced to seven days' imprisonment in 1849, for 'refactory conduct and wilfully breaking the windows' at Ledbury

Goode for assaulting her on 20 June 1849, 'but the evidence not being at all creditable on the part of the complainant, the Justices, after examining the Constable of the parish as to the general character of Hannah Goode, who had stated she bore a very indifferent one, dismissed the case'. See HJ: 4 July 1849.
[56] HRO: Q/SR/137. HQS: Epiphany, 31 December 1849.
[57] HJ: 22 April 1840.
[58] HRO: Q/SR/132. HQS: Epiphany, 1844. HJ: 4 December 1844.
[59] HJ: 5 February 1845.

Workhouse. The riotous behaviour of these women originated in the refusal of the workhouse master to let them take their 'breakfast bread' away from the table for later consumption.[60] A similar act of protest was committed in 1856 at the Hereford Union Workhouse when Elizabeth Taylor broke twenty-one panes of glass in an effort to draw attention to her plight. On being sentenced to seven days at the County Gaol she complained to the magistrate that:

> She slept on cold stones without any shoes on – that the master only gave her swedes and salt for dinner – had no supper – and that the whole of her food for the day was only seven ounces.[61]

Although the magistrate 'strongly inveighed against such treatment of paupers and strongly reprimanded the complainant' such treatment was probably far from unusual, nor was this sort of response by the inmates.[62]

Whereas the criminal actions of the workhouse inmates may be seen as social crimes it is difficult to categorize all acts of wood- and crop-theft under the same heading. While research has failed to uncover any overt acts of wood-gathering or leasing that were carried out to defend customary rights it is clear that the farmers' hedges and crops were prone to vandalism. In many cases the vandalism or damage occurred during the theft of the crops or wood. For example, when Mary Davies was committed to gaol in 1838 for 'trespass and maliciously cutting, and destroying and carrying away a quantity of wheat there growing', it is clear the cutting and destroying were an integral part of the theft.[63] In short, it was necessary for Davies to cut, and therefore destroy, the wheat to steal it. Similarly, many cases of wood-theft involved 'malicious damage' to hedges and fences; the vandalism was inevitable. Quite frequently, however, many acts of malicious damage to crops and hedges did not involve theft, suggesting that the perpetrator's motive was not simply food or warmth.

Historians all too often equate rural terrorism with the rick fire and the maimed pony.[64] Research soon shows, however, that there were many other crimes that could be regarded as acts of protest. These acts were often less conspicuous; nevertheless, they were committed with the same aim: to cause the farmer or landowner a degree of financial hardship and to illustrate his vulnerability in the face of an attack by the disaffected rural poor. Indeed,

[60] *HT: 24 August 1849.*

[61] *HJ: 9 January 1856.*

[62] Such acts of protest against the Union Workhouses were not confined to Herefordshire. See Roger Wells, 'Resistance to the New Poor Law in the Rural South', in Rule and Wells, *Crime, Protest and Popular Politics in Southern England* and John Knott, *Popular Opposition to the 1834 Poor Law*, Croom Helm, London (1986).

[63] *HJ: 21 November 1838.*

[64] See Chapter 7 for a discussion of incendiarism and animal maiming in Herefordshire.

hedges, gates and fences were often targeted as objects for vandalism. For example, 'some evil disposed person or persons' tore up a quantity of fencing, placed them across an adjacent hedge and set them alight at Hampton Bishop in 1801, 'whereby the said hurdles and hedge were consumed and burnt', endangering many of the farmer's buildings. Despite the offer of a free pardon and the added incentive of a twenty-guinea reward the perpetrators escaped detection.[65] In 1820 the *Hereford Journal* reported that 'a great injury was done to the stiles and fences in the neighbourhood' of Bishopstone when a 'number of gates were thrown from their hinges, (and) cattle and horses (were) thus admitted into wheat grounds causing great damage'.[66] Similarly, in 1846 a farmer from Credenhill offered a £5 reward following 'the wilful and malicious destruction of a gate' which let his cattle into a field of crops.[67] Shrubs and trees were also the occasional target of rural terrorists. It was reported in 1840 that 'some evil-disposed persons maliciously cut and injured a quantity of fine shrubs growing upon the lawn at Grayton Hall, the residence of Higford Burr esq MP'.[68] In 1845 it was reported that 'some malicious scoundrel cut off three young elm trees and an oak growing at Bradlow. . . . The trees were left on the ground.' Crops were also destroyed and the contemporary press frequently records instances where fruit trees had been 'injured', quantities of peas and beans had been 'spoiled', growing wheat had been 'destroyed' and hop bines 'maliciously' cut.[69] It would be possible to argue that there was not a crop that had not been vandalized at one time or another.

It is unfortunate that we will never discover the reasons for these attacks. Indeed, even the very few cases that reached the courts fail to throw any light upon the offender's motive. When, in 1845, Robert Lane was questioned about his part in destroying eight of John Arkwright's apple trees at Hope-Under-Dinmore, he said nothing in his defence, despite being sentenced to six months' hard labour and ordered to be whipped.[70] This may have been to protect his accomplices, although it is more likely he knew that a protest from the dock was not only futile but would also invite a harsher sentence. Lane, and the unknown perpetrators of the other crimes mentioned above, were moved to commit these crimes for a reason. They were aware that the punishment for these types of crime was harsh yet they still carried them out, despite the possible consequences. Essentially we can only speculate as to why these crimes were committed; however, that the offenders

---

[65] *HJ: 13 May 1801.*

[66] *HJ: 27 December 1820.*

[67] *HJ: 5 August 1846.*

[68] *HJ: 25 March 1840.*

[69] See *HJ: 1 December 1830, 16 February 1831* for reports of damage to fruit trees, *20 June 1831, 16 July 1834* and *20 December 1834* for reports of crop destruction and *HJ: 23 August 1826* for a report on an attack to a hop yard where 'upward of 4,000' bines were cut.

[70] HRO: Q/SR/133. HQS: *Trinity, 25 June 1845. HJ: 2 July 1845.*

did not carry away the crops or wood suggests that they were deliberately left as a reminder of their discontent.

As in other rural crimes, poverty was the usual cause of wood- and crop-theft. When David Hyde was fined 10s, plus costs, or a month's hard labour for causing wilful damage to a hedge in 1843, he told the magistrate that he had no money and 'I suppose I must have the month' in gaol.[71] In 1846 Noel Jones, described by the court as 'a poor man', caused 2d worth of damage to a fence and was subsequently fined 6d, plus 9s 6d costs. After gathering 'all the money he could muster' – 10s – Jones was still 2d short. The magistrate gave him two days' grace to find it.[72] Similarly, in 1847, 'an elderly woman named Green' was charged with breaking and carrying away a part of a fence and while the value of the wood was 'trifling' the court still imposed a 7s 6d fine. Green was unable to pay and said 'mun gi'e her credit till she got some (money)'. The court gave her three days.[73] Green and Jones were probably not unusual hedgebreakers because they were both old and poor. Yet poverty caused by age and infirmity were not the only reasons why people resorted to this kind of theft. Unemployment, either through redundancy or illness, also drove men and women to break fences and raid crops for food and warmth. In 1838 William Morris, on being sentenced to fourteen days' hard labour for stealing turnips, 'pleaded distress as the cause of the theft'.[74] In 1850 Moses Cooper, a potato-thief, claimed in his defence that 'want drove me to it. I could not get any employment'. In the same year Sarah Pember, on being fined for wood-theft, claimed that 'her husband had been ill . . . and unable to earn a livelihood'.[75] These were crimes committed by desperate people. When Harriet Green of Wellington was sent by her mother to collect wood for the family hearth in 1853 she chose to break a farmer's fence to get it. This led to a court appearance and when the magistrate asked Green's mother 'if she was not ashamed' of her daughter's behaviour her mother replied:

> She certainly ought not to have done it, but I did not know anything of it. If any of the farmers in the parish will take her and clothe her, they may have her. I have seven of them at home, and they may have them all. If they won't I will take them all to the workhouse. My husband gets but seven shillings a week, and it is impossible we can support them.[76]

Although the family's financial situation was made clear to the magistrate he still found it necessary to impose a fine of 7s, her husband's weekly wage,

---

[71] HJ: 24 May 1843.
[72] HJ: 18 February 1846.
[73] HJ: 20 January 1847.
[74] HJ: 21 November 1838.
[75] HJ: 28 September 1850 and HT: 15 June 1850 respectively.
[76] HT: 5 March 1853.

plus costs. Undoubtedly many magistrates did their best to stamp out the crime by fining and imprisoning offenders. Not all magistrates, however, were as uncompromising as those cited above. In fact there is evidence to suggest that they were able to exhibit some compassion, especially if the prosecutor requested mercy. In 1849 the *Hereford Times* reported the story of a wood-thief who walked free from the court with the proceeds of her crime. The newspaper reported that:

> Ann Williams, a poor old and miserable looking woman, was charged with stealing some palings, the property of Dr Gilliland, who caught her in the act . . . although much injury had been inflicted upon his property . . . he (Dr Gilliland) should not like to be instrumental in punishing one so old and poor. His request was met and the magistrates dismissed her. She (then) left the court carrying the burdens of broken palings in her arms. Mr Davies (one of the magistrates) thought it too bad she should be allowed to carry away the spoil.[77]

Moreover, magistrates, once guilt was established, occasionally charged the perpetrator with the costs and expenses of the trial only. This was especially true if the examining magistrate could extract a promise from the offender that such an act would not be repeated. William Bruton and Hannah Moore were ordered to pay 'expenses only' in 1849 after giving the bench at Bromyard such a promise on being found guilty of 'injuring certain trees' at Wolferlow.[78] In the same year Mary Child gave an undertaking not to offend again and was merely ordered to pay costs and damages by the Wigmore magistrates for 'destroying part of a dead fence'.[79]

Many cases of wood- and crop-theft were dismissed in this way, though research suggests that the magistrate's reluctance to clog up the courts of Quarter Sessions played a part in their generosity. Yet while these displays of mercy may have freed the courts for more weighty cases it failed to free the County Gaol of inmates. Quite often even the 6s or 7s costs imposed by the courts could not be met by the offenders and defaulters were gaoled from periods of one to six weeks, depending upon the circumstances of the crime. For example, Mary Lines, aged 6, and Sarah Moss, aged 12, were found guilty before the Bromyard magistrates in 1846, of 'picking two handfuls of pease (*sic*) in a field'. Although the magistrates fined them only 6d each the costs of the case and the damages to the prosecuting farmer meant that the total came to a further 13s 6d each. Neither of the children's parents could pay. Mary was fortunate as she was sent home following a promise by her parents to pay the money. Sarah, however, was not so fortunate because either her

---

[77] *HT: 17 March 1849.*
[78] *HT: 12 May 1849.*
[79] *HT: 29 September 1849.*

parents could not, or would not, undertake to pay the amount. Thus she was 'committed to gaol for fourteen days'.[80]

To see children among the lists of convicted crop- and wood-thieves was not unusual. A few contemporaries believed that children were put up to these crimes by adults. Following the apprehension of four boys, 'the eldest not more than twelve', for stealing onions from a garden at Holmer in 1829, the *Hereford Journal* remarked that 'this is too common a practice and the children, we sometimes feel, are instructed to commit such acts'.[81] If the parents of crop-thieves felt the magistrates would take a softer line with youthful delinquents however, they were very often mistaken. The Hereford magistracy were never afraid of making examples, even if they were children pilfering fruit from orchards, as 12-year-old George Stevens found out when he was sentenced to fourteen days' imprisonment for stealing a few walnuts at Brampton Abbots.[82]

Predictably, where the courts were particularly severe on wood- and crop-thieves was when the offender had a previous conviction or an indifferent reputation. In such cases a gaol sentence, rather than the usual fine, was handed down by the bench. In 1847 Charles Williams, an 11-year-old who the village constable claimed was of 'irreclaimably vicious habits', was gaoled for two weeks for wilfully damaging a hedge at Bromyard.[83] Also at Bromyard, but in 1849, William Smith, 'a notorious poacher', received the same sentence for damaging a fence.[84] Another way to ensure a gaol sentence, or a hefty fine, was for the offender to 'give vent his feeling' when being apprehended. At the 1845 autumn Ross Petty Sessions it was reported that 'a man named Mutlow was fined 1s for stealing turnips . . . and an accomplice, of the name of Nutt, was committed to prison for one month, he having used an abusive tongue besides committing the offence'.[85] While the magistrates were hard on Nutt, a labourer named Nicholas Griffiths felt the weight of the law to a greater extent in 1840. After being found guilty of 'stealing a quantity of potatoes' it was revealed to the court that he had a previous conviction for 'stealing wheat two years ago'. He was sentenced to fourteen years' transportation, again showing that the courts had little time for re-offenders.[86] These were sentences to deter, and who better to make an example of than those with bad reputations, disrespectful tongues and previous convictions?

[80] HRO: Q/SR/134. HQS: *Trinity, 1846. HJ: 5 August 1846.*
[81] *HJ: 19 August 1829.*
[82] HRO: Q/SR/137. HQS: *Epiphany, 3 January 1849.*
[83] *HJ: 19 May 1847.*
[84] *HT: 30 June 1849.*
[85] *HJ: 5 November 1845.*
[86] *HJ: 8 April 1840.*

To be apprehended stealing wood or crops was not only expensive for the criminal, in fines or in time spent in gaol, but also for the county itself. In 1846, for example, the *Hereford Journal* reported:

> A young girl, named Mary Floyd, was charged with having stolen a small quantity of chips, valued at one and a half pennies, from a field at Marden, the property of George Wanklyn. The defendant admitted the charge upon which J S Gowland esq, one of the magistrates on the bench, said, it was necessary that some punishment should be inflicted, with the hope of deterring her in the future from the commission of dishonest deeds, but he could not consent to send the case to trial at the Sessions, thereby imposing upon the county an expense of some £10 or £12. – The Rev J Eckley and M Newton esq. concurred in these remarks, and it was agreed to punish her for trespass. Ordered to pay for expenses only, amounting to 6s.[87]

The £10 or £12 cited by Gowland was not an unusual figure and the cost of justice often ran high for the county. At the Epiphany Quarter Sessions of 1850 the bench allowed over £20 in expenses to a farmer from Much Marcle who had accused three of his labourers of stealing 'a small quantity of wheat'.[88] They were acquitted. Similarly, in 1853, the theft of five sally poles, valued at 10d, cost the county nearly £15 in expenses awarded to the prosecution.[89] In most cases of wood-theft the value of what was stolen was trifling. In 1836 James Davis was convicted of 'having injured and damaged a stick', the property of Caleb Hill of Bosbury, the value of which defied pricing.[90] Edward Jones, a 45-year-old labourer from Aymestrey, was sentenced to three days' hard labour in 1853 for stealing an ash pole, 'valued at one penny'.[91] The crime of crop-theft also involved pathetically small amounts. In 1849 John Wheeler (alias Powell) found himself in court charged with stealing 2oz of potatoes, valued at 1d and in 1860, William Bough was found guilty of stealing a 'double handful of beans' and was sentenced to one month's hard labour.[92]

The thefts of small amounts of wood and crops was certainly illegal but the magistrates occasionally wrung their hands in anguish at the sheer number of 'petty' cases finding their way to the Quarter and Assize courts. In 1836 the Chairman at the Epiphany Quarter Sessions expressed his concern about the numbers of 'time-wasting' cases cropping up on the calendar and he drew attention to the plight of a prisoner who had been 'lying in gaol for

---

[87] *HJ: 19 August 1846.*
[88] HRO: Q/SR/138. HQS: *Epiphany, 30 December 1850.*
[89] HRO: Q/SR/141. HQS: *Easter, 18 March 1853.*
[90] *HJ: 30 November 1836.*
[91] HRO: Q/SR/141. HQS: *Epiphany, 3 January 1853.*
[92] HRO Q/SR/137. HQS: *Epiphany, 31 December 1849* and HRO: Q/SR/148, *Trinity, 2 July 1860* respectively.

a month' waiting to be tried for the theft of a single post.[93] Despite the magistrate's complaints this was the way the law concerning wood- and crop-theft was administered and many miscreants had to appear at the next Sessions. The *Hereford Journal* pointed out in 1839 that:

> As a warning to those who think they can trespass upon the outdoor effects of the farmer with impunity, we inform them that in many cases of wood stealing the magistrate has not the power of summary conviction, but we are obliged to send such deprivators for trial to the Sessions, when, after having probably suffered an incarceration of several weeks, they are sent back to gaol for a month or two of hard labour.[94]

While the local magistrates may have complained of the numbers of wood- and crop-thieves reaching the higher courts it is easy to see why victims were sometimes eager to prosecute. At certain times of the year, farmers were subjected to continual attacks to their fences, hedges and crops. A magistrate in 1844, on sentencing 'two lads' named Lewis and Powles to a month's hard labour for stealing 'a quantity of pease (sic)', noted that 'if these crimes of robbery were to be allowed with impunity, a field of pease would soon be swept away'.[95] Indeed, the usual excuse given to the bench by the victims of these criminal acts was that they hoped the prosecution of a few individuals would deter the rest of the rural poor from theft. A Wellington farmer named Godsall prosecuted a 'wretched-looking' 14-year-old girl in 1839 for stealing some withy stakes. The reason he gave the magistrate for bringing the case to court was that 'having caught the prisoner in the act of stealing those (stakes) remaining he was determined to make an example of her, in order to deter others'.[96] In 1840 a farmer from Holmer, William Jones, stated to the magistrates following the prosecution of 'a boy' for stealing apples that all 'he wanted was protection'. He further pointed out to the magistrates that 'he had been at considerable expense in setting persons to watch' and that 'deprivations to a great extent had been committed on his property'.[97] If farmers were willing to prosecute then magistrates were generally only too keen to oblige. A magistrate made it clear he was 'making an example' of Hannah Powell and Martha Field in 1847 when he fined them 15s each, plus costs, for stealing peas from a field at Withington. The relatively harsh sentence was without doubt applauded by the prosecution as they noted that 'the defendants were only two of a party that made a regular sortie . . . very early in the morning . . . being actively

---

[93] *HJ: 6 January 1836.*
[94] *HRO: Q/SR/127. HQS: Epiphany, 1839. HJ: 2 January 1839.*
[95] *HJ: 17 July 1844.*
[96] *HJ: 2 January 1839.*
[97] *HJ: 16 August 1840.*

engaged in filling their aprons' with his peas.[98] Moreover, victims sometimes went to great lengths to secure the proof needed for a successful prosecution. In 1834 a Pembridge farmer, after losing several hop poles from his yards, 'marked one and placed it as a trap'. The farmer did not have long to wait because the following day Joseph Goodwyn, a labourer, was seen crossing some nearby fields with five of his poles across his shoulder. He was apprehended and when the poles were examined the one previously marked came to light. After reminding Goodwyn that this sort of act was 'a serious offence' the magistrate sentenced him to one month's hard labour.[99]

While magistrates occasionally seemed reluctant to prosecute wood- and crop-thieves it is clear that they did not hesitate to deal harshly with grain-thieves. Throughout the period, although this was especially true prior to the 1830s, men, women and children apprehended stealing wheat from fields could expect to feel the full weight of a magistrate's or judge's sentencing powers. Because of the value of wheat its theft was an act of felony and thus a transportable offence. The threat of transportation, a lengthy period in gaol and whippings, however, did not deter the theft of wheat from where it stood in a field, from 'stooks' where it lay on the ground after the harvest, or even from barns. The length of a sentence depended upon the scarcity of grain. The theft of wheat following a poor harvest, or during periods of shortage, saw the harshest sentences handed down. In 1800, an infamous year of wheat shortages, John Lucy was sentenced to seven years' transportation for stealing a small quantity of wheat.[100] And at the 1801 Epiphany Quarter Sessions James Stokes and John Davis were both ordered to be 'whipped at the carts tail on the next market day' for separately 'stealing wheat in the chaff'.[101] Although the sentences of Lucy, Stokes and Davis were warnings to other potential grain-thieves it was clearly believed that examples needed to be made. The importance of wheat as a source of food for the rural population during the first quarter of the nineteenth century cannot be underestimated. Riots in the county's market towns over the price of bread still occurred.[102] Again, women were prominent in these disturbances and

---

[98] *HJ: 28 July 1847.*

[99] *HJ: 22 October 1834.*

[100] *Summer Assize: 1800. HJ: 13 August 1800.*

[101] HRO: Q/SR/89. HQS: Epiphany, 15 January 1801. HJ: 21 January 1801.

[102] The historiography of grain riots is quite extensive, although research concentrates upon the eighteenth century. Arguably, however, these studies are applicable to the early nineteenth-century grain riot. The seminal piece of work in this field has to be E. P. Thompson's 'The Moral Economy of the English Crowd in the Eighteenth Century', *Past and Present*, No. 50 (1971), Dale Williams' 'Morals, Markets and the English Crowd in 1766' *Past and Present*, No. 104 (1984), for a critique of Thompson's work and Thompson's 'The Moral Economy Reviewed', in *Customs in Common*. See also Andrew Charlesworth, 'Comment: Morals, Markets and the English Crowd in 1766', *Past and Present*, No. 116 (1987) for an overview of the debate. For reading more relevant to the grain shortages of

they were not afraid to exert their own moral economy.[103] In the summer of 1800, when wheat was being sold at an unprecedented 27s per bushel, the *Hereford Journal* noted:

> An inclination to disturb the peace has discovered itself in several county markets, by persons, generally women, riotously assembling and taking flour and meal and selling them at their own price.[104]

Later in the year the same newspaper reported:

> We are sorry to find, that some disposition to riot, manifested itself at Ross on Thursday last. While every considerate man laments the high price of the necessary articles of food we must condemn the folly of those who aggravate the evil by violent measures.[105]

Action was not confined to overt protest during 1800, nor was it confined to urban women. Indeed, during 1800 there were a number of reports concerning the theft of wheat from granaries and barns throughout the county. In January it was reported that three bags of wheat had been stolen from the barns of Mr Bonnor of Eccleswall Court, Linton, and four bags from the Weir End Farm. These crimes, speculated the *Hereford Journal*, were the work a 'banditti' that came from 'near the Forest of Dean' who even had the affrontery to steal the farmer's horses to carry their booty away.[106] In the same month it was reported that twelve bushels of grain were stolen from a corn mill at Burton, near Ross, and in the following November a barn 'belonging to John Jones was robbed of a large quantity of wheat'.[107]

The organized theft of grain from barns by gangs was rare and essentially confined to periods of high prices or scarcity. Usually the theft of wheat was far less glamorous and the crime was overwhelmingly carried out by hungry individuals or small groups of women. To what extent the theft of grain by these female groups may be interpreted as an assertion of extinct leasing rights is open to conjecture. The evidence produced by the court records does little to clarify whether these women were asserting a right or that they simply felt their chances of apprehension decreased if they operated in groups. Groups of women did pillage ripening wheat fields; however, since

---

1800 see Roger Wells, *Wretched Faces* and 'The Revolt of the South West, 1800–1801: A Study in English Popular Protest', *Social History*, Vol. 5 (1977) and A. Booth, 'Food Riots in the North West of England: 1790–1801', *Past and Present*, No. 77 (1977).

[103] John Bohstedt, 'Gender, Household and Community Politics: Women in English Riots, 1790–1810', *Past and Present*, No. 118–21 (1988).

[104] *HJ: 19 February 1800.*

[105] *HJ: 29 October 1800.*

[106] *HJ: 1 January 1800.*

[107] *HJ: 15 January 1800* and *12 November 1800* respectively.

they also raided pea and turnip fields in small groups, it is difficult to place such offenders in the ranks of defenders of custom.

A whipping followed by a period of imprisonment seemed to be the usual penalty for the theft of wheat and even later in the period, when wheat lost some of its importance as a source of basic food for the rural poor, the crime was still met with a relatively harsh penalty. As late as the 1850s to be caught stealing wheat from the fields would still bring a gaol sentence of one to two months with hard labour and to steal wheat from out of a barn was to be imprisoned for up to twelve months, again with hard labour. Bearing in mind these stiff sentences, confrontations between wood- and crop-thieves and farmers did, perhaps inevitably, take place. Moreover, these confrontations occasionally resulted in violence. In 1810 the magistrate for the Wormelow Hundred issued a summons for the apprehension of Elizabeth and Thomas Jones, for assaulting William Hill when he 'detected them stealing wood' from land 'in his occupation'.[108] A similar attack took place in 1825 when George Preece discovered Mary Higgs and William Price stealing firewood from Rough Hill Wood, Aconbury. Both Higgs and Price were later committed, Higgs for wood-theft and Price for 'violently assaulting' the wood's owner.[109] Such cases were not uncommon. Violence, however, could, on occasions, go beyond 'resisting arrest', as the following extract from the *Hereford Journal* of 1842 illustrates.

> Stabbing – A serious offence of this description . . . occurred on Friday last, at Monnington-on-Wye . . . two persons of the names of James Garstone and Matthew Williams (on) being detected by Mr Richard Langford in the act of stealing cherries called upon them to desist . . . (however, they) continued their work of plunder. At length Mr Langford procured some assistance, and proceeded to eject them forcibly from his premises, when Garstone stabbed him in the side with a knife.[110]

Injury was not only dealt out by the wood- and crop-thieves and although reports of beatings being handed out by enraged farmers never made the contemporary pages of the press it would be naive to believe they did not occur. As we have seen it was fairly commonplace for farmers to set guards, especially over ripening fruit. Moreover these guards were often armed, and at times responded over-zealously. In 1814:

> a labouring man . . . was discovered at night in the orchard of a farmer. . . . A person on the watch with a loaded gun on him, so near as to lodge the whole of its contents into the poor man's loins . . . his recovery is extremely doubtful.[111]

---

[108] HRO: AF/67. *Magistrates Meetings: Wormlow Hundred, 1810–11.*
[109] *HJ*: 9 March 1825.
[110] *HJ*: 20 July 1842.
[111] *HJ*: 19 October 1814.

Such violence, however, was rare, and compared to the struggles between poachers and gamekeepers confrontations were usually mere scuffles.

While the theft of wood and crops lacks the 'glamour' of poaching and the covert expression of hatred that is incendiarism and animal-maiming the crime is worthy of study. The study of these insignificant crimes exposes the grinding poverty of the rural working class in nineteenth-century Herefordshire. Moreover, it exposes the illegal contribution rural women were prepared to make towards the domestic economy. Although the other chapters in this book concentrate on the male rural labourer and his response to their plight the female response should not be overlooked. If Joseph Stephens, the 1834 overseer of Credenhill, is to be believed, a labourer's wife and children could match his earning over the period of a year. In this respect they were equals. They were also equally at the mercy of the county's employing farmers and landowners and as likely, if not more so, to be laid off at a moment's notice. It is little wonder, in these crimes at least, that they showed scant regard for the farmer's property.

6

'Give him a good un'

Social crime, poaching and the Game Laws

> The pleasure it is to an expert poacher to steal a march, not only on the game, but on the men who claim it as their own.

> Make a net as I have done then when bad times come use it against the class that causes the bad times.[1]

Game – that is, hares, pheasants, partridges and deer – were perceived in different lights by the gentry and the rural poor. The gentry saw the hunting of game as a privileged and prestigious pastime; a pastime that should be reserved for those who could legally indulge in the pleasures of the field. The rural poor, on the other hand, saw game species either as food or as a means to supplement an often inadequate income. The gentry saw their quarry in terms of private property and believed that they were both legally and morally entitled to protect it from the ravages of poachers. Yet much of the rural population simply saw game species as wild animals which defied ownership and the humble cottager felt that he was as morally entitled to hunt as the Lord of the Manor. These differing perspectives resulted in conflict. Indeed, the conflict between the gentry and their game-keepers and poachers on the Herefordshire preserves occasionally resembled class warfare. Moreover, as in a war both sides employed various methods to gain supremacy in a bid to win what Hopkins has called 'the battle of the hedgerows'.[2] Both sides were prepared to use violence, the extent of which occasionally left men maimed or even dead. The gentry were also able to utilize legislation, the courts and propaganda, and did so freely. The poacher, conversely, enjoyed a certain amount of covert, if not overt, popular support by plundering the game preserves of the privileged. As George Monboit has pointed out the whole history of game preservation 'can be understood as the struggle of the upper-classes to secure and preserve the exclusivity of the hunt, and the attempts of the lower orders to undermine their efforts'.[3]

---

[1] Garth Christian (ed.), *James Hawker's Journal: A Victorian Poacher*, Oxford University Press (1979). 95 and 108.
[2] Hopkins, *The Long Affray*.
[3] George Monboit, 'Hunting for an Answer', *Guardian*, 3 March 1995.

The crime of poaching is not a crime of any particular age. It has been committed ever since men of wealth and influence have sought to retain the 'pleasures of the hunt' for themselves. Poaching has continued unabated, to a greater or lesser extent, from the time of the Saxon kings to the present day.[4] The poacher is one of the English countryside's most enduring figures. Despite the persistent nature of the crime this study will benefit from an examination of its extent in Herefordshire between 1800 and 1860. Such an approach will show not only that poaching was endemic during this period but also that the crime was linked, in part, to economic distress.

To argue that hunger was the sole inspirational force behind poaching activity, however, is too simplistic. That the crime occurred in the good years of full employment, reasonable prices and good harvests, as well as the lean years of high food prices, poor harvests and unemployment, suggests other reasons for its prevalence among the rural working class of Herefordshire. One explanation may be that many poachers did not regard the taking of game as a criminal activity, despite legislation to the contrary. Equally poaching could be seen as a protest activity. Indeed, to poach was in itself a protest against class-based legislation. The notion then that poaching was a social crime, a crime that was 'openly or tacitly' supported by local communities, will be discussed below.[5]

The purpose of the English Game Laws was to guarantee that the rural pleasure of the shoot remained the unshared privilege of the landed gentry and aristocracy. Rights to hunt via 'rights of park, chase and free warren' had been granted to landowners since the Middle Ages and 'Royal Gamekeeperships' had been bestowed (upon those who held influence) since the Stuarts. This selectivity was buttressed by the Qualification Acts which ensured that only men of landed property could enjoy the hunt. While the first Qualification Act was passed as early as 1389, the act that is relevant to this study dates from 1671 and remained in place until 1831. Under the Qualification Act of 1671 the pursuit of game was allowed only to those who fulfilled at least one of four categories. Essentially the law defined those who were entitled 'to keep or use guns, bows, greyhounds, setting-dogs, ferrets, cony-dogs, lurchers, hays, lowbels, hare-pipes, gins, snares, or other "engines" to take game or conies'. Hunting was permitted only for those who held 'Lands, tenements, or other estate of inheritance of the value of £100 p.a.', for those who were the 'son and heir apparent of an esquire, or other person

---

[4] Poaching in Herefordshire continues. Although the crime is not as common as it was in the early nineteenth century the taking of game without permission, or licence, is still a matter for the courts, and the penalties are still relatively severe. For example, the *Ledbury Reporter* of 14 March 1996 reported upon the conviction of a poacher who 'lamped' a rabbit and was fined £220. Similarly, the *Hereford Times* reported the conviction of Wye salmon poachers on 7 March 1996 and 21 March 1996 who received £2,200 in fines and 200 hours' community service respectively.

[5] Rule, 'Social Crime'. 139.

of higher degree' and for the 'owners and keepers of forests, parks, chases or warrens, stocked with deer or conies for their own use'.[6]

The Qualification Act restricted the pleasures of the field to the gentry which, in effect, excluded the majority of the rural population. Munche argues that 'the vast majority – perhaps as high as 99 per cent – of the population were not permitted to own a gun or keep a lurcher'.[7] The 1671 Act, however, did not stop poaching and law upon law covering every conceivable danger to game was passed to deter and punish miscreants. Indeed, by the early nineteenth century the Game Laws themselves would have filled a weighty volume. Sharpe argues that the English Game Laws were 'a tangled mass of confused and often contradictory legislation'.[8] He emphasizes this point by citing Blackstone, who wrote in 1783 that the preservation of game was controlled by:

> A variety of acts of parliament, which are so numerous and so confusing, and the crime itself of so questionable a nature, that I shall not detain the reader . . . the statutes for preserving game are many and various, and not a little obscure and intricate.[9]

Blackstone's obvious boredom and Sharpe's reluctance to get entangled in any lengthy discussion on the English Game Laws are perhaps understandable for, until 1831 when the Game Laws were rationalized, the subject remained a legal minefield. Despite its labyrinthine nature, however, it will be necessary to explain the law during this period for the purpose of this study. Poachers would not have been poachers without the Game Laws; therefore any discussion of poaching necessitates a discussion of the relevant laws.[10] Legislation came thick and fast between 1796 and 1831 and no less than twenty-four separate acts were passed in an attempt to cope with increasing poaching activity. If Blackstone himself could not keep up with the ever-changing legislation, then pity the poor poacher who may have been unaware of a new law until he faced a magistrate. As 'Nimrod' argued in the *Sporting Magazine* in 1825: 'it is very well for a judge on the bench to say "all men are bound to know the laws of the land"; but the fact is all men do not know the laws of the land.'[11] Ignorance of the law, however, was little excuse. Moreover, there is no evidence to suggest that poachers generally

---

[6] The Preservation of Game Act. 22 and 23 Charles II, C.9 (1671).

[7] Munche, *Gentlemen and Poachers*. 28.

[8] J. A. Sharpe, *Crime in Early Modern England: 1550–1750*. Longman, London (1987). 125.

[9] Sharpe, *Crime in Early Modern England*. 125.

[10] The list of Game Law offences dealt with in this chapter is by no means definitive. Munche, *Gentlemen and Poachers*, is arguably the definitive work on the English Game Law system. For a catalogue of the legislation for the period 1671 to 1831, see pp. 169–86.

[11] Cited in, *HJ: 12 December 1825*.

expressed any interest in the complexities of the Game Laws, or that they would have stopped poaching if they had.

Although poaching was illegal and the punishment severe for those who were caught, it seems that it was endemic in Herefordshire during the first half of the nineteenth century. As with other crimes its full extent cannot be determined and those unfortunate enough to stand before a magistrate or Assize judge made up a mere fraction of those who regularly plundered the preserves of the mighty. Attempts to determine the extent of the crime in Herefordshire, using recorded convictions, has been able to focus only on Quarter Sessions convictions between 1815 and 1822, and those petty convictions returned by the county's magistrates to the Quarter Sessions between 1822 and 1860. Herefordshire is not alone in this respect; other historians dealing with other counties have faced similar problems. Douglas Hay explains that:

> Most of the Game Laws were part of that large and growing body of legislation that was executed by individual Justices of the Peace, acting in their own neighbourhoods, hearing cases more often than not in their own houses, and neglecting almost always to record the conviction. Hence game offences figure hardly at all in most legal records.[12]

For David Jones the problem of sources was not confined to the eighteenth century, and he experienced similar difficulties when discussing the nineteenth-century poacher.

> Estate papers usually provide us with little information . . . and comparatively few cases were brought before the Quarter Sessions. We have therefore to rely mainly on newspaper evidence which is often selective, Petty Session files that are frequently incomplete, and Parliamentary Papers which provide us with only the bare statistics of summary trial after 1856.[13]

After the act of 1671, and until 1831, a poacher could be convicted before a single JP and one 'credible' witness. This system was open to abuse. It was not inconceivable that a poacher would be convicted by the very victim of his crime, with the victim's employee acting as the credible witness. A great many JPs also had game preserves and, as Hay argues, they may well have 'abandoned' the virtues of impartiality and integrity under such circumstances.[14] While some magistrates undoubtedly abused their position others were beyond reproach. Sir Edwyn Stanhope, for example, 'retired from

---

[12] Douglas Hay, 'Poaching and the Game Laws on Cannock Chase', in Hay et al. Albion's Fatal Tree. 192.
[13] Jones, 'The Poacher'. 829.
[14] Hay, 'Poaching and the Game Laws'. 241.

the bench, at his own request, during the hearing', of two men who were found poaching on his estate at Holm Lacy in 1846.[15] There were exceptions to 'drawing-room justice'. Poachers charged with a more serious offence were committed to appear at the next Quarter Sessions or Assize. Thomas Greenold, Thomas Lawton, William Lillo and Thomas James fell into this category when they were committed for being 'found on enclosed ground, in the night, with intent to kill and take game' at Yarpole in 1815.[16] From 1770 Sunday poachers did have the right to appeal to a higher court against summary conviction, as did night poachers prior to 1816, and after 1828. Between these dates night poachers had to face the Quarter Sessions but after 1828 the procedure reverted to facing two JPs with the charged having right of appeal.[17] Although the chief purpose of this chapter is not to discuss the impartiality or otherwise of the law we must be aware that most poaching cases were dealt with by a JP who was not obliged to register or record such convictions and, as Hay puts it, 'even when he did, the bare record tells us nothing much of interest'.[18]

The poacher may have also found himself facing a Quarter Session magistrate when the victim of the crime sought compensation via a civil suit. After 1772 the 'informer', the person who laid the information before a justice, was presented with two options. An Act of that year enabled the aggrieved party either to pursue the case in the usual way before a JP, or to sue for his share of the fine.[19] Most game legislation ordered that the fines collected for game offences be split between the informer and the local overseer of the poor; moreover, the complainant could sue 'by action of debt in any court of record'.[20] If the victim won his case he could claim his share of the fine and, as a bonus, double the costs of the prosecution. This course of action, however, could be seen as precarious. Failure to win the case before the criminal law was reformed placed the financial burden of the total costs on the plaintiff.[21] Nevertheless, victory for the plaintiff brought other benefits. Most labourers could not afford the £5 fines doled out by magistrates and an inability to pay the fine meant imprisonment; and one less poacher to worry the keepers. This sort of case may have been motivated more by keeping poachers out of circulation than seeking financial compensation.

Despite the lack of a full statistical picture fragments of information do exist. As Jones noted, the newspapers of the period give us a great deal of insight into the conflict between the poachers and the gentry. They also

[15] HRO: Q/SR/134. HQS: *Michaelmas, 1846. HJ: 28 October 1846.*
[16] HRO: Q/CM/4: *Returns of Convictions under the Game Laws, 1815–21. Epiphany 1815.*
[17] 10 Geo III, c. 19 (1770), 56 Geo III, c. 130 (1816) and 9 Geo IV, c. 69 (1828).
[18] Hay, 'Poaching and the Game Laws'.
[19] 8 Geo I, c. 19 (1772).
[20] P. B. Munche, 'The Game Laws in Wiltshire: 1750–1800', in Cockburn (ed.) *Crime in England.* 212.
[21] For a discussion of the reform of the criminal law see Chapter 3.

list many Petty Session convictions before 1822, although the number of cases reported are but a fraction of the real total. An example of this was the conviction of John Hoskins, who was fined £5 before the Revd John Bissell for 'using a gun in pursuit of game' at Lyonshall in 1811.[22] Hoskins was just one of many poachers during this period who were punished by JPs and whose convictions went unrecorded except for a line in a local newspaper. Similarly, a few notebooks kept by rural magistrates still exist and they give details of warrants issued and fines dealt out to offenders. These valuable books are fragmented, apart from the odd year in a particular parish, and only two such books exist for Herefordshire within the period of study.[23] The years 1800 to 1814 for Herefordshire, however, do not have to remain a blank. Using a mixture of the materials available we can attempt a tentative assessment of the nature and extent of poaching in the county. Figure 6.1 shows that between 1822 and 1860 a total of 1,381 petty convictions relating to breaches of the Game Laws were returned to the Hereford Quarter Sessions by the county's magistrates.[24]

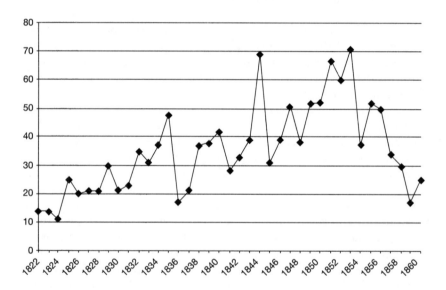

Figure 6.1 Petty Session Returns: Convictions for Game Law offences, 1822–60[25]

[22] *HJ: 18 December 1811.*
[23] See HRO: BB/88/1. *Magistrates Examination Book of the Reverend Henry Gorges Dobyns Yate, c1801–1803* and HRO: AF/67. *Minute Book of Magistrates Meetings: Wormlow Hundred, c1810–1811.*
[24] These figures include convictions for 'Illegal Fishing', 'Stealing Conies' and 'Trespass in Pursuit of Game'.
[25] HRO: Q/CM/4. *Petty Session Returns: Convictions, c1822–51* and HRO: Q/CE/1. *Petty Session Returns: Convictions, c1852–60.*

As Figure 6.1 shows, until 1853 the trend for poaching prosecutions was generally upward. It has to be accepted that changes to the way the criminal law was administered, the Game Laws and improved policing pushed up the numbers of petty poaching convictions. The rise in convictions, however, mirrors the rise in rural crime in general and reflects the decline in the fortunes of the agricultural labourer. Although the reduction in poaching convictions after 1854 may suggest that opportunities for rural employment had increased it is possible that the gentry adopted other laws. At first glance the number of petty convictions for Game Law offences may seem modest, with an average of just over thirty-six cases per year; but poachers were not only brought to the courts for infringements of the Game Laws. Indeed, the charge of trespass was also used frequently in the war against poaching. As Figure 6.2 shows, the county's magistrates dealt with 469 cases of trespass between 1822 and 1860.

To categorize all cases of trespass as potential Game Law infringements is impossible. The court records give little indication if the trespassers were in pursuit of game, intent upon stealing wood, fruit, crops, or merely taking a

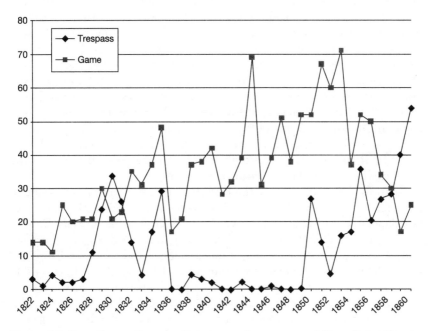

Figure 6.2 Petty Session Returns: Convictions for trespass and Game Law offences, 1822–60[26]

[26] HRO: Q/CM/4. *Petty Session Returns: Convictions, 1822–51* and HRO: Q/CE/1. *Petty Session Returns: Convictions, c1852–60.*

short cut home. Although poaching was a male-dominated crime, women made up just under 20 per cent of all trespassers, and we cannot use gender as a yardstick. There were female poachers but research for this period has unearthed only two: a Hannah Phillips of Ledbury, who was committed to the House of Correction for three months in 1811 for 'using an engine for game', and Sarah Suff, who was committed to gaol in 1840 'for using a wire' at 'The Park' Bolstone.[27] Nor can we assume that a 'known' poacher was actually in pursuit of game when apprehended for trespass. An example of this was John Smith of Ledbury, who was convicted at the Petty Sessions no less than eleven times between 1823 and 1830. Ten of the convictions were indeed for poaching, but since one conviction was for stealing hedgewood we cannot be quite certain of Smith's motives every time he trespassed. Despite these reservations many of the trespass cases were likely to have been brought against those who intended to break the Game Laws.

Poachers also appeared before the Quarter Sessions and Assize judges and these courts sat in judgment over the most serious cases which involved long custodial sentences, transportation and even capital punishment. Third offences, armed poaching at night, assault or the murder of a gamekeeper saw such punishments handed out. Herefordshire had its share of all these types of poaching cases and the Oxford Circuit judges occasionally passed transportation sentences on poachers who had the misfortune to stand before them. The poacher was dealt with by various agencies of the law. He could be fined or gaoled by a JP in his drawing-room or at a formal Petty Session (by far the most popular option), by a magistrate at Quarter Sessions or by the full majesty of an Assize court; all utilizing a confused mass of legislation which attempted to protect the gentry's sport. The result, for the historian, is an often inadequate picture of the extent of poaching and its frequency. We do know, however, from the available evidence, from the court records that still exist, from contemporary comment and from newspaper reports, that the crime was endemic in Herefordshire during this period.

Apart from preserving game the English Game Laws were also an exercise in social control. It would seem that the landowning and employing classes harboured a deep distrust of the labouring man. Unless the rural labourer was at work or in church, it was assumed he was up to no good. Poaching, among other illegal activities, encouraged independence and a lack of deference. After all, if a man could sustain himself and his family without visible employment he was unlikely to show the respect his betters felt they deserved. The act of 1671, apart from endorsing the privilege of the gentry, was also directed at those who sought to subsist at the expense of the shooting classes. While the selling of game had been, since 1603, a 'back door', 'no questions asked' trade, an act of 1707 attempted to shut this door altogether. It made the buying or selling of game by any 'higgler, chapman, carrier, innkeeper,

---

[27] *HJ: 18 December 1811* and HRO: Q/SR/128. *HQS: Easter 1840.*

victualler or alehouseperson' illegal, essentially trying to cut out the middle-man, between the field and the plate.[28] This act was endorsed in 1755 and was extended to cover 'any person'; meaning that all English game, apart from that which the gentry provided, was poached.[29]

Until 1831, when licences were again granted to dealers, the trade in game was pushed underground. The Acts of 1707 and 1755, however, failed to halt the popularity of poaching. However, these acts not only encouraged poaching but may also have encouraged poachers to become more violent in the face of arrest. The gentry, in seeking to preserve their stocks of game, had inadvertently created a lucrative black market. What was previously destined for the poacher's table became a potential source of income. Munche provides evidence from the 1823 Game Report which shows that in 1820 a poacher could collect up to 2s for a hare and 3s 6d for a brace of pheasants from a black-market higgler.[30] Four pheasants and a hare, perhaps the result of a single night's poaching, could bring in the equivalent of a week's wages for a Herefordshire farm labourer in 1813.[31] It is little wonder that many were tempted, if not to be independent altogether, then to supplement inadequate incomes.

While Munche concedes that 'a hare in the pot' was always welcome in a labourer's home, he argues that the 'traditional image of starving peasants snaring game in order to keep body and soul together' has little evidence to support it.[32] Undoubtedly professional poachers who traded with higglers and other middlemen existed in Herefordshire as they did in other counties. Merely because research has uncovered only a few cases of supplying in the county does not mean a black market for game was not in operation; it would be naive to suppose otherwise. It is possible to prove that habitual poachers did exist and one suspects, judging by their frequent court appearances, that poaching was their career rather than their pastime. Thomas Stinton and James Alcott were referred to, on their committal to Hereford Gaol in 1844, for setting wires at 'The Venn Cover', as 'notorious poachers'.[33] Similarly, in 1846 Thomas Bufton of Much Cowarne, when being convicted of Game Law offences, was described as 'a notorious stealer of game'.[34] Between 1800 and 1860, certain names, or families, continually arise over short periods;

---

[28] 5 Ann, C. 14 (1707).

[29] 28 Geo II, C. 12 (1755). Considered 'bad form' by the purist to sell the product of their sport, game was often given away, usually to those whose favour and influence was sought. Much of the gentry, however, were not 'above' such ideals and found the trade in game a profitable by-product of running an estate.

[30] Munche, *Gentlemen and Poachers*. 61.

[31] Duncumb, 'General View'. Duncumb put the weekly wage of a farm labourer in Herefordshire at 7s 6d, summer rate in 1813.

[32] Munche, *Gentlemen and Poachers*. 62.

[33] *HJ: 9 October 1844*.

[34] *HJ: 30 September 1846*.

notably the Smith, Morris and Woodyatt families from the Ledbury area. The most prominent members of these families, in terms of court appearances, were John Smith, mentioned above, William Morris and Thomas Woodyatt. These three men amassed nineteen convictions between 1820 and 1834 and were a thorn in the side of the preservers of the Eastnor estate, their usual hunting ground.[35] The sheer numbers of convictions amassed by these men suggest three possible explanations. The first – and this explanation can be immediately discounted – was that they were, as poachers, inept and kept getting caught; second, that these men were marginal to society. Unwilling, or unable, to survive by legitimate employment, they existed by 'mouching', scratching a living, how and when they could. Mouchers, according to Richard Jefferies, were men who 'sneak about the hedgerows on Sundays with lurcher dogs and snap up a rabbit or a hare'. To the moucher, poaching was 'not a precise profession . . . (but a way of life for men who) loiter along the roads and hedges picking up whatever they can ever lay their hands on'.[36] As shown above, Smith may have fallen into this category as he had convictions for wood-theft and later turned to petty crime. This may suggest he lived a 'scratch-as-scratch-can' existence. Finally, they could have been members of a highly organized gang. They had all worked together at one time or another and it is possible they had connections with the game trade. It is clear that the £5 and £10 fines, as well as the odd spell in prison, did little to deter them from poaching. The number of times they stood before a magistrate suggests that they saw the fines and gaol as an occupational hazard. Moreover, they did not confine their activities to their locality. Although most of their convictions came from offences committed in the Ledbury area, Smith and Morris were apprehended in 1828 for poaching in the parish of Weobley, some twenty-three miles from their home.[37] To travel such distances for game suggests that they may have been professional enough to do so and that a ready market existed; a market that could support themselves and their families.

Professional, and semi-professional, gangs did exist during the period who poached to sell rather than to consume, although the evidence from Herefordshire to suggest it was widespread is thin on the ground. There is, however, evidence that poachers from outside the county did make hunting forays on to the Herefordshire estates in order to take advantage of the abundant game. Again, we can only speculate if the poachers poached for food or to trade for cash at a later date. On 4 August 1818, the *Hereford Journal* described one such attempt at poaching by professional outsiders:

[35] See HRO: Q/CM/4. *Returns of Game Convictions, c1815–21* and *HQS: Convictions, c1822–51*.

[36] Richard Jefferies, 'The Gamekeeper at Home', in Walsh (ed.) *The Poacher's Companion*. 17.

[37] *HJ: 2 April 1828*.

A daring attempt at deer stealing was made . . . in the park of the Duchess of Norfolk, at Holm Lacy [sic]. About twenty wires were laid by two men, colliers, in dirty flannel dresses, and a third person wearing a blue coat and glazed hat, and riding a small black mare. The keepers were aware of their operations and got possession of their dog, which was young of a dark bridle color and of the lurcher breed. The gang escaped but without their booty.[38]

Although on this occasion the poachers were unsuccessful the attempt does suggest a certain amount of professionalism. The number of wires and the man riding the horse, who was clearly the leader of the gang, all point to a degree of organizsation. Indeed, if the two men were colliers they probably came down the River Wye (Holme Lacy is situated alongside the river) on their barges and no doubt they would have taken the carcasses of the deer back, either to the Forest of Dean or to Monmouthshire. We have also seen, from the section concerning sheep-stealing, that the bargees regularly plundered the countryside to support themselves.

Apart from the Smith, Woodyatt and Morris families other names crop up with regularity. We have to determine, however, whether this suggests that they stole professionally, habitually or only when economic conditions forced them to do so. Professionalism, the selling of game on a regular basis for money, existed in Herefordshire but not to the extent suggested by Munche. Basing his thesis upon the price of wheat in relation to the number of poaching convictions, Munche argues that the 'principal element in the labourer's diet' was bread rather than meat. He further claims that 'in times of dearth, game was more valuable to him as a source of money with which he could buy bread'.[39] He is undoubtedly right: bread was the most important food item of the agricultural labourer until the late 1830s. Wheat prices, however, are but one variable. If we expect poaching conviction figures to correspond with the price of bread we will be disappointed. First, an arrest may have taken place some time after the crime had been committed. An offence that took place in the winter may not have been recorded by the courts until the following spring, or even the summer. Second, a reaction to rising food prices may have been adjourned, as the labourer and his family used up their meagre savings; money put by for the yearly rent, clothes and so on. The game-related cases appearing before the Hereford Quarter Sessions rose from two in 1817, to twenty-two in 1818. Wheat prices soared in 1817, but the increase in game convictions did not become apparent until the following year. This is shown clearly by the Quarter Session convictions recorded in the winter and spring of 1818. Thirteen of the poaching offences were committed between the Trinity (summer) 1817 and Epiphany (winter) sessions of 1818 and the remaining nine infringements against

---

[38] HJ: 4 August 1818.
[39] Munche, Gentlemen and Poachers. 63.

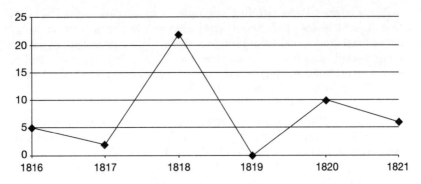

Figure 6.3 Convictions at Hereford Quarter Sessions for Game Law offences, 1816–21[40]

the Game Laws were committed between Epiphany and Easter (spring) 1818 (see Figure 6.3).

Employment, or the lack of it, also played an important role in determining the numbers of game convictions. The year was 1817 when the post-war agricultural depression gripped Herefordshire and, as farms became vacant, labourers found themselves underemployed at best, and unemployed at worse. Throughout the first half of the nineteenth century winter employment was scarce and the winter of 1817 to 1818 was to prove no exception. Indeed, the winter and spring months between 1800 and 1860 were the busiest periods for the poacher and the magistrate alike. Between 1822 and 1860 magistrates returned no less than 444 individual convictions relating to the Game Laws to the Epiphany sessions (32.15 per cent), compared to 235 cases at Trinity sessions (17.01 per cent), out of a total of 1,381 cases (see Figure 6.4).

While the evidence indicates some relationship between food prices, unemployment and increased poaching we do not know if the poacher intended to sell the game to a 'higgler' or if it was destined for the pot. We cannot doubt, however, that the majority of these crimes were committed to solve the immediate problem of want. It seems hair-splitting to argue whether the product of his crime was intended to fill his belly, or his pocket and then his belly. After all it is the criminal's ultimate motive which should be of paramount importance rather than how he disposed of his booty. The lean years, the years of hardship, saw an increase in the desperate amateur. This is shown by the 'one-off' offenders who appeared once before a magistrate, never to reappear in the court records. Such poachers were more typical than the Smith, Woodyatt and Morris family members. Desperate amateurs took game as and when it was needed. Poaching was, as Hopkins

---

[40] HRO: Q/014/253. *Hereford Quarter Session: Game Convictions, c1816–21.*

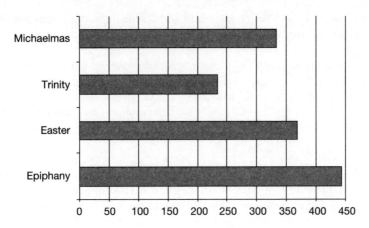

Figure 6.4 Petty Session Returns: Convictions for Game Law offences, by session, 1822–60[41]

argues, 'a good way to stay off the overseers books'.[42] The proceeds from a night spent poaching on a local estate put food on the table without the need to resort humbly to 'parochial aid'. Poverty was the motive behind many a poaching career; as the infamous Norfolk poacher James Hawker wrote: 'poverty made me poach.'[43]

For Hawker, poaching was a craft; a craft perfected through necessity. Hawker may have been an unusual figure, especially when we bear in mind that he was an intelligent, politically aware teetotaller; a far cry from the gentry's perception of the typical poacher. Poaching was hard and occasionally unpleasant work. The romantic image of one man and his dog outwitting the landowner's servants and his quarry under a moonlit sky was often far removed from the reality. He was often up all night, often wet, often cold and always in danger of being caught, yet he was often described as an idle drunkard. Much of the eighteenth-century gentry, argues Munche, imagined that 'the only thing which stood between the poor and "immorality" was the necessity of having to work for a living'.[44] Poachers were seen as immoral because they could survive without visible means of support. Their perceived immorality was such that William Taplin described poachers in 1772 as 'abandoned ruffians'.[45] This perception of the poacher was still

[41] HRO: Q/CM/4. *Petty Session Returns: Convictions, c1822–51* and HRO: Q/CE/1. *Petty Session Returns: Convictions, 1852–60.*
[42] Hopkins, *The Long Affray.* 19.
[43] *Hawker's Journal.* 77.
[44] Munche, *Gentlemen and Poachers.* 53.
[45] William Taplin, 'Observations on the State of the Game Laws', in *The Poacher's Companion.* 10.

commonplace over a century later and Lord Walsingham's comments are typical of the shooting classes, arguing in 1892 that the poacher was:

> Without scarcely an exception, a cowardly, drunken ruffian. He and his wife and children are clothed in rags; his idleness and loafing habits are habitual to him, for he will not accept honest well-paid work. . . . His restless, suspicious leer, hollow eyes, alehouse face, and his stooping, shambling gate (*sic*) proclaim him at once. . . . He drinks and sleeps by day like a great fat cat, and like a cat he prowls by night.[46]

It could be argued that Walsingham was describing the effects of poverty rather than providing a picture of desperate criminality. He described those who needed to poach; namely the hungry agricultural labourer and his family. As a class they were all under suspicion as potential poachers anyway and Walsingham was simply repeating the jaundiced views of most of the gentry. After all they found it useful to propagate such myths. The picture portrayed by eighteenth- and nineteenth-century commentators was a conscious attempt to undermine the community support enjoyed by poachers, and to push them to the margins of what was accepted as 'decent' behaviour. The rural working class, it was suggested, should survive by honest toil, touching their caps and showing deference to their masters while accepting their station in life, not by raping the local gentry's game preserves. The wretched picture portrayed above, however, is but one side of the coin. Poachers, according to some poachers themselves, were not an underclass. They were working men who sought to supplement inadequate wages while enjoying a degree of independence from the constraints of a working life that increasingly demanded regulation. In 1880 Richard Jefferies described the poacher as:

> Often a sober and, to all appearances, industrious individual, working steadily during the day at some handicraft in the village, such as blacksmithing, hedge-carpenting – i.e. making posts and rails etc – cobbling, tinkering, or perhaps in the mill; a somewhat reserved, solitary workman of superior intelligence and frequently advanced views as to the 'rights of labour'.[47]

While accepting that Jefferies' view of the poacher was somewhat romanticized one feels his description is more acceptable than that of the gentry. In reality, the poacher probably fell somewhere in between the two extremes. Socially irresponsible poachers would not have been at large for long and they would soon have been candidates for conscription, gaol or even transportation. At village level, keepers would frequently visit such

---

[46] Lord Walsingham, 'Shooting', in *The Poacher's Companion*. 14.
[47] Jefferies, 'Gamekeeper at Home'. 17.

men's cottages, destroying nets, dogs and confiscating firearms. Such men were generally known and the authorities kept a close eye on their activities. The magistrate at Bromsberrow, the grandly named Revd Henry Gorges Dodyns Yate, between 1801 and 1803, drew up a list of 'poor people who kept dogs' with the name of the owner and 'cur' written alongside.[48] These dog owners were all seen as potential poachers. We could also argue that those men whom Walsingham described as 'drunken ruffians', who were too idle to dress and feed their families, would not necessarily have enjoyed community sanction. Poaching was not for the work-shy. Hours would have been spent tramping the countryside, locating game, maintaining nets and snares before his sport could commence.

Another myth propagated in the war against the poacher was that this criminal act was the first step to the gallows. Condemned men, making their (dutiful) last speeches on the scaffold, often gave the myth more substance than it was worth. These speeches often related woeful tales of the evils of drink, neglect of religious duties and falling in with bad company. Poaching was, if they were to be believed, the first criminal action for many a condemned man. William Scrope, writing in 1839, also believed that a poacher's career inevitably had but one ending. Often the poacher:

> proceeded from crime to crime, till at last, their career ends either on the gallows or transportation. I have fined and imprisoned scores of these vagabonds, and some of them two and three times over, and I never yet heard of one that was reclaimed. They are absolute thieves.[49]

The Revd William Daniel attempted to offer an explanation why this was so. He believed failed night-time poaching led to property theft, and argued in 1812 that after:

> confining their first nocturnal excursions to the snaring of hares and the netting of partridges, whenever they have less booty than usual they are tempted to compensate the deficiency by petty plunder of some other kind, and the log-pile, the stack, the fold, the hen-roost, all in turn pay tribute to the prowling vagabond, who fills as he can that void in his 'capacious bag' which has been left by his want of success as a poacher.[50]

Scope and Daniel may have had a point. Poachers did 'diversify', and again we can turn to the Smith, Morris and Woodyatt families of Ledbury. Thomas Woodyatt and William Morris fell foul of the law when a joint venture involving the theft of five turkeys saw them transported for seven

---

[48] HRO: BB/88/1. *Magistrates Examination Book, c1801–03.*
[49] William Scrope, 'The Art of Deer Stalking', in *The Poacher's Companion.* 31.
[50] Revd W. B. Daniel, 'Rural Sports', in *The Poacher's Companion.* 11.

years in 1832.[51] No doubt their lengthy poaching careers ensured a relatively harsh sentence and the Assize bench saw this as an ideal opportunity to relieve the Ledbury gentry of two persistent offenders. A year earlier a similar case saw the transportation of John Smith who, with a John Baynham, conspired to 'steal a quantity of wheat in the chaff' from a Donnington farmer.[52] Once again the Assize judge handed down a seven-year sentence to Australia and relieved the county's gamekeepers. Judges and magistrates saw any extension of operations by known poachers as an excuse to ship them overseas and the sentences were unusually harsh. Compare the fate of Smith, Woodyatt and Morris with the sentence handed down to William Underwood in 1833 who in broad daylight violently robbed a man in front of his helpless wife in Ledbury. Although Underwood was well known as a 'vicious ruffian', he received a relatively light six months with hard labour.[53] Although Underwood, who had only one leg, would never had been a success as a poacher, we can see the difference in sentencing. It is significant that while the Smith, Morris and Woodyatt families kept to poaching they escaped long custodial sentences. Once they crossed the boundary, separating poaching from other forms of property theft, they brought down the full weight of the law. The gentry created the myth that poaching was the first step to the gallows or Australia and their sentences, when known poachers stepped off the estates, gave the myth substance.

Undoubtedly poaching, perhaps along with wood- and crop-theft, was the crime that was most likely to be community sanctioned. In short, poaching was a social crime. Indeed, poaching was, and perhaps still is, the best example of a 'conflict of laws . . . between an official and an unofficial system'.[54] The Game Laws were created to protect gentlemen's game, yet game was considered by the mass of the rural population as an advantage of living in the countryside. Magistrates and the shooting classes were aware that this conflict of interests existed. They also realized that they faced dogged resistance. As early as 1772 William Taplin noted:

> it appears that, amongst the lower classes, the act of poaching is considered a crime of very little consequence, merely because it is in opposition to laws against which they have the most unprincipled and unqualified aversion.[55]

Taplin was further convinced that the 'rustics prostituted (their) ideas of integrity' to justify their poaching activities.[56] But did they? Religion,

---

[51] Lent Assize 1832. HJ: 15 February 1832.
[52] Lent Assize 1831. HJ: 30 March 1831.
[53] HRO: Q/SR/121. HQS: Michaelmas 1833. HJ: 23 October 1833.
[54] Hobsbawm, 'Distinctions'. 5.
[55] Taplin, 'Observations'. 10.
[56] Ibid.

and subsequently the scriptures, were, for the ruling classes, an important tool for exercising social control.[57] The Bible was held up as a rule book by which an ordered society was governed and as a guide to the punishment of miscreants. 'An eye for an eye' is the prime example and this philosophy was used to justify capital and corporal punishment. The same rule book, however, stated clearly that animals were 'created by God for the use of all men' and not only a privileged few.[58] While it is difficult to evaluate fully the stance taken by the clergy, at parish level it would seem that they were prepared to bow to the demands of the landed elite. Moreover, we have to remember that the Church itself was a major landowner. Many parsons were also magistrates. The Reverends Dobyns Hunt, Bissell and Hunt actively convicted poachers in their role as magistrates in Herefordshire during the period under study. But it should not be assumed that because parsons carried out the letter of the law they necessarily agreed with the law's sentiments. 'Nimrod', writing for the *Sporting Magazine* in 1825, complained that: 'I have listened to a good many sermons in my time, but I never remember to have heard one word from the pulpit on the crime of, and evils attending, poaching.'[59] Although it is possible that some parsons covertly condoned poaching it seems more likely that they were sympathetic to the views of the local gentry, rather than those of the local labouring population.

The proletarian logic of poaching was simple. Their actions could be justified by arguing that it was not possible to own a hare of the fields or a salmon of the river. Such creatures knew no masters nor were they naturally constrained by boundaries, either physical or legal. This attitude to game was noted by W. H. Woolrych who wrote in 1858:

> It has been found difficult, if not impossible, to imbue the common people with the idea that creatures *ferae naturae* – here at one hour of the day and many miles off at another – are not a legitimate source of profit.[60]

Game animals, in their natural state, were regarded as a gift from God and could not be owned by any man. God had given the poor man a gift and they felt that they had a moral right to supplement their income and diet by helping themselves to the fruits of the land. A poacher may well have been a criminal in the eyes of the magistrate or Assize judge, yet he was not breaking God's law. The poacher could still command respect from his

---

[57] Louis Althusser argued, historically, that the Church was the most important of all the 'Ideological State Apparatuses' (ISA). The Church, later replaced by education, through its sermons, scriptures and so on, taught workers to 'accept and submit to their exploitation'. See Haralambos, *Sociology*. 180.

[58] Frank McLynn, *Crime and Punishment in Eighteenth Century England*. Oxford University Press, Oxford (1991). 202.

[59] Cited in *HJ: 12 December 1825*.

[60] H. W. Woolrych, 'The Game Laws', in *The Poacher's Companion*. 60.

community simply because he had not stepped outside the bounds of what was perceived to be reasonable behaviour. The poacher did not steal from his neighbours; he merely ignored an unreasonable set of laws that sought to deprive families of a means of putting food on the table. The Game Laws were seen as unfair and unjust by the majority of the rural population. Yet it was not only the labourers who fell foul of the Game Laws. The occasional farmer was not adverse to a bit of poached game. Taplin remarked in 1772 that he often 'visited many farmers, and never saw one that could not take me into his Pantry, and produce a Hare or more, and two or three Brace of Birds'.[61] In 1814 two unnamed farmers from Bosbury were convicted and fined £10 each for 'laying wires in a wood belonging to Lord Somers', suggesting that poaching was not confined only to the poor labourer, although we have to concede that they too may have fallen upon hard times.[62] Undoubtedly the rural labourer and tenant farmer alike understood that the gentry claimed game as their own but there is little evidence to suggest that the Game Laws were universally accepted.

The animosity felt by many tenant farmers towards the Game Laws was probably on a par with that of the agricultural labourer. There were several areas of potential conflict. The landowner and his guests, having access to hunt over the whole manor, were able to roam anywhere to pursue their sport. Crops could be trampled underfoot, hedges and fences holed and broken and farm stock endangered by worrying dogs. Hares are especially fond of turnip tops, and the young shoots of wheat and barley were equally susceptible to foraging game. Sporting birds, notably pheasants and partridges, ate grain of all sorts in abundance, while deer could cause enormous damage to crops and young trees. Legally the tenant farmer could do little to stop game ravaging his crops. Munche has shown that landlords often reduced rents in lieu of the damage done by game species; moreover, he argues that some landlords were 'sensitive' to their tenants' complaints. Research, however, has failed to find this generosity practised in Herefordshire.[63] Farms became an extension of the preserve and a farmer complained to Taplin in 1772 that:

On my farm I breed yearly, on the most moderate calculation, thirty Braces of Hares and one hundred and twenty Brace of Birds; I am not permitted publicly to kill any of these for myself or to oblige an absent friend or relation. My landlord and his gamekeepers almost daily refresh themselves at my expense; and for two seasons past have never offered me Partridge, Hare or Pheasant. There may as well be no game if I, who am in reality the breeder, and in whose power it is to be the

---

[61] Taplin, 'Observations'. 39.
[62] HRO: Q/SR/103. HQS: Epiphany, 1815. HJ: 23 November 1814.
[63] Munche, Gentlemen and Poachers. 47.

preserver, am not permitted to enjoy the pursuit in common, with those who enjoy it by oppression.[64]

In retaining the exclusivity of hunting the landowning gentry created a great deal of bitterness between themselves and one of their natural allies, the tenant farmer.[65] Middling farmers, those usual stalwarts of law and order, prostituted their own integrity by often turning a blind eye to poaching, and thereby gaining a vicarious revenge. It is possible that such tenants, covertly at least, were sympathetic to poachers. Haggard's *King of the Norfolk Poachers* noted that 'a good many Farmers shut there (*sic*) eyes to the Poacher, they know he will shut gates after him, besides getting them a brace of birds now and again'.[66] Farmers may have even encouraged rural labourers to vandalize game. Taplin pointed out in 1772 that:

They (the farm labourers) will, with a smile of satisfaction, destroy a nest of eggs ready to hatch, or a brace of leverets, and with the noble spirit of revenge, tell their employer. 'They had better be killed so, than bred for gentlemen; for they'll take care to give nothing to the poor, that they can keep for themselves.'[67]

That the Game Laws were unpopular among the mass of the rural population is clear, and it is little wonder that those who did poach game were often respected and even admired. 'True he is an outlaw against the laws of the land,' wrote Haggard's poacher, 'but that do not disturb him much but rather give him more encuragment (*sic*) than not.'[68] Those who sought to preserve game were aware that many poachers enjoyed community support. The gentry were also aware that these attitudes undermined their attempts to eradicate poachers from their estates. This community support was still commonplace in the late nineteenth century, as Lord Walsingham lamented in 1892 when he wrote:

A poacher is often regarded as a 'bold outlaw', a sort of revival or descendant of Robin Hood. The feebly sympathetic man who is ignorant of country life will be apt to say, 'poor fellow, he has a wife and family to support after all'. . . . There is still something of a halo of romance thrown around the poacher. His silent, stealthy expeditions by night, his risk of apprehension and other dangers from keepers and mastiffs, court a feeling of sympathy in the minds of many who do not

---

[64] Taplin, *Observations*. 40.
[65] For a late nineteenth-century discussion on the conflict between landowning game preservers and their tenants see Allan Fletcher, 'Game Laws in the Late Nineteenth Century: A Case Study from Clwyd', *The Local Historian*, Vol. 26 (1996).
[66] Haggard, *King of the Norfolk Poachers*. 150.
[67] Taplin, *Observations*. 40.
[68] Haggard, *King of the Norfolk Poachers*. 150.

know him as he is, who are inclined to consider him 'a gallant, clever robber, a *Claude du Val* of the preserves'.[69]

Walsingham's description fits Hobsbawm's concept of the social bandit.[70] Such men, according to Hobsbawm, are those within a community who are 'unwilling to bear the traditional burdens of the common man in a class society'.[71] Poachers often fit this model. Rider Haggard's poacher and James Hawker were such individuals who, although often employed, retained some independence by pursuing the game of those who sought to dominate them completely. Whether poachers actually saw themselves as '*Claude du Vals* of the preserves' is open to debate but we cannot doubt that the crime was community sanctioned because it was not seen as a particularly criminal act. That many poachers' careers were lengthy (Haggard's poacher and James Hawker took game all their adult lives) and that they were respected suggests that their communities gave them protection. This was an absolute necessity for a social bandit. Hobsbawm argues that such a person was: 'naturally protected by the peasants and by the weight of local conventions which stands for "our" law – custom . . . against "theirs", and "our" justice against that of the rich'.[72]

In reality there were very few ways in which a community could protect its poachers or other social criminals. Physical protection was out of the question, as indeed was any form of overt defiance, so they used the only weapon they had at their disposal – silence. As Hopkins argues, in 'denying all aid to the authorities, it was the silence of protest'.[73] The refusal to cooperate with the authorities meant efforts to track down poachers were hampered at every turn. As early as 1772 Taplin had seen this unwillingness to comply with the authorities, by refusing to give information against poachers, as an obstacle to more convictions. He argued:

> The laws for the protection and preservation of game are, in a degree, deprived of their intended effect, by want of the very information by which only they can be rendered effectual; and this is the true and fundamental basis upon which the practice of poaching is so largely carried on with the most exulting impunity.[74]

Taplin argued, albeit clumsily, that because poaching was a social crime, and therefore community sanctioned, informers were often elusive. 'Tip-offs' were often needed for prosecutions. They were also needed for searches of suspected poachers' cottages, in which nets, wires and other 'engines for the

69 Walsingham, 'Shooting'. 13.
70 Hobsbawm, *Primitive Rebels*.
71 Ibid. 13.
72 Ibid. 16.
73 Hopkins, *The Long Affray*. 60.
74 Taplin, 'Observations'. 10.

destruction of game' could be used as incriminating evidence. 'Information laid' was an important weapon yet the majority of informers were game-keepers. A typical entry in a magistrate's notebook for the Wormlow district in 1811 reads: 'Summons for Richard Wall for keeping and using three nets for the destruction of game, information by Thom Price gamekeeper for the Governors of Guy's Hospital.'[75] Admittedly the gamekeeper may have received a tip-off about Wall's activities, but that so few informants were ordinary labourers suggests the benefits to be derived from a share of a fine were outweighed by the possible backlash of feeling towards an informer. Community feeling in such circumstances could run high. In September 1808 Hereford experienced a riot in which the house of an unnamed man was besieged. His 'crime' was that he 'laid information' against 'people who served in shops on a Sunday'.[76] Sunday trading was against the law but it was community sanctioned. Admittedly this is an urban, rather than a rural, example but it clearly illustrates the strength of community feeling and perceptions of 'our' law against 'theirs'. Research has failed to uncover any examples of rural community backlash against those who informed on poachers in Herefordshire. There may quite simply have been none, or at least none who did it openly. However, just because it has been impossible to prove that the mechanisms for dealing with those who informed on poachers were used does not mean these mechanisms did not exist. [77]

Violence was part and parcel of everyday life in the early nineteenth century. Life was still 'nasty, brutish and short' for the vast majority of the population. Violence was also a fact of life for the poacher and the game-keeper, his immediate adversary, and to poach was to invite confrontation. The history of the preserves is littered with tales of exchanged shots and beatings, handed out on both sides. Affrays were commonplace and men were maimed, sometimes even killed, as both sides fought over the right to hunt. Undoubtedly, much of the violence that took place between poachers and gamekeepers was the result of fear. On the poacher's side, sentences, if he was apprehended and convicted, were relatively severe and they acted as a great incentive to avoid capture. Fines were heavy and failure to pay them inevitably resulted in gaol. For example, to be discovered in possession of a pheasant, hare or engines between 1711 and 1831 resulted in a mandatory £5 fine per hare or bird. Failure to pay this fine meant three months' gaol,

---

[75] HRO: AF/67. *Magistrates Note Book: Wormlow Hundred, c1811.*

[76] *HJ: 7 September 1808.* There is little indication of the riot's size or its seriousness. A 'riotous assembly' (*sic*) reported in a newspaper could, essentially, be composed of anything from two to three drunks arguing on a street corner to a full-scale mob. Nevertheless there is little to suggest that this was a drunken squabble. That the informer was targeted suggests that the disturbance was an organized show of displeasure rather than a spontaneous outburst of anger.

[77] For a discussion of community justice see Chapter 1.

with a month added for subsequent offences.[78] To be caught poaching at night brought heavier sentences. Game was more vulnerable at night; hares could be netted in numbers and pheasants could be plucked off their night-time roosts with ease. Unsporting, certainly, but effective nevertheless. Equally unsporting was the fact that the night hampered the detection of poachers and the protection of game by keepers. It seems that harsh sentences for night-time poaching, however, were meted out primarily as a result of the landowner's insecurity. The thought of the lower orders skulking around their estates at night armed with guns was too much for landowners to tolerate. Between 1773 and 1816 heavy fines were the order of the day for night poachers: up to £50, depending on the number of previous offences, with gaol and public whippings for defaulters.[79] Armed night-time poachers were dealt with even more severely. From 1800 they could expect six months' hard labour for a first offence, graduating to spells of up to six years, with whippings and forced enlistment in HM services.[80] As far as the gentry were concerned, forced enlistment was useful on two counts. It was probably assumed that being sent to fight the French would dampen any revolutionary ideas, and it was a useful tool for keeping known poachers off their estates. Several Herefordshire poachers were sent to fight in a foreign war, as the following piece in the *Hereford Journal*, dated 5 February 1811, shows:

> A CAUTION TO POACHERS: At our . . . Sessions, last week, Richard Bridgewaters, received sentence as a 'rogue and a vagabond', which was that he be imprisoned for six month's [sic], publicly whipped and sent to serve in the navy.[81]

The gentry's fear is reflected further by treating group poaching as a new category after 1800. To poach as part of a gang after this date was to risk receiving the same penalties as the lone armed poacher.[82]

It is significant that the measures taken against armed night-time poaching increased immediately after the Napoleonic wars. The onset of the post-war agricultural depression, demobilized soldiers returning home and the effects of wartime enclosure all spelt unemployment and poverty. Despite the penalties it is little wonder that, with a meal, or something that could be converted into cash roosting on the nearest estate, many men thought the risk was worthwhile. It was under such conditions that a harsh but short-lived Act of 1816 was passed, threatening seven years' transportation or 'any other punishment as may by law be inflicted for a misdemeanor'.[83] Although

---

[78] 9 Ann, C. 25 (1711). Repealed 1 and 2 Will IV, C. 32 (1831).
[79] 13 Geo III, C. 55 (1773).
[80] 39 and 40 Geo III, C. 50 (1800).
[81] *HJ: 5 February 1811*.
[82] 39 and 40 Geo III, C. 50 (1800).
[83] 56 Geo III, C. 130 (1816).

this act was repealed before the year was out, transportation was still a possibility if a poacher was apprehended armed or at night or, after 1828, if he was in a group.[84] It is indicative, perhaps, that the Act of 1816 was passed at the time of the 'Bread or Blood' riots in East Anglia. Punishments for those poachers apprehended were generally harsh, but for those who poached armed and under the cover of darkness, or in groups, the penalties were positively draconian.

The above catalogue of penalties for poachers is by no means complete. It merely illustrates the legislation used most widely against the Herefordshire poacher and why he was often compelled to resist arrest. There were many other pieces of legislation that were used more sparingly. Legislation existed to protect game out of season, 'tracing hares in the snow' and stealing the eggs from game birds, to name but a few. In short, the Game Laws evolved to cover every eventuality. The Waltham Black Act was still on the statute books until 1827, which prescribed that poachers being found 'in disguise and armed . . . in any enclosed ground' were technically liable to be hanged.[85] The 'Black Act' was, however, as McLynn has argued, 'too blunt a weapon' to be used against poachers.[86] Juries were loath to send a man to the gallows simply for poaching game.

Faced with relatively heavy fines, gaol, whippings or transportation, the poacher was often prepared to fight for his freedom. For a Herefordshire poacher to stand in the dock charged not only with game offences, but also with assault or resisting arrest was not unusual. John Freeman and Thomas Whitefoot received seven years' transportation in 1820 for 'poaching on the lands of W Handbury esq of Shobdon, armed with sticks and resisting'.[87] Thos Payne and John Jones from Kingsland received one year's gaol each for assaulting a gamekeeper with sticks in 1831.[88] Thomas Prosser from Aymestrey was fortunate enough to receive the relatively light sentence of six months plus hard labour for a similar offence in 1822. Prosser, it was argued by the prosecution, 'beat Stephen Rose (the gamekeeper) dreadfully and (he) was torn by (Prosser's) dogs'.[89] Some of the injuries incurred in resisting arrest were horrific, as the following piece, published in the *Hereford Journal* in 1806, shows:

> Committed to our House of Correction as rogues and vagabonds (were) John Price and Edward Probert, two poachers belonging to a gang who have infested the neighbourhood of Leominster for some years past, being found . . . in Croft Park,

[84] 57 Geo III, C 90 (1817) and 9 Geo IV, C. 69 (1828).
[85] 9 Geo I, C. 22 (1723).
[86] McLynn, *Crime and Punishment*. 209.
[87] HRO: Q/SR/108. HQS: *Epiphany 1820. HJ: 19 January 1820.*
[88] HRO: Q/SR/119. HQS: *Easter 1831. HJ: 30 March 1831.*
[89] *HJ: 23 January 1832.*

belonging to our present High Sheriff, Somerset Davis esq, and having with them two dogs. . . . They also had with them large sticks, or bludgeons, with which they violently assaulted and beat Mr Davis' gamekeeper, and his assistants, who secured them after a very violent contest. Thomas Price, one of the gang . . . had his ear nearly severed from his head in the struggle and was otherwise so much bruised before he would surrender, that he was unable to attend before the magistrate to be examined with his associates.[90]

In 1844 the 'notorious' Thomas Stinton beat a gamekeeper's assistant over the head with a spiked club of 'a most dreadful description'.[91] In the following year 'three watchers were beaten so badly by a gang of ten poachers on the Stoke Estate' that 'they have been obliged to keep to their beds ever since'.[92] Such resistance to apprehension was not unusual and other examples could be cited to show the extent of the violence between gamekeepers and poachers. Bruises and bloody noses were occupational hazards for both keepers and poachers, yet to meet a violent death on the Herefordshire preserves was exceptional. Such an event did occur in 1834, however, when an assistant gamekeeper on the Clive estate died as a result of being shot by a poacher at Kingstone.[93] There can be little doubt that the death of James Davis, locally known as Boulter, was, to some extent, due to the enthusiasm of the gamekeeping posse. Indeed, it was this enthusiasm that went some way in acquitting his suspected assailants, Richard Addis, John Evans, Charles Nash, and the brothers Edwin and Allen Smith, of 'wilful and felonious murder'. This case, discussed more fully below, shows that the preserves of the rich could be violent places. In a similar vein, and in the same week that Davis lost his life, Jasper Davis and John Duggard were committed to Hereford Gaol 'charged with going armed at night, in the pursuit of game, and threatening to shoot gamekeeper John Rudd in the parish of Weobley'.[94] Unlike the Kingstone gang Davis and Duggan kept their heads and did not discharge their guns. At their trial Justice Patterson remarked that if the gun had gone off they would have been 'left for the hangman', instead of sentencing them to hard labour for a year.[95] These two cases, perhaps more than all the others, illustrate the potentially explosive situations that existed when gamekeepers confronted poachers. It would also seem that the Herefordshire poacher showed little deference for class in such a confrontational situation. Although it was unusual, landowners themselves could come under attack if they tried to intervene in poaching activities, as the following incident which took place in 1811 shows:

[90] HJ: 15 October 1806.
[91] HJ: 9 October 1844.
[92] HJ: 15 January 1845.
[93] HJ: 29 January 1834.
[94] Ibid.
[95] Lent Assize 1834. HJ: 26 March 1834.

Last Saturday night, as J Kenward esq, of Westhide . . . was returning home from Tarrington . . . (he) heard some dogs, and immediately a hare they were pursuing ran into a purse-net laid in the fence. . . . He got off his horse and took up the animal when three men in waggoners frock coats directly advanced, knocking him down, and on his attempting to rise repeated their blows, leaving him senseless in the road. One of the cowardly ruffians whilst committing this outrage exclaimed 'do him, give him a good one'.[96]

William Scrope argued in 1839 that the poacher's courage came from a bottle. English poachers, according to Scrope, were men 'who screw up their courage at the beerhouses, asserting with imprecations that they will shoot any keeper rather than be taken'.[97] Many poaching gangs probably did meet in the village beer-house before a hunting foray, but to argue that they were all drunken bullies is simply propaganda. James Hawker, as mentioned above, did not drink alcohol, while Richard Jefferies noted later that the successful poacher had a clear head at all times.

It was not only the landowner and his keepers who ran the risk of suffering violence. The reverse was also true although, not surprisingly, when keepers and the gentry handed out arbitrary beatings to poachers their actions did not make the newspapers. The gentry who sought to protect their game had not only the law at their disposal but also a range of machinery that could maim, or even kill, an unwary poacher. Until 1827 man traps and spring guns were employed legally upon estates.[98] Man traps, the metal jaws of which could lacerate and break a man's leg, and spring guns, mounted and fixed guns that were set off by the unwary tripping a wire, had to be negotiated, although it is possible that they claimed more innocent lives than those of poachers. It seems that the reason they were outlawed was because they were a greater danger to 'respectable' citizens out on a Sunday stroll than to a vigilant poacher. Although both poachers and keepers were often armed, the keeper could use his weapon in an affray without fear of prosecution. Effectively this was a licence to kill because between 1693 and 1831 gamekeepers could 'oppose and resist night poachers' and they would 'be indemnified from prosecution if offenders (were) killed'.[99]

Despite the gamekeeper having the advantage in this war it is difficult not to feel some sympathy for his plight. Within a rural community a game-keeper was generally an unpopular figure because, as Munche notes, he was 'both an agent and the symbol of game preservation'.[100] Gamekeeping as a profession, however, did have its financial advantages. As early as 1772 Taplin had estimated that the average wage of a gamekeeper was as much as

---

[96] HJ: 11 December 1811.
[97] Scrope, 'Deer Stalking'. 31.
[98] 7 and 8 Geo IV, C. 18 (1827).
[99] 4 and 5 Will and Mary, C. 23 (1693).
[100] Munche, Gentlemen and Poachers. 45.

£20 per year.[101] His wage was also boosted by bounties on vermin, the sale of rabbit skins, a supply of fresh meat and a share of the poacher's fines. He was far better off than many of his class. In return for these advantages it was necessary to protect his master's game, often at the expense of his neighbour's goodwill. There is some evidence to suggest, in Herefordshire at least, that a few gamekeepers were willing to overlook a limited amount of poaching activity. Indeed, the gentry, from time to time, had to place warning notices in the local press making the situation perfectly clear to gamekeepers and poachers alike. An example of this is the piece below, which appeared in the *Hereford Journal* in 1820, composed by Richard Arkwright, landowner of Hampton Court.

GAME.

In consequence of the destruction of game in the manors of Hope-Under-Dinmore, Bodenham, Stoke-Prior, Newton Warton and Ivington, keepers are directed immediately to lay information against all unqualified persons sporting therein.

Hampton Court, 13 October 1820.[102]

Although this notice was a clear warning to poachers it was also a reminder to his keepers to do their duty. Perhaps Arkwright's keepers were exceeding their authority; equally 'the destruction of game' may have been the keeper's own doing. This is gamekeeper turned poacher. Taplin observed in 1772:

The greatest poachers, are the pretended Preservers' Deputies, called Gamekeepers. It is a notorious Fact that these worthy Servants kill one brace for their Employers and two for themselves. The extensive Game Trade that is carried on . . . with the Road Waggoners, would to those unacquainted with it, surpass Belief.[103]

He may have had a point, as this newspaper report from the *Hereford Journal* in 1834 illustrates:

William Shiers, convicted of being out at night, armed with a gun and provided with a sporting dog, was last week committed to Hard Labour for three months in our County Gaol. A brace of partridges, four hares and twelve rabbits, were found in an unoccupied house in Mordiford, which Shiers had made his depot for plunder, and nine wires for snaring hares, were taken from his pocket on searching him in prison. We understand the above man's name to be Shyer, not Shiers, and

---

[101] Ibid. 43.
[102] *HJ: 23 October 1820.*
[103] Taplin, *Observations*. 41.

he was a gamekeeper to a gentleman who resides near Ross till within the last few months; after his discharge he was fined two pounds for poaching on the property of his late master!![104]

Undoubtedly some gamekeepers did poach but it would be safe to assume that most did their utmost to protect their master's sport. Generally the gamekeeper was in an unenviable position. To perform his duties to the letter often brought ill-will from the local labouring population, while if he sought to appease the locals he ran the risk of incurring his employer's displeasure. However, the potential financial rewards from holding such a post meant that most gamekeepers would follow the safest course: to protect the game placed in his charge.

William Taswell, Lady Rodney's gamekeeper, was an enthusiastic preserver of his ladyship's game at Berrington Court. Indeed, his enthusiasm for his job upset the local poaching fraternity to such an extent that an anonymous letter expressing their displeasure was found stuffed into the mouth of an ornamental brass canon at the front of Berrington House in 1811. It promised:

Birrington [sic] shall shine in the dark the keeper shall dy by the gun . . . you had better send bridgewaters hom a gane if you dont wee will put three in his place that keeper has got a fu hars now wee will Let them bee till a nother yer and Get our Engines mended and you shant have one hare by this time next year that keeper had Better Go back in to Derbyshire for if he stays hear he shall Surely dy he is not Going to be Master of Us tradesmen we always did Get Master and wee will do birrington will have a fine Lamp some dark night.[105]

Taswell, the gamekeeper, had been brought in from Derbyshire to put a stop to the poaching on the north Herefordshire estate. Moreover, it would seem he was successful, or at least successful enough to make himself and his employer the centre of a hate campaign. Cottages had been visited and 'nets and engines' had been destroyed and a local poacher, Rodney Bridgewater, the subject of the above letter, had been gaoled, whipped and conscripted for assaulting Taswell the previous winter. That Taswell had upset the local poaching fraternity is evident, as the day before the letter was discovered 'some person discharged a gun, loaded with Duck Shot' at him.[106] Taswell was only slightly wounded in the attack but this prompted Lady Rodney to offer a reward of one hundred guineas, a huge amount, for information leading to the arrest of his assailant. The would-be assassin, however, was never arrested despite the reward; neither was the composer of the letter, despite

---

[104] *HJ: 29 October 1834.*
[105] *HJ: 6 March 1811.*
[106] Ibid.

a further offer of another hundred guineas. We can only suppose that both the letter and Taswell's treatment was community sanctioned, and not only by the poaching community. That the two hundred guineas – a small fortune for a labourer – remained unclaimed indicates a significant degree of solidarity. Once again a wall of silence was erected to meet those who sought the perpetrators.

The imprisonment and treatment of Bridgewater was the beginning of the campaign which led to the letter of protest and the attempt on the keeper's life. It was evident that the local inhabitants had, until Taswell's appointment, enjoyed game from the estate at will and they were not prepared to let this advantage slip from their hands without a fight. The letter clearly asserts that Taswell's victory would be short-lived and that any further interference in their poaching activities would see Berrington Hall burnt to the ground and the keeper murdered. The incendiary letter was psychological terrorism *par excellence*. Indeed, the delivering of the letter to her very front door presumably showed Lady Rodney how vulnerable her home was. This vulnerability was reflected by the size of the reward.

Arson, as a tool of protest, was not confined only to buildings and haystacks. Coppices were also vulnerable to attack in Herefordshire.[107] On 3 May 1820 an advertisement was published in the *Hereford Journal* offering a twenty-guinea reward for information which would lead to the apprehension of the 'arsonist' who set fire to one of his coppice woods.[108] No doubt the size of the reward, offered by John Braithwaite Esq. of Brockhampton Court, although small in comparison to that offered by Lady Rodney, played a part in the committal of James Waller, alias 'Ironsides', to Hereford Gaol. Three days after his incarceration, however, on 24 May, another fire was reported in a coppice wood in the same parish. This time the wood was the joint property of E. F. Foley and Edward Poole Esq.[109] Again no culprit was ever discovered and 'Ironsides' was acquitted 'no bill found' on 9 August 1820.[110] While there may have been a link between the two incidents research has failed to discover it. Indeed, apart from an arson attack in 1832 on a coppice wood belonging to Sir Charles Morgan's Risca estate the two incidents were in isolation.[111]

Coppice woods served several purposes. Mainly they provided materials for fencing, hop poles and so on. They were also important for game preservation and whoever were responsible for the attacks could not have picked a more destructive time of year. May, the month of the attacks, would have seen an abundance of game in coppice woods. Ground nesting birds, the

[107] For a discussion of incendiarism see Chapter 7.
[108] HJ: 3 May 1820.
[109] HJ: 24 May 1820.
[110] HJ: 9 May 1820.
[111] HJ: 25 April 1832.

mainstay of the sporting gun, would either be sitting on eggs or feeding young, while the furred variety of game, hares and deer used the cover to hide their young and for daytime cover. The attacks could be seen as an attempt not only to destroy the animal's habitat and their young but also to destroy future sport for those who were qualified to hunt it legally. Because nobody answered for the above crimes we can only speculate as to the motivation behind the attacks. The fires may have been started by a disgruntled labourer. It could, on the other hand, be argued that in destroying coppices the poachers, if indeed the fires were the work of poachers, would be destroying their own livelihood. Game in coppice woods, however, were easier to protect by keepers. Pheasants, for instance, would be drawn to them for night-time roosting. The coppice woods were also suitable territory for the gamekeeper's spring guns and man traps. To fire a coppice was to spread and expose game, making it much easier and safer to poach.

Another poaching case from Herefordshire that had overtones of protest was the case of the colliers who were disturbed while deer poaching on the Duke of Norfolk's estate in April 1832. According to the newspaper report the poachers were 'dressed in dirty flannel dresses'. Cross-dressing, for want of a better expression, and criminal acts are synonymous with protest and there was certainly a tradition of it in this part of the world, as Albert's article suggests.[112] Rebeccaism, turnpike rioters and even male food rioters have worn, at one time or another, women's clothes. Several explanations could be offered as to why this was the case. Stevenson speculates that men who were dressed as women would be less likely to be selected for arrest from a rioting crowd.[113] Edward Thompson, however, argued that this was not necessarily the case. While women may have been less likely to be prosecuted for their part in a disturbance, for reasons of putting whole families on the parish, they were still arrested and committed to gaol.[114] Although the above poachers were undoubtedly in 'disguise' they were instantly recognized as colliers. Similarly, Richard Addis, one of the accused in the Kingstone poaching murder, reportedly wore 'a dark dress' at the time of the offence.[115] Arguably an early nineteenth-century collier dressed as a woman simply looked like a man dressed as a woman. One also has to raise questions as to the point of being disguised in this manner, in a wood, on a dark night. To 'black up', to cover the face in soot or burnt cork, made sense, since nothing shone better on a dark night than a pale face. Such a disguise helped to avoid detection, but the loose-fitting nature of dresses for a poacher would be impracticable, suggesting that their garb had some other, perhaps symbolic, meaning.

---

[112] William Albert, 'Popular Opposition to Turnpike Trusts in Early Eighteenth Century England', *Journal of Transport History*, Vol. 5, No. 1 (1979).

[113] Stevenson, *Popular Disturbances*. 126.

[114] Thompson, 'Moral Economy'. 305–36.

[115] *HJ: 2 April 1834.*

Cross-dressing was not confined to poaching jaunts. The Ledbury turnpike riot similarly saw colliers dressed as women. A witness described the mob of 1735 as 'a great number of persons armed with guns and axes, some of them disguised with black'd faces and women's cloathes (sic)'.[116] One of the turnpike protesters, James Bayliss, convicted and hanged under the Waltham Black Act of 1723, said under examination that 'the gown, apron and straw hat' worn at the time of the riot belonged to his wife.[117] Indeed, it is unfortunate for the historian, although fortunate for the poaching colliers, that they were not apprehended, for it was possible they would then have been tried under this particularly savage piece of legislation. Perhaps they may have explained under examination why they were dressed in such a manner. Their escape forces us to speculate; however, it seems there was a tradition among protesting colliers and others undertaking criminal activity to cross-dress.

Engels called the English Game Laws a 'barbaric cruelty'.[118] He was right, but his claim that on capture the poacher 'goes to jail, and for a second offence receives at the least seven years transportation' is clearly a non-sense.[119] Engels' mistake was understandable, given the complicated nature of the Game Laws as they stood in the early nineteenth century. Nor was Engels alone, and Munche points out that the Hammonds also mis-interpreted sections of the Game Laws, and he argues further that such misinterpretations have added to the Game Laws' reputation for 'savagery'.[120] Punishments meted out to poachers were, by today's standards, 'barbaric' but it must be recognized that punishments for shoplifting, sheep-stealing, fraud, and a multitude of other crimes, were equally harsh, if not more severe. The poacher who was unfortunate enough to face an Assize judge, however, enjoyed the same privileges as other prisoners. He was often defended by professional and able men. He was able to call upon witnesses and his ultimate fate rested upon a jury's decision. It is accepted that arbitrary 'drawing-room' justice continued to be the main way poachers were dealt with. However, those who elected, or were committed, to await a Quarter Session or Assize could be safe in the knowledge that they would see 'fair play' within the constraints of a harsh system.

During research for this book it soon became apparent that poachers, sheep-stealers and other felons were often assigned excellent defence lawyers.

---

[116] Thompson, 'Moral Economy'. 332.

[117] Waltham Black Act: 9 Geo I, C 22 (1723). See E. P. Thompson's *Whigs and Hunters*, Penguin, Harmondsworth (1990) for a full analysis of the Black Act of 1723. The book also contains a reference to Reynolds' trial, and subsequent execution. See also Albert, 'Popular Opposition to Turnpike Trusts' for a discussion of the Ledbury Turnpike Riot of 1735.

[118] Engels, *The Condition*. 266.

[119] Ibid. 267.

[120] Munche, *Gentlemen and Poachers*. 8.

In many cases their knowledge of the law and their unbiased professionalism ensured that poachers often received sentences far less severe than the law prescribed. Moreover, in some cases they secured an acquittal, even when the accused was guilty. The perceived savagery of the Game Laws and their complexity were useful tools for the defence. The case of James Eckley is a good example of this. Eckley stood accused of having 'been found in the night of 14 December 1824, in a close, in the parish of Much Cowarne, armed with a gun, for the purpose of killing game'.[121] Eckley, argued Powell for the prosecution, was indicted 'under the statute 57th George c. 90' under which 'any person convicted of this offence (shall be), liable to be transported for seven years, or any other punishment as may be inflicted on persons guilty of misdemeanor'. Eckley was clearly guilty. He had been caught red-handed as he climbed over a hedge in the close, gun in hand. He also chose to compound his crime by assaulting Palmer, an assistant gamekeeper for F. H. Thomas Esq., with a blow to the head, while the nets found upon his person and the nets already set in the hedge compounded his guilt.

A lawyer named Armitage, who acted in Eckley's defence, clearly thought that to defend Eckley by protesting his innocence would be a hopeless tactic. Thus he chose to attack the Game Laws themselves, arguing that the punishment far outweighed the crime and suggested that Eckley was sure to be transported if he was found guilty, despite protests to the contrary from the prosecution. He also claimed that the way 'gentlemen sent out their game-keepers, armed like footpads . . . with pistols, to watch for poachers (was) calculated to provoke violence'.[122] Armitage's defence must have exceeded Eckley's wildest dreams. He was acquitted.

It is clear that Eckley was guilty but the Hereford Jury were not prepared to see him transported for this crime. Indeed, despite assurances that 'the court had also the power (to inflict) any punishment, or fine, or imprisonment, or both', the jury, perhaps sensing the judge's mood, refused to gamble with Eckley's future. Furthermore, as the nineteenth century wore on, juries consisted more and more of the 'middling sort', who were as unable to hunt legally as Eckley. One senses an element of tenant farmer protest here. Finding Eckley not guilty, despite overwhelming evidence to the contrary, may have been their way of expressing their feelings towards a system that prevented them from hunting over land they may well have rented. More simply, however, it may have been the jury's way of denying the judge an opportunity to impose an unjust sentence. Whatever the reason for its decision the *Hereford Journal's* comment that the verdict 'excited considerable surprise' was an understatement. Following the verdict, Powell, the prosecutor, attempted to have the jury 'discharged', having lost confidence in their ability to pass judgment. The judge, who was equally enraged at the

---

[121] *Lent Assize 1825. HJ: 22 December 1824.*
[122] *HJ: 21 March 1825.*

jury's decision, commented that 'the jury have given their verdict in opposition to the most direct and positive evidence'. Addressing them he said: 'I do not know how you can reconcile your consciences.'[123]

Perhaps the judge's anger was understandable when faced with a jury that would not convict on indisputable evidence. Some judges, however, would not urge a jury to find a defendant guilty unless the evidence was totally conclusive. The Kingstone poaching gang not only escaped the poaching charges through the defence lawyer's ability, but Addis was acquitted of the charge of the 'wilful murder' of James Davis.[124] It was clear that one of the gang had fired the fatal shot into Davis' neck and it was also clear that Addis was the chief suspect. Moreover, statements made by two of the gang who had turned 'King's evidence', Nash and Evans, claimed that he had indeed fired the fatal shot. The absolute proof that Addis was the murderer, however, was absent. On the evening before the trial at the Assize banquet, Justice Patterson warned in his speech that:

> Proof of who fired the weapon is not absolute. I am not, gentlemen asking or advising you to throw out the bill, but it will be better for you to do so than you should find it (so), and the *petite jury* compelled to acquit (Addis).[125]

Patterson was clearly arguing that it would be better to release Addis now rather than his being acquitted by a jury. It seems likely that he was guilty, but the failure of the prosecution to prove this would damage the credibility of the courts. The bill was not 'thrown out' and, as Patterson had predicted, Addis walked out of the court a free man. The bulk of the prosecution's evidence came from Nash and Evans who claimed that Addis had fired the fatal shot and the discovery of a hat, said to belong to Addis, which was found in a nearby field. The hat, on its own, was insufficient to convict Addis and, as we have seen in the chapter concerning sheep-stealing, juries were loath to believe the words of men who would accept a pardon for giving evidence. After all, the threat of the rope could compel men to say almost anything and a question mark hung over everything they said under examination.

The Smith brothers, Edwin and Allen, had to face the lesser charge of poaching by night but even here the prosecution was deprived of a victory. Speaking for the defence, Sargent Ludlow, argued the gamekeepers, in following the gang, had exceeded their authority. Their enthusiasm for making an arrest had taken them outside 'Mr Clive's manor, free warren or chase', and they had no authority where the arrests were finally made. Moreover, to add insult to Mr Clive's injury, he also pointed out that some of

---

[123] Ibid.
[124] *Lent Assize 1834.*
[125] *HJ: 2 April 1834.*

his keepers were not even licensed.[126] Again an acquittal and, again, the credibility of the prosecution was damaged. Patterson's misery must have been compounded when one of the Smith brothers began laughing as he was summing up:

> His Lordship instantly addressed him in the most serious manner, and told him, he might laugh, but it was right he and the other prisoners should know that they had escaped only through the absence of that strict and legal proof which the jury, in a spirit of leniency, deemed necessary to their conviction; there could, however, be no doubt that they were all present on the night referred to, and conscious as they must be of having been concerned in an affair in which the life of a fellow creature was inhumanely sacrificed, the present behaviour too fully demonstrated the depravity and baseness of their hearts, and (this) would be remembered if they should ever be brought to court again as offenders against the laws of their country.[127]

Acquittals were rare, and for every poacher who walked free many more did not. The above examples have been used simply to illustrate that the legal system sometimes worked to the poacher's advantage and that they often enjoyed fair representation in court. As Hay argues, the ruling elite sought credibility, and to ensure this the law had to be seen to be impartial.[128] To let the odd poacher slip through the net was a small price to pay to retain that credibility. To send every night-poaching labourer to Australia for his crime was equally damaging and, although the ultimate penalties were harsh, they were rarely employed. Fragments of the eighteenth-century Bloody Code lingered into the nineteenth century yet the basis of the code was that it was meant to deter rather than punish. To make examples of all poachers who stood at a higher court would have been counter-productive. As a result transportation was used relatively rarely as a punishment for poaching. The reality for a poacher caught armed and resisting in Herefordshire was that he would be forced to spend a period in the local gaol, at hard labour. If a convicted poacher was sent to the hulks to await transportation he could consider himself unlucky that the magistrate, or judge, had chosen him to be held up to his peers as an example. Equally, to gaol every poacher who stood before a magistrate would have filled the county prison. It is noticeable, therefore – and this is particularly true after the Act of 1831 – that magistrates often gave convicted poachers every opportunity to pay rather than be gaoled for non-payment of fines. Henry Mints, John Hicks, Thomas Tingle and William Stevens, for example, were given two weeks to find £1 each by the magistrates of the Harewood End Petty Sessions for 'destroying

---

[126] *HJ: 2 April 1834.*
[127] Ibid.
[128] Hay, 'Property, Authority and the Criminal Law'.

conies' in 1840.[129] Similarly, Henry Powell was also given two weeks to pay a £2 fine, plus 6d costs, at Ross Petty Sessions in 1845, after he was found guilty of 'laying wires in the Penyard Wood'.[130] Occasionally, poachers escaped solely with a dressing down by the Bench and a bill for the costs only. Charles Nicholls was caught laying 'night lines for trout in the River Pinsley' in 1846 and, after promising the Leominster Petty Session magistrate that 'he would not do it again', was discharged 'after paying the costs'.[131] A year later, Alfred Preece, 'a lad', was found guilty of a similar offence on the River Wye and was released with a reprimand, after his father paid a nominal fine and fees amounting to 13s 6d. Preece's father, in seeking his son's freedom, told the magistrates that 'he would be answerable to his son's future conduct', and while the magistrate agreed to this he commented that the boy's father 'was a greater poacher than the son'.[132]

We have to remember that to some extent at least the gentry relied upon the goodwill of their tenants, the local tradespeople and the *hoi pol'loi*. To hand out draconian sentences, to enforce laws that many were opposed to, was to stretch the sinews of deference to breaking point. Some landowners were more severe than others, and while they all saw the necessity of prosecution to protect their sport, it is clear that not all the gentry agreed with the severity of the Game Laws. At the 'request of the representatives of the late T Bird esq', Richard Smith received only a 10s fine for poaching at St Martin's with a dog in 1838.[133] In 1845 Sir E. F. S. Stanhope asked the magistrates at the Harewood End Petty Sessions to treat James Haines 'leniently' after he was caught laying wires on his preserves. Haines escaped with a paltry 5s fine.[134] In 1844 William Unett Esq. persuaded his gamekeeper to drop a charge of assault against Thomas Stinton who had hit the keeper on the head when attempting to escape. Stinton was indeed fortunate, for instead of facing a transportation order he was gaoled for two months.[135] Unett, perhaps knowing the reluctance of Herefordshire juries to have poachers convicted for transportable offences, felt it more prudent to pursue the lesser charge of poaching at night and advised his gamekeeper to follow this course. Nevertheless, Unett's intervention, as well as the appeals made by Bird and Stanhope, were not simple acts of compassion. Such displays of mercy and compassion probably did more to further the cause of public relations between themselves and the local labouring population than any post-harvest feast or winter time act of charity coals and blankets.

---

[129] HJ: 26 February 1840.
[130] HJ: 20 August 1845.
[131] HJ: 11 June 1846.
[132] HJ: 30 June 1847.
[133] HJ: 14 November 1838.
[134] HJ: 27 August 1845.
[135] HJ: 9 October 1844.

Following the murder of James Davis, the *Hereford Journal* and the *Hereford Times* received several letters and printed some articles denouncing the Game Laws as they then stood. Typically, explanations for the increase in poaching violence were varied. Low beer-shops, 'which by their establishment in retired country districts, have afforded a convenient rendezvous to organised gangs', was a favourite reason given.[136] The lifting of restrictions of the sale of game in 1831 was another. It was argued, by a correspondent to the *Hereford Journal*, that 'game would become so cheap no poacher would find it worth his while to pursue his trade, but how different has been the result'.[137] Indeed, the restrictions on the sale of game meant the crime was potentially quite lucrative. Most commentators, however, agreed that: 'It therefore becomes a question (of) whether something ought not to be done to put a stop to these lawless proceedings, and to place the Game Laws upon a more just and equitable footing.'[138]

Hereford's letter-writing class, the majority of whom were tenant farmers and landowners, agreed that poaching would not, and perhaps could not, be stopped. They recognized that 'our peasantry are apt to look upon all wild animals as their own, and to regard poaching as a very trivial offence'.[139] Arguably the motivation for poaching lay deeper than that. 'The English peasantry', Engels explained in 1844, 'according to the old English custom and tradition, sees in poaching only a natural and noble expression of courage and daring.'[140] James Hawker would have certainly agreed with this sentiment, writing that poaching 'is in our nature as Englishmen'.[141]

---

[136] *HJ: 5 February 1834.*
[137] Ibid.
[138] Ibid.
[139] Ibid.
[140] Engels, *The Condition.* 267.
[141] Christian, *Hawker's Journal.* 104.

7

'Vile' and 'evil-disposed persons'

Incendiarism and animal-maiming

There can be little doubt that certain rural crimes were committed with the sole intention of striking terror into the victim's heart. The crimes of arson and animal-maiming fall into this category. The destructive, sadistic and threatening nature of these crimes, crimes that gave no material benefit to the perpetrators, simply carried a message of hate. We can only imagine the horror of the farmer upon the discovery of a mutilated mare, or the helplessness as he watched his wheat rick burn to ashes. Moreover, following such an attack we can imagine his feelings of vulnerability and isolation. Incendiarism and animal-maiming were acts not simply of rural terrorism but psychological terrorism *par excellence*.

Of all the crimes examined in this book, incendiarism and animal-maiming were by far the most serious. Other rural crimes against property carried the death sentence prior to the 1830s, but incendiarism and animal-maiming often brought down the full weight of a judge's sentencing powers.[1] Their seriousness was reflected by the possible sentences a court could impose upon those found guilty. Between 1723 and 1837, arsonists, if convicted, could be tried under the Waltham Black Act.[2] This infamous Act laid down that to maliciously or wilfully set fire to any 'house, barn, out-house, hovel, cock, mow, stack of corn, straw, hay or wood', whether in disguise or not was 'to be punished by death without benefit of clergy'.[3] Although, after 1837, the death sentence for arson was retained only for those who deliberately set fire to a 'habituated dwelling-house', transportation for a rural incendiarist was still the most likely outcome of a successful prosecution.[4] Between 1722 and 1823 the crime of animal-maiming also came under the Waltham Black Act and was technically punishable by death.[5] Moreover, despite the relaxing of

---

[1] Other rural crimes that carried the death penalty, relevant to Herefordshire, c.1800–60, were sheep-stealing, until 1832 and animal-maiming, until 1823.

[2] Waltham Black Act: 9 Geo. I, c. 22 (1722).

[3] Radzinowicz, *English Criminal Law*, Vol. 1. 68–9.

[4] Burning of Buildings Act: 7 Will. 4 and 1 Vict. c. 89 (1837).

[5] John Archer argues that the death penalty for animal-maiming was not repealed until 1832; see 'By A Flash And A Scare'. 200. Radzinowicz, however, points out that the Waltham Black Act was repealed; that is, apart from 'setting on fire and maliciously

the law, an animal-maimer, like an incendiarist, could still expect a lengthy spell in gaol or even transportation.

Both crimes were grave offences and, although they were clearly different, they did share some similarities. Apart from poaching, the crimes of animal-maiming and incendiarism lend themselves easily to the concept of social crime and crime as protest. The firing of farm property has long been associated with rural protest. Hobsbawm and Rudé's definitive study of the 1830 to 31 agrarian disturbances has fixed firmly in the minds of social historians the idea that rural arson was a crime of the discontented and displaced.[6] The fires that lit up the rural south, south east and east, however, were not confined to the 'Swing' years of 1830 to 1831. Roger Wells has shown that the malicious destruction of farm property by fire pre-dated 'Swing', while Jones, Archer and Muskett have indicated that the crime continued well into the 1840s.[7] These studies, none the less, have concentrated upon incendiarism in the south and east of England, with East Anglia being the most heavily researched region of them all. Similarly, the study of animal-maiming has centred largely on East Anglia and the subject has been the sole domain of one historian, John Archer.[8] Rural arson and animal-maiming were also committed in Herefordshire and there is some evidence to suggest that they were carried out with the same intention; that is to convey a message of discontent. This chapter will examine the extent to which these crimes were committed in Herefordshire between 1800 and 1860 and will also discuss the extent to which they might be classified as crimes of protest, rather than crimes borne of personal malice.

Incendiarism

With 101 reported attacks to farm property between 1800 and 1860 rural incendiarism in the county was not commonplace, although it certainly increased after 1831. This is especially true when Herefordshire is compared to other counties such as Norfolk and Suffolk during the same period.[9] As

---

shooting at persons' in 1823. The relevant Act is 4 Geo 4, c. 54 (1823). See Radzinowicz, *English Criminal Law*, Vol. 1.

[6] Hobsbawm and Rudé, *Captain Swing*.

[7] Wells, 'The Development of the English Rural Proletariat', in Reed and Wells, *Class, Conflict and Protest*, and Jones, 'Thomas Campbell Forster'. See also Muskett's article on incendiarism in Suffolk during the 1840s, 'The Suffolk Incendiaries', and Archer, 'By a Flash and a Scare'.

[8] Archer, 'By a Flash and a Scare' and 'A Fiendish Outrage?'.

[9] David Jones, for instance, argued that in 1844 alone, eighty-five suspects of incendiarism were committed to local goals in Norfolk and Suffolk. Compare this to Herefordshire, the same year, with five arson attacks and no committals. Jones, 'Thomas Campbell Foster'. 38.

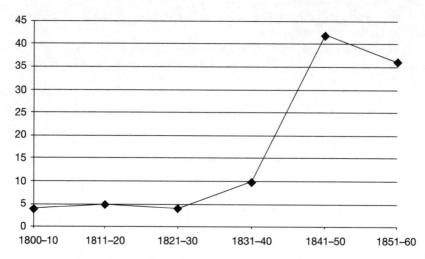

Figure 7.1 Reported cases of rural incendiarism: Herefordshire, 1800–60[10]

Figure 7.1 shows, the peak period was between 1843 and 1850, with forty reported attacks to farm property.

As Figure 7.1 suggests, incendiarism to farm property prior to 1830 was an unusual crime and expression of discontent. These findings are similar to those of Archer, who claimed that incendiarism in Norfolk was 'of a relatively low order' prior to 1830.[11] Incendiarism in Herefordshire prior to the 1830s was also rare, with only 1801 being conspicuous by having two reported attacks. The peak periods for rural incendiarism in the county were undoubtedly from March 1843 to September 1844, with fifteen reported attacks, and from February to December 1849, with twelve reported incendiary attacks on farm property (see Figure 7.2).[12] While rural arson undoubtedly increased in the county after 1834 the crime was never as prevalent as it was in the east of England.

Why incendiarism should have been a more frequent expression of discontent in Norfolk and Suffolk is open for debate. Herefordshire, however, was (is) geographically smaller than both Norfolk and Suffolk. The 1851 census noted that the rural acreage of Norfolk and Suffolk was 1,268,286 and 899,428 acres respectively, while Herefordshire consisted of a mere 415,994 rural acres. The rural population of these eastern counties was greater, with Norfolk having a rural population of 276,891 and Suffolk 239,802 in

---

[10] *HJ*: c.1800–60 and the *HT*: c.1832–60.

[11] John Archer, '*By A Flash and a Scare*'. 73. Moreover, Hobsbawm and Rudé, in *Captain Swing*, argue that incendiarism only gained in popularity as a form of protest 'after 1830'.

[12] See Appendix VIII for a complete list of reported incendiary attacks to farm property, c.1800–60.

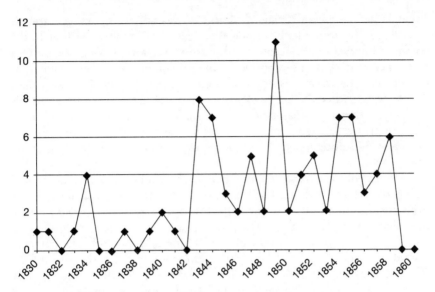

Figure 7.2 Rural incendiarism in Herefordshire, 1830–60

comparison to Herefordshire's 74,703.[13] Arguably, then, the agricultural discontent that was a feature of the first half of the nineteenth century may have been proportionately greater in Norfolk and Suffolk. It could also be argued that the Herefordshire labourer simply had fewer targets to attack. During the first half of the nineteenth century the economic geography of Herefordshire differed to that of eastern England. Whereas the east concentrated more upon cereal production, and therefore had more easy targets for the incendiarist to burn, agricultural production in Herefordshire was generally more mixed. Indeed, incendiarism in the north of the county and in the west of the county, which bordered Wales and was largely given over to sheep farming, was extremely rare.

Despite the number of incendiary attacks to farm property in Herefordshire, between 1800 and 1860, there were only nineteen committals to Hereford Gaol on suspicion of incendiarism. That these committals led to only seven convictions, two of which were of boys, illustrates the difficulty the authorities had in detecting those responsible. Incendiarism, and animal-maiming, were probably the most difficult of all the rural crimes to guard against. By their very nature they were secretive acts, usually committed under cover of darkness. Where the time that an incendiary attack occurred is given, either by the contemporary press or in the court records, it was invariably reported as being carried out in the dead of night, with 11 p.m. to

[13] BPP: *1851 Census: Population*, Vol. 6. 642–3.

2 a.m. being the favoured time.[14] Moreover, incendiary attacks were usually carried out by individuals rather than gangs or groups. Although the committal and conviction rate for this crime was low, it is significant that the suspects arrested in ten out of the eleven committals either acted alone or in pairs. Courtroom testimony by defendants not only gives an insight into what motivated the fire but also his or her attendance in court invariably left details that are invaluable for the student of historical criminology. Because of the deficiency of court cases for incendiarism we are forced to rely upon the contemporary press for any type of meaningful analysis of the crime.

Undoubtedly the reported numbers of incendiary attacks, illustrated in Figures 7.1 and 7.2, are but a fraction of the true number. First, it has been possible to count only those fires that were reported as the work of incendiaries rather than those which were started by children, tramps having a smoke or by accident. With the benefit of hindsight it is probable that a fire started in a wheat rick, away from the farmhouse, in the early hours of the morning, was the act of an incendiary. However, unless the contemporary press stated that the evidence suggested it was arson it is unsafe to class the fire as a crime. Not all fires were lit with malicious intent, or even by a human hand. Ricks, if the wheat or straw had not been properly dried out before stacking, could combust. They could also be struck by lightning or lit by a carelessly knocked-over lamp. Exactly how many incendiary fires were lit only to be extinguished by an alert farmer, or had harmlessly burn themselves out before they caused any extensive damage, we will never know. Moreover, we will never discover how many farmers were victims of incendiarism yet chose not to report the attack to the authorities for fear of further repercussions. The dark figure of incendiarism in the county of Herefordshire between 1800 and 1860 is, in keeping with other crimes, much greater than the research for this project has been able to reveal.

While the contemporary local press frequently reported incendiary fires immediately, there were instances where they were not reported until some weeks later. During 1843, for example, the farmers of Madley were the target of eight incendiary attacks. The local press, however, reported only half that number at the time and the higher figure came to light only when, a month later, the *Hereford Journal* made a passing reference to the fact that these fires had occurred at all.[15] Although only the barest of details of these attacks were ever given it seems quite likely that some fires were never reported. Furthermore, the editors of the local press tended to avoided speculation as to the causes of fires and generally stuck to the facts. Indeed, this was often the way fires were reported, although quite often the reader

---

[14] During 1849, five of the seven incendiary fires in Herefordshire were reported as being started between 11 p.m. and 2 a.m. See *HT: 6 January to 29 December 1849*.
[15] *HJ: 10 May 1843*.

is left in little doubt as to whether or not the fire was the work of an incendiarist. The time a fire began, its proximity to the farmhouse and the popularity of the victim all provide clues as to whether or not a fire was started deliberately. It is also clear that newspaper editors did not always regard an act of incendiarism as worthy of a headline. An incendiary attack may have been given only a line or two in the press, and this was especially true if the editor decided a local ball or the death of a local dignitary was more newsworthy. Generally, an incendiary fire was only given column inches if it was part of a spate of attacks. If a bigger story presented itself then quite often editors chose to report those events rather than an arson attack on a remote farm. It could also be argued that editors deliberately chose not to devote too much newspaper space to incendiary attacks, feeling it was not in the public's interest to draw attention to such acts. Archer has argued that one of the main attractions of incendiarism was the amount of publicity a fire would attract from the local press, but the evidence from Herefordshire suggests that this may not have been the case.[16] Editors may have felt that to report an incendiary attack was not only to glorify crime but was also likely to invite copy-cat fires. It was suggested at his trial that John Jones, a 14-year-old farm servant of Preston Court, fired his employer's farm buildings in 1849 because he had been influenced by a similar attack in a neighbouring village.[17] It is impossible to discover if the editors of the local press consciously under-reported incendiary attacks. What is certain though is that they gave far more space to acts of sheep-stealing and poaching.

The severity of the potential sentences for the crimes of incendiarism not only illustrates the draconian nature of eighteenth- and early-nineteenth century criminal law, but also illuminates the fear that this crime instilled in their victims. Arson was especially feared. Rural dwellings of the period were full of combustible materials. The thatched roof of the more humble home or the panel-lined rooms of the great country house meant that it was prudent to treat fire with a great deal of respect. Meals were often cooked over naked flames and candles and lanterns lit the way after dark, and the pages of the contemporary press were littered with tragic stories of women and children who had burned to death after their clothing or bedding caught fire. Accidents were relatively common and a knocked over candle or lamp could reduce a humble home to ashes in a very short time. Admittedly fire services existed in the county but they were essentially an urban service. In addition, while there is evidence to suggest that they would willingly attend a fire in a country district, by the time their appliances had reached the scene of the fire it was usually too late. By the time the Hereford appliance had arrived at a incendiary fire at Madley, in 1843, not only had the barn been reduced to ashes, but it had also spread to a 'beest-house (*sic*)

[16] Archer, '*By A Flash and a Scare*'. 163.
[17] HRO: BG/11/8/9. *Summer Assize 1849*. HT: *4 August 1849*.

and wheat rick'.[18] In 1849, another incendiary fire at Madley, which started between midnight and one in the morning, was not attended to until 3 a.m. and 'too late for their services to be of much avail'.[19] This fire caused damage valued at over £300 and, as the property was uninsured, it proved to be particularly damaging for the farmer concerned. Fire was an excellent weapon in the armoury of the rural terrorist. A strategically placed ember or match had the power to bankrupt an uninsured farmer, or at the very least cause him a substantial amount of financial discomfort.

As Archer has argued, insurance against arson on farm property was relatively rarely taken out before the 1830s.[20] Indeed, when reporting incendiary fires the contemporary press of Herefordshire made no reference concerning the insured state of the property until after 1839. After that date the *Hereford Journal* and *Hereford Times* did occasionally report if the victim was covered by insurance, though this was more likely to be stated if the loss to the farmer was substantial. Only twenty-one of the incendiary attacks reported in the press mentioned if the property was uninsured, part-insured or wholly insured. Because incendiarism was a relatively uncommon crime in the county it is possible that tenant farmers were disinclined to secure insurance for their property. Landowners, on the other hand, seemed more prudent. In 1849 the landlords of Church House Farm of Madley, the Governors of Guys Hospital, were proved to have been wise in insuring their property against an incendiary attack when they lost a barn and outbuildings, but the tenant, John Smith, did not insure his produce and had to sustain the financial loss of 100 bushels of barley and a hayrick.[21] It would also appear that farmers often underestimated the value of their property. The tenant of Verry's Farm, near Ross, despite being insured for £600, 'still sustained a loss of £800' damage following an attack in 1847.[22] Similarly, in 1849 a farmer named Davies from Preston-on-Wye suffered over £1,000 worth of fire damage, yet he was insured for only half that amount.[23] If the victim was uninsured an act of incendiarism had the ability to reduce a farmer to the level of the local labouring population, a point probably not wasted upon the incendiarist.

As Figure 7.3 shows, the most frequent object of attack by the Herefordshire incendiarist was a rick, constructed either of wheat, hay, clover or oats. Ricks were favoured targets for obvious reasons. First, they were easy to ignite and, once started, difficult to extinguish. Second, and more significantly, ricks were often situated in a field, some distance from the

---

[18] *HJ: 15 March 1843.*

[19] *HT: 24 March 1849.*

[20] Archer, *'By A Flash and A Scare'. 162.*

[21] *HT: 24 March 1849.*

[22] *HJ: 22 September 1847.*

[23] *HT: 7 April 1849.*

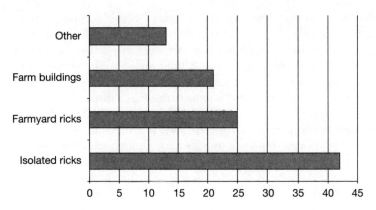

Figure 7.3 Targets of rural incendiarism in Herefordshire, 1800–60[24]

farmhouse, giving the incendiarist time to make his escape. Moreover, isolated fires were difficult to deal with, especially if the rick was located away from a source of water or too remote for the fire service to reach. Ricks, however, as Figure 7.3 shows, were often lit under the very nose of the farmer. Generally, these acts of incendiarism were far more destructive and costly for the farmer. Not only was the farmyard the site of many of the farmer's assets but a fire, once under way, had the potential to spread to other ricks and buildings. The incendiary attack at Verry's Farm in 1847, which was started in a wheat rick, soon spread and consumed thirteen other ricks, a barn, a stable, two wagons and two carts before it could be put out.[25] Similarly, in 1858, a fire lit in the yard of a farm owned by Lord Somers quickly destroyed two large wheat ricks, a rick of oats, one of straw and a large barn full of straw.[26]

Incendiarism could also prove costly to animal and, occasionally, human life. An incendiary attack to a barn at Bolstone in 1834 left some horses 'much singed'.[27] 'Some livestock' was destroyed in a fire at a Madley barn in 1843 and during an arson attack in 1849, again to a barn at Madley, a farmer lost seven sheep, five cows and six lambs.[28] The greatest loss through an incendiary attack, however, occurred in 1843, when a fire lit in four hayricks and two corn ricks at Eaton Bishop spread swiftly to some buildings and burned Peregrine Morgan, a sleeping tinker, to death.[29]

[24] 'Other' means unspecified 'farm property', woods and coppices.
[25] *HJ: 22 September 1847.*
[26] *HJ: 3 February 1858.*
[27] *HJ: 16 April 1834.*
[28] *HJ: 16 August 1843* and *HT: 31 March 1849* respectively.
[29] *HJ: 15 November 1843.*

Research has made clear that incendiarism became more pronounced in the county after 1834. Why this was the case is less clear, especially as the conditions for the agricultural labourer were often as unbearable prior to 1830 as they were after that date. Archer argues, quite simply, that the increase in incendiarism may be explained by the availability, after 1830, of the 'Lucifer' match. As he rightly argues, the mechanics of starting a fire before their availability were difficult. Using a tinder-box in high winds, or on a wet night, must have been frustrating and the impracticalities of carrying a brazier of hot coals across fields are obvious. To leave a brazier behind was to leave a clue, while to attempt an escape while carrying it was to be slowed down.[30] The availability of the match after 1830 caused concern and the *Hereford Journal* noted that:

> The superabundance of these articles (matches), no less than the ready means which they afford for the commission of crime, calls for some preventative check, and laying on a duty in the same way as on patent medicines seems well calculated to effect that object.[31]

Undoubtedly 'Lucifer' matches were used to start incendiary fires. Fourteen-year-old farm servant John Jones was sentenced to fifteen years' transportation in 1849 after using a match to burn down his employer's farm buildings.[32] Following an incendiary fire at Kington in 1847, the *Hereford Journal* argued that the fire was 'deliberate as portions of a box of "Lucifer" matches were discovered nearby'.[33] Spent matches discovered at the scene of a rick or barn fire were seen as evidence that the blaze was the work of an incendiary, as was the case at Newton Farm, south of Hereford, in 1849.[34] Indeed, to be in possession of a box of matches was to throw suspicion upon the owner. Following an incendiary attack in 1848 upon the ricks of Mr Pitt, a farmer of Kimbolton, a 30-year-old local labourer, John White, was committed to the County Gaol on suspicion of starting the fire. Although there was insufficient evidence to secure a conviction against White it is clear that the prosecution at his trial made a great deal of the discovery of a box of matches in White's cottage.[35] Similarly, John Owens, a 44-year-old labourer, found himself facing an Assize judge in 1849 partly because he had bought a box of matches from a village shop on the day of an incendiary attack to Thomas Dunn esquire's corn stacks. Owens did have a previous conviction for poaching upon Dunn's preserve and he may have harboured a grudge

---

[30] Archer, 'By A Flash and a Scare'. 73–4.
[31] HJ: 24 January 1844.
[32] HRO: BG/11/8/9. *Summer Assize 1849. HJ: 7 April 1849.*
[33] HJ: 21 April 1847.
[34] HT: 7 April 1849.
[35] HRO: BG/11/8/9. *Lent Assize 1848. HJ: 29 March 1848.*

against Dunn, but the evidence presented by the prosecution was far too circumstantial to secure a conviction.[36] It is clear that the advent of the 'Lucifer' match was a great help to the would-be incendiarist. Moreover, it is also clear that the contemporary police and prosecution counsels believed that the ownership of matches was a factor when suspected incendiarists faced the courts. The evidence suggests, however, that if the prosecution was forced to rely upon the ownership of matches as proof of being an incendiarist then the jury was likely to acquit the defendant.

Incendiarism, after 1837, no longer carried the death penalty unless the target was an inhabited dwelling. The abolition of the death penalty for rural incendiarism possibly went some way towards increasing its popularity among those who wished to express their discontent. Moreover, the fate of some of the Swing activists would, even in the late 1840s, have been fresh in the memories of many rural labourers. Despite the repeal of the death penalty, sentences were always harsh where a conviction was secured. Between 1800 and 1837 the jury at the Hereford Assizes were able to find only one person guilty of incendiarism and he was unfortunate enough to feel the full weight of the law. John Barlow, a farm servant, was tried and convicted of 'wilfully' setting fire to a hay house belonging to his master in 1818 and suffered the ultimate sentence. The exact circumstances under which Barlow started the blaze, which also burned his master's horse to death, remain a mystery, but it is clear he lit the fire in a fit of pique after being castigated by his master for some misdemeanour. If Barlow had hoped that the judge would change his death sentence to one of transportation for life, as often was the case in other felonies, he was to be disappointed. The sentence was left to stand; the judge was clearly in a hanging mood, perhaps feeling that an example needed to be made. Despite a vigorous local campaign, by all sections of Herefordshire's population, to have Barlow transported rather than hanged, and appeals to the Home Office for clemency, he was 'launched into eternity' on 15 April, just twenty-three days after he committed the offence. Barlow was naturally 'much effected' by his plight and pitifully attempted to barricade himself in his cell. It seems that his last desperate efforts to stave off his executioners left its mark upon the local population as, apart from a coppice fire, there were no reported incendiary acts for seven years.[37] It seems likely that Barlow's execution, similar to the execution of the sheep-stealer James Webb in the same year (see Chapter 4), acted as a short-term deterrent.

On the four occasions after 1837 when the authorities secured convictions for incendiarism the perpetrators all received harsh sentences. Two men named Tudor and Trillo, a labourer and mason, were each sentenced to fifteen

---

[36] HRO: BG/11/8/9. *Lent Assize 1849. HT: 24 March 1849.*
[37] *Lent Assize 1818.* See also *HJ: 23 March 1818* for Barlow's committal, *HJ: 30 March 1818* for a report of his trial and *HJ: 15 April 1818* for a report of his execution.

years' transportation in 1845 for burning down a rick containing 900 faggots of wood belonging to a farmer named Cooke from Pipe and Lyde. The evidence against Trillo and Tudor was weak, being based upon a trail of broken footsteps to their cottages from the scene of the fire. However, it was brought to the jury's attention that they were strongly suspected for being responsible for another blaze the previous September, which had destroyed 500 bushels of wheat on the same farm. This and the common local knowledge that Tudor held a grudge against the farmer sealed their fate to penal servitude overseas.[38] Of the other convictions, the previously mentioned 14-year-old John Jones, who committed the 'copy-cat' incendiary attack at Preston Court in 1849, causing over £1,000 of damage to his master's farm, was also sent to Australia. Because Jones confessed to his crime, and because of his 'tender years', the judge showed some 'compassion' and did not transport him for life but for fifteen years.[39] In 1855 Tamar Walby, a 28-year-old single woman, received a similar sentence when she pleaded guilty to setting fire to her former master's rick yard after being dismissed 'for misconduct'.[40]

The most interesting convictions during the period, however, was that of two 21-year-old unemployed labourers in 1857. Starving and unable to find work these two men, called Shelwood and Jones, set light to 'a wheat rick and other farming produce' at Little Foxhall Farm, near Ross, with the sole intention of being apprehended. Following the fire they approached a policeman and Shelwood said 'we did it . . . we want to give ourselves up'. The *Hereford Journal* also reported that the two men, under examination, had said to the police that they 'had very little to eat during the past week and (they) was nearly starved and one country was as good as another'.[41] Further questioning revealed that they had committed the crime with the sole intention of being transported to Australia where, they believed, they would be allowed to mine for gold and make their fortunes. They did not get their wish because the judge gave them six years' imprisonment each. In his summing up he explained that:

> Hunger was a bad thing, but there was a proper place for them to go to, the workhouse; if they imagined that to be (convicted of incendiarism) was a means by which they might get to the gold-fields and dig for gold, they were mistaken. He would send them to prison where they would not have too much food and have to work hard.[42]

---

[38] HRO: BG/11/8/9. *Lent Assize 1845*. See also *HJ: 2 April 1845*.

[39] HRO: BG/11/8/9. *Summer Assize 1849*. For a report of Jones' trial see *HT: 4 August 1849*.

[40] HRO: BG/11/8/9. *Special Winter Assize: 19 December 1855*.

[41] *HJ: 22 April 1857 and 6 May 1857*.

[42] HRO: BG/11/8/9. *Summer Assize 1857*.

Judges, however, were not always the unfeeling dispensers of harsh justice. Nine-year-old William Farley was acquitted of arson after he burned down a wheat rick at Little Marcle, because the judge felt that one so young could be neither 'wilful or malicious'.[43] And Joseph Philpotts, a labourer from Kingstone, who burned down two of his ex-employer's wheat ricks in 1852, was given the benefit of the doubt and committed to the lunatic asylum at Abergavenny, despite a history of bad feeling between Philpotts and the farmer.[44]

It is significant that, with the exception of Tudor and Trillo, the only convictions for incendiarism during the period were against the young, foolish or desperate. Arguably, incendiarism was a difficult crime to detect. This is reflected by the poor committal rate and the even poorer conviction rate. During the period 1800 to 1860, out of the total of 101 reported incendiary attacks to farm property, investigations led to only eleven committals and of these the authorities secured just five convictions. This low rate of committals and convictions presents problems when attempting to discover the motives for incendiary attacks to farm property. Without the courtroom testimonies of the accused and the evidence of the prosecution we are often left with only the newspaper reports of the attacks, if they were reported at all. Acts of incendiarism, however, can be linked to periods of acute economic and social hardship. The period March 1843 to September 1844, for example, coincided with yet another agricultural malaise which led to loss of employment or reduced wages. Between those dates fifteen incendiary fires were lit throughout the county. Although the number of fires was small when compared to East Anglia, that half of the incendiary attacks were centred around the Madley area, an area that concentrated upon cereal production, predominantly wheat, suggests that a link existed.[45]

Rebecca also raised her head in 1844 and there is some evidence to suggest that Welsh feelings spilled across the border into Herefordshire. In January 1844 the *Hereford Journal* reported that a clergyman in the village of Credenhill 'received through the Post Office a letter which was posted in Hereford signed 'Rebecca', stating that there were to be three fires in his parish, three in Brinsop and three in the adjoining parish within a month.[46]

---

[43] HT: 31 March 1849.
[44] HRO: BG/11/8/9. *Spring Assize 1852*. There was some debate in the contemporary press about Philpotts' mental state. The prosecution argued that he was sane. If accused of incendiarism it may have been wise to fake insanity, since lunatics were released as soon as they were 'cured'. In short, Philpotts may have been back in Kingstone within months, rather than spending the rest of his life in Australia. Arguably, prisoners convincing the authorities that they were insane did occasionally happen. See e.g. Richard Ireland, 'Eugene Buckley and the Diagnosis of Insanity in the Early Victorian Prison', *Llafur*, Vol. 6 (1993).
[45] See Appendix VIII.
[46] HJ: 24 January 1844.

Just how seriously we can take this letter as a genuine part of the Rebeccaite movement is open to conjecture. It is true that Welsh Rebeccaism reached as far east as Breconshire and a short distance from the Herefordshire border.[47] Moreover, the county, especially the west, had a certain 'Welshness' about it and Herefordshire itself had a large contingent of Welshmen within its population.[48] Indeed, some of the remaining peasant farmers who worked the English side of the Black Mountains may have felt an affinity with the Rebeccaite cause. Although the letter did not deliver all its proposed threats, the warning was not entirely hot air. In the same week that the Credenhill clergyman received this anonymous letter there was indeed an incendiary attack upon some 'farm buildings' at Brinsop.[49] Research has failed to discover, if, or why, Rebeccaism should have reached as far east as Credenhill in Herefordshire, or if further incendiary attacks took place in the neigbouring villages as the letter promised, or why this particular clergyman received the letter. Nevertheless the fact that this fire occurred in the middle of a spate of such fires suggests that it was probably a reaction to local conditions rather than an expression of Welsh Rebeccaism.

The following outbreak of concerted incendiarism in the county took place in 1849. Again it could be argued that this was linked to local social and economic pressures because 1849 was yet another poor year for agriculture. Although farmers undoubtedly suffered, it was the agricultural labour force that suffered the most, through unemployment, underemployment and wage cuts. After 1847 the prices of cereals began to plummet and between the years of 1848 and 1851 the prices of wheat had fallen to lower levels than in 1822 and 1834 to 1835.[50] Arguably, this collapse in prices was due to Peel's repeal of the Corn Laws in 1846, which permitted greater imports of foreign grain. However, if this was indeed the case, the good harvests of the late 1840s simply added to the farmer's misery. Fifty years previously, when bread made up the bulk of their diet, the rural labouring population would have benefited from the reduction in grain prices. Indeed, Caird has argued that the price of bread, the 'principal' item of the labourer's consumption, had fallen by 30 per cent. However, as we have seen in Chapter 2, the rural poor had shifted from a bread diet to the potato as their main source of

---

[47] Charlesworth (ed.), *An Atlas of Rural Protest*. See also David J. V. Jones, *Rebecca's Children: A Study of Rural Society, Crime and Protest*, Clarendon Press, Oxford (1989).

[48] The 'Welshness' of Herefordshire is reflected, in part, by the many villages with Welsh names. Llanwarne, Llangarren and Llangunnock, for example, are all Herefordshire villages to the south and west of the River Wye. Moreover, there is evidence that some of the population, even as late as the nineteenth century, spoke Welsh; indeed, the authorities felt it was necessary to employ a Welsh-speaking Clerk of the Court as late as 1855. Fletcher, *Herefordshire*. 9.

[49] *HJ*: 24 January 1844.

[50] Armstrong, *Farmworkers*. 84.

nourishment.[51] In appealing to the incendiary's conscience following the firing of 'sixteen stooks of wheat' at Kington in 1847 the *Hereford Journal* lamented that the 'wanton destruction of property is at all times reprehensible but the wilful burning of the food of man merits the most condign punishment'.[52] Although the principle may have been the same, times had changed, as had the labouring population's diet, and while such an appeal may have carried some weight at the beginning of the century, by 1850 stomachs were more used to potatoes than bread. The labouring population's shift from a cereal-based diet to one of potatoes may be a further reason why incendiarism became more popular after the 1830s. After all, the displaced labourer who lit a wheat rick after the 1830s was not adding to the price, or scarcity, of basic food but simply damaging his target – the farmer. In essence his conscience was clear and the farmer's wheat ricks became a legitimate target.

There is some evidence to suggest that incendiarism was also linked to seasonal unemployment. Indeed, the crime was most prevalent during the months of winter and spring when agricultural employment was hardest to find (see Figure 7.4).

That incendiarism to farm property peaked during the winter and spring months suggests that discontent over seasonal unemployment was a factor. Following the destruction of a barn and seven ricks at Little Cowarne in December 1855, the *Hereford Journal* remarked that 'it is our painful duty to state that incendiarism has begun to show itself in this county thus early in the winter', suggesting that it was regarded as a winter crime.[53] It is somewhat

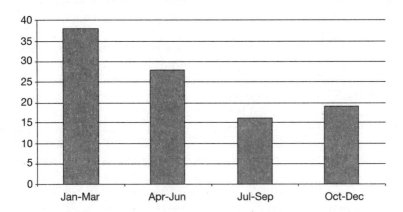

Figure 7.4 Reported cases of incendiarism by season in Herefordshire, 1800–60

---

[51] J. Caird, *English Agriculture in 1850–1851* (2nd edn), Frank Cass, London (1968). 518.
[52] *HJ: 8 September 1847.*
[53] *HJ: 5 December 1855.*

surprising that incendiarism was more frequent during that time of the year. Rural arson, apart from the satisfaction that could be gained from seeing a farmer's property burn to the ground, gave the perpetrator no material benefit. The theft of wood, crops, sheep and game provided either food or warmth. Incendiarism, on the other hand, did little to ease the agricultural labourer's plight. We can only reason that incendiarism became more frequent during those months because that was when the agricultural labourer was most aggravated by his helplessness to find work.

The principal problem in being forced to rely upon the contemporary press as a source is that the newspapers were often the voice of 'respectable' society. This was especially true of the *Hereford Journal* which sought to reflect traditional Tory values. However, both the Tory *Journal* and the more Whiggish *Hereford Times* were united in their feelings towards rick-burners. Incendiarists were inevitably portrayed as 'vile', 'wanton' or even 'depraved' by both newspapers and there was little or no attempt to discover what may have been behind such attacks. The poverty of the rural workforce was essentially hidden from view unless extreme conditions, such as wheat or potato shortages, made their plight apparent to all. Moreover, farmers who were the victims of incendiary attacks were never portrayed as contributing to their own downfall by shedding workers or reducing wages. Both the *Journal* and the *Times* would not reason that a certain farmer had his wheat ricks burnt because he had sacked half of his workforce. To do so would have alienated many of their readers.

It is difficult to ascertain the extent to which an incendiarist would enjoy community support, or how far the act was 'legitimised by popular opinion'.[54] Essentially this can only be done by judging the reaction of the crowd at the site of an incendiary attack. When a straw rick at Llangarren was discovered alight in 1846 the editor of the *Hereford Journal* went to great lengths to explain that the fire was not the work of an incendiary. Moreover, the rural working population of the village helped in trying to extinguish the blaze. Similarly, an incendiary attack in 1833 upon the barn of a Mr Jones, a tenant farmer of Much Dewchurch, prompted the *Journal* to report that the incident was not popular with the local labouring community. The editor stated that while the fire was the work of 'a vile and cowardly incendiary . . . no labourer of Mr Jones is suspect'. He also went on to claim that: 'it is creditable to the working class in the vicinity that they loudly express their vehement abhorrence of the fiend-like act.'[55] Undoubtedly somebody with a grudge against Mr Jones lit the fire, yet it was clear that the act was not legitimized by popular opinion. Presumably this was either because Mr Jones was seen to be a good employer or because the general conditions for the labouring population in Dewchurch were tolerable.

[54] Rule, 'Social Crime'. 138.
[55] *HJ: 4 September 1833*.

The opposite was the case at the scene of an incendiary fire at Newton Farm in 1849. Here a crowd not only stood by and watched 'an extensive range of stabling' burn to the ground, offering no assistance at all to the fire services, but some even took the opportunity of getting a free meal. As the editor of the *Hereford Times* explained:

> A disgusting scene occurred at the fire. Mr Preece had some fowls of a particularly fine kind and many perished in the flames. Several of the humbler spectators seized some of the fowls, which but a few moments before had been alive, and, thus curiously roasted, they tore them to pieces and voraciously devoured them.[56]

Again it is difficult to establish why this particular farmer was so unpopular. Nevertheless, his unpopularity among the local labouring population was evident by the crowd's unwillingness to help the fire service put out the conflagration, their willingness to capitalize upon Preece's misfortune by eating his chickens and their unwillingness to help the police with their enquiries. 'Evidence was given in a very reluctant manner', reported the *Hereford Journal*. What information was given was insufficient to lead to any arrests, despite the attraction of a £100 reward.[57]

It is also conceivable that some farmers, by continually pursuing prosecutions for petty thefts of crops and wood, incited local outrage and subsequently an incendiary attack. A Goodrich farmer in 1850 had a rick, holding 200 bushels of wheat, destroyed by fire soon after he evicted some crop-thieves from his pea fields. The crop-thieves 'used threats of revenge', claimed the *Hereford Times*.[58] In a like manner, Daniel Theyer, a farmer from the troubled parish of Whitchurch, had a barn and a 'quantity of straw' destroyed by fire in 1855. The *Hereford Journal* speculated as to why Theyer had become a victim and noted that he had been:

> subject to a series of petty robberies for the last two years, but though individually small collectively amounted to a good sum, and it is supposed because he had put the law in force against some of the offenders on several occasions, he is persecuted in the most ruthless and vindictive manner. On the very night of the fire his stable was robbed.[59]

Later in the same year, following a fire on a farm at Little Cowarne, the *Hereford Journal* reported 'that threatening language has been written on other premises signifying that persons are going about for their object; the

[56] HT: *7 April 1849*.
[57] Ibid.
[58] HT: *29 June 1850*.
[59] HJ: *13 June 1855*.

firing of ricks'.[60] A few farmers frequently suffered at the hands of incen-diarists and maimers. 'The work of an incendiarist' which destroyed a haystack on a Dorstone farm in 1856, occurred a few days before the site of an animal-maiming attack when 'a capital horse, belonging to Mr Bannister (the farmer) was stabbed in the fore-part of the belly'.[61] It is clear that individual farmers could become the focus of discontent.

The farmers of Madley suffered more incendiary attacks than any other village or parish in the county: a total of thirteen fires between 1800 and 1860. Why the parish of Madley should account for 12.87 per cent of all the fires in the period is a mystery. A great many of the fires lit around the Madley parish were put down to the work of one man. Between March and August of 1843 the parish of Madley experienced six incendiary fires and, while no culprit was ever brought to book, suspicion rested heavily upon a local man named John Price. The authorities, however, were unable to prove, or disprove, that he was the Madley incendiarist. Suspicions were so strong that Price was kept under constant surveillance and the local magistrates even went so far as introducing two policemen from London 'to watch his motions'. Price was aware of this surveillance and when he was informed in a local beer-house that he was being watched he waggishly replied, 'I know – I'm watching them too.' Described by the local press as a 'mysterious being', or 'insane', and occasionally 'maddened by drink', the police beat a frequent path to his door every time an incendiary attack was carried out in the area.[62] Consequently, when another outbreak of incendiarism took place six years later, in 1849, Price was again the prime suspect. Price's arrest came on 14 April 1849 when he was charged with setting fire to the property of John Waltham, one of Madley's farmers.[63] Waltham had claimed that Price had visited the farm a few days before the farm buildings holding sheep, lambs, cows and wheat were set on fire. It transpired that Price had come begging for cider which Waltham refused. Following Waltham's refusal Price became 'saucy', a scuffle ensued, the police were sent for and Price was eventually arrested and forced to spend the night in the City Gaol. The prosecution argued that the incendiary attack was Price's revenge.[64] The evidence presented against Price by the prosecution was, however, entirely circumstantial and he was acquitted.

It is open to debate whether Price was indeed the incendiarist respon-sible for this, or any other attack to farm property. It is clear that he was a marginal character, who took employment only when he was forced to do so through necessity. It was also reported that he spent much of his time

[60] HJ: 5 December 1855.
[61] HJ: 23 July 1856.
[62] HT: 14 April 1849.
[63] Ibid.
[64] HRO: BG/11/8/9. Summer Assize 1849. HT: 4 August 1849.

the worse for drink or attempting to beg food and cider from the local population. In short, Price was his own worst enemy by refusing to conform to the norms of rural society. Thus, when discontent exploded into covert action he was regarded as an obvious suspect by the respectable, and fearful, farmers of the district. Price became the target of their insecurity, not least because he was unpopular and feared. Indeed, his reputation as an incendiarist remained with him. Every time an outbreak of incendiarism took place in the vicinity of Madley the local press informed readers of his current whereabouts, as the following piece, published in 1855, shows:

> The Madley Fire-King – During the lamented days of incendiaries which our fair county has from time to time been the theatre of, there lived on the other side of the River Wye, in the locality of Madley, an individual who has rendered himself unenviable notorious; and though blessed by his Godfathers and Godmothers with the Christian name of 'John' in addition to the patronymic of 'Price', was better known to all in the neighbourhood as 'The Fire-King'. If really not a dangerous man, he was a very foolish one, and his body has frequently had to suffer, and severely too, for the waywardness of his tongue. We cannot exactly tell how many years of Price's life has been spent inside a gaol, but letting the incendiary commitments out of the question, he has, we believe, suffered three years and a half imprisonment for threats . . . (this) has again been the cause of his incarceration for threatening to do (a local farmer) some grievous bodily harm.[65]

The farmers' prejudice aside, it is difficult to see how Price was responsible for the incendiary attacks of 1843 and 1849. First, as Price was such a marginal character, he was less likely to be affected by the periods of agrarian depression with which these fires coincided. His scratch-as-scratch-can existence was untouched by periods of unemployment, since he was always essentially unemployed. Local hardship would merely manifest itself by Price having less to show from his begging. That the incendiary attacks did coincide with downturns in agrarian capitalism suggests that disgruntled workers rather than a lone local beggar may have been responsible. Second, there were claims that Price was mentally unbalanced, suggesting that his state of mind played a large part in the lighting of these fires. If, however, Price was suffering from some kind of pyromania, why was there a gap of six years between the two incendiary outbreaks? Arguably, if Price was a pyromaniac, his illness, or compulsion, would have forced him to light fires until he had been either cured, apprehended or died. Admittedly, if Price was the culprit, he might have stopped his incendiary behaviour when he was being watched by the two London policemen. This would not, however, have been the response of a man driven by compulsion. Finally, it was well documented during the trial that Price was more often drunk on cider than

[65] *HJ: 19 September 1855.*

sober. This would not have been the ideal condition in which to start a fire undetected. Incendiarists were well organized; they had to be. By the time a fire was discovered an incendiarist needed to be well away from the scene of the blaze if he was to escape detection. It is improbable that Price could have done this in his usual inebriated state. Arguably, if the local drunkard had undertaken a programme of incendiarism he would have been apprehended soon after it had began. The thought of a drunken Price lighting fires all over Madley without detection belies belief.

It is apparent that some of the men (and women) charged with incendi-arism in Herefordshire were, indeed, guilty of their crimes. But incendiarism, because of its secretive nature, was a difficult charge to prove. This was especially true in the absence of a witness, and considering the primitive nature of detective work it is understandable that the authorities often made mistakes by arresting the wrong person. The main criterion, when looking for a likely suspect, was to find somebody with a grudge against the victim. This was understandable and generally made sense. Indeed, the police were sometimes right to follow this course of action. Tudor, convicted in 1845 for incendiarism at Pipe and Lyde, held a grudge against his victim because he claimed that he had owed him 5s for some mowing he did the previous summer.[66] At other times, however, the authorities got it completely wrong. In 1834 a woman named Milborough Brown was arrested and committed to the City Gaol after being accused of burning down a wheat rick, the property of a man called Lane who was a farmer and a local overseer of the poor at Yarpole. Brown was the chief suspect in this case solely because she had 'abused Lane after he had refused her further relief' a day or so before the fire took place.[67] As no witnesses could be brought forward the accused was acquitted, but not before she had spent a considerable period of time in gaol awaiting trial. Similarly, in 1849, as Thomas Nicholas was being examined after being arrested on suspicion of setting fire 'to the barns of Mr Wm Preece of Newton Farm . . . Sergeant Griffiths (of the Hereford City police) entered the courtroom and announced a second fire on Mr Preece's property'.[68] Admittedly the second fire may have been the work of Nicholas' friends and family in providing him with an alibi. Nevertheless, it is interesting to note that Nicholas was the chief suspect simply because he was a former farm servant of Preece and they had 'parted on bad terms'.[69]

It is evident that incendiarism in Herefordshire during the period 1800 to 1860 was relatively infrequent. Predictably, the local press never mentioned rural pay levels or employment levels when reporting incendiary attacks but merely saw the crime as an act of malice. In a way they were right to do so.

[66] HJ: 12 February 1845.
[67] Lent Assize 1834. HJ: 26 March 1834.
[68] HT: 7 April 1849.
[69] Ibid.

Incendiarism was an act inspired by malice. Not the malice, however, of personal revenge or spite but a malice born of despair. That the attacks to farm property coincided with periods of agrarian depression resulting from poor harvests or falling grain prices suggests that these attacks were initiated by those who would suffer most: agricultural labourers and their families. What the incendiaries hoped to achieve by their actions is open to discussion. Nevertheless, fire was a great leveller, and a well-placed match might relegate an unpopular employer to the ranks of the impoverished.

Animal-maiming

Animal-maiming was even more uncommon in Herefordshire than incendiarism. Only twenty-six reported attacks in Herefordshire in sixty years gives credence to Archer's claim that 'animal maiming was an East Anglian specialty'.[70] In some ways incendiarism and animal-maiming were similar. Both crimes were difficult to detect, usually because they were the work of embittered individuals operating at night under cover of darkness. Moreover, as with incendiarism, the crime of animal-maiming was more prevalent after 1830, 1831 being the peak year with nine reported attacks (see Figure 7.5).

Again, it is unclear why animal maiming should have been so popular as an expression of discontent with the East Anglian agricultural labourer and not with his Herefordshire counterpart. We can immediately discount any notion that the county's labourers were more sentimental about the welfare of animals. The pages of the local contemporary press frequently reported

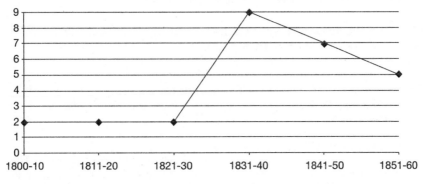

Figure 7.5 Reported cases of animal-maiming in Herefordshire, 1800–60

[70] Archer, 'By a Flash and a Scare'. 202.

cases of cruelty to livestock and pets. At Ross Petty Session in 1832, a short-tempered wagoner named Bingham was fined £5 after abusing and ill-treating a mare which had proved difficult to handle.[71] Also in 1832 another wagoner, Edward Carpenter, beat his master's horse so severely that it tried to break free of the wagon and disembowelled itself in the process.[72] A year later, in 1833, Thomas Jenkins, a farm servant, was gaoled for one month for 'ill-treating a cart mare, beating the poor animal about the head'.[73] Domestic pets were often treated little better. In 1837 a 'boy was dressed down by the magistrate' for throwing quicklime in a dog's face at Ross and, a month later, Thomas Williams, who was the worse for drink, was fined £1 for throwing 'a whelp onto the fire' at an inn near Hereford.[74] This was an age when cock- and dogfights were still a common pastime for the rural population and animal life was not held in high regard. Indeed, with this thought in mind, it is surprising that animal-maiming was not employed more frequently by the rural protester in Herefordshire.[75]

As with incendiarism it is difficult to discover the true extent of animal-maiming. Many acts of animal cruelty that seem to fall into the realm of the maimer, may, in fact, be categorized more accurately as theft. The docking, or cutting, of horses' manes and tails may seem to be a simple act of maiming but horsehair was a saleable commodity and theft cannot be ruled out. While this was not a common crime it did, nevertheless, break out from time to time. In June 1826, for example, the *Hereford Journal* reported that:

> A gang of wretches have been committing a description of deprivation in this vicinity during the last week, rather uncommon in this county. On the night of the 30 ult they cut the hair from the manes and tails of three horses, the property of Mr Pendry, of Ailstones Hill and on Saturday night they affected the same wanton deprivation on seven horses, belonging to Mr Jones of Breinton, and three to Mr George of Wareham, in a field near Broomy Hill.[76]

Moreover, the newspaper felt it prudent, in August of the same year, to warn other horse-owners to be on their guard:

---

[71] *HJ: 22 February 1832.*
[72] *Lent Assize 1832.*
[73] *HJ: 14 August 1833.*
[74] *HJ: 20 September 1837 and 4 October 1837.*
[75] For example, the *Hereford Journal* of 23 December 1829 reported that a large crowd which had gathered to watch a dogfight at Red Hill was broken up by the magistrates. Such plebeian sport, if it can be called that, was not only illegal but also frowned upon by the county's more respectable inhabitants and magistrates were only too keen to enforce the law. For example, a man named Tyler was fined 5s by the City magistrates in 1836 'for putting two dogs to fight' for the 'amusement of his friends'. See *HJ: 5 October 1836.*
[76] *HJ: 7 June 1826.*

to caution our agricultural friends against a set of vagabonds who are now traversing this county, engaged in cutting hair from the tails and manes of any horses they can conveniently meet with. We have been reliably informed that no less than twelve or fourteen valuable horses were mutilated in this manner last week.[77]

Further outbreaks of horsehair theft followed in 1830, 1840 and 1843; there were also committals and the occasional conviction for the crime.[78] What is made clear from the subsequent prosecutions, however, was that the crime was regarded as petty theft rather than anything more sinister. Indeed, horsehair thieves were not sent to the Assize or even the Quarter Sessions but were dealt with summarily by two magistrates. John Price, for example, pleaded guilty to horsehair docking at the Hereford City Sessions in 1840. He was sentenced to one year's hard labour, despite his 'excuse for his conduct (saying) at the time of stealing the hair he had nothing to eat for three days'.[79] Similarly, it is possible to compare some methods of sheep-stealing with animal-maiming and, while some of the methods employed by sheep-stealers were brutal in the extreme, the theft of mutton was the aim of the attack. In 1839 a sheep-stealer 'destroyed a lamb by cutting off the shoulder, leaving the remaining part in the meadow' where it presumably died in agony.[80] This was, similar to docking, a form of mutilation; however, it was maiming that provided a benefit for the perpetrator; in this case a leg of lamb. It remains debatable whether such acts were simply thefts or acts of maiming. For the animal's owner, however, the message would often be the same.

The animals (and occasional tinker) that died by way of an act of incendiarism may have been unintentional victims, yet there was nothing unintentional about the maiming of farmyard beasts and pets. As Archer has argued, maiming 'could be a bloody business' and while the details of such crimes may offend our twentieth-century sensibilities it did occasionally occur.[81] Moreover, when maiming did occur, it was often suggestive of social crime or rural protest. Although animal-maiming has often been associated with the hamstringing of cattle it soon becomes apparent to the researcher that a wide range of beasts could become the object of attack, as Figure 7.5 shows.[82] Horses were by far the most common object of attack in Herefordshire. Maimers subjected horses to some horrifyingly sadistic

---

[77] HJ: 23 August 1826.
[78] See HJ: 8 December 1830, 8 January 1840 and 24 May 1843.
[79] HJ: 11 October 1840.
[80] HJ: 14 August 1839.
[81] Archer, 'By a Flash and a Scare'. 198.
[82] For example, the hamstringing, or 'houghing', of cattle has often been associated with early eighteenth-century rural protest in Ireland. See S. J. Connolly, 'Law, Order and Popular Protest in Early Eighteenth Century Ireland: The Case of the Hougher's', in

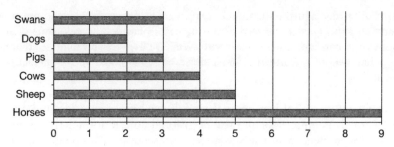

Figure 7.6 Targets of animal-maimers in Herefordshire, 1800–60

attacks. In 1809 a maimer attacked three horses, forcing the end of a cart whip into the womb of a mare. Not content with that he attacked another mare 'with foal' in a similar fashion, before cutting out the tongue of a third.[83] It was reported by the *Hereford Journal* in 1818 that 'some barbarous savage' beat a mare 'severely upon the head, and then cut her throat', leaving the beast to bleed to death in the road.[84] The stomach of a valuable pony belonging to Mr Archibold of Barr's Court was slashed open in 1839, while in 1857 'some unmitigating scoundrel' entered a field at Marden and 'cut off the ears and tails of a couple of fine colts' belonging to a farmer.[85]

The second most common object of attacks were sheep (20 per cent), the usual method being to slash the animal's throat or mutilate it with a knife. In 1839 someone, 'with fiendish malignity . . . mangled and killed a fine sheep' belonging to a butcher.[86] Similarly, a maimer entered a field on the Chandois Estate in 1857 and slaughtered 'three lambs by cutting their throats'. Not content with this he returned the following night and slaughtered 'a fat wether in a similar manner'.[87] Further examples of animal-maiming could be provided; however, the above cases are adequate to illustrate the grisly and sadistic work of the maimer.

While incendiarism was both threatening and economically damaging to the victim, animal-maiming was sheer intimidation. The cutting, stabbing, beating and poisoning of farmyard beasts and domestic pets was an expression of hatred towards the animal's owner. It was, as Archer argues, 'symbolic murder'.[88] The editor of the *Hereford Times* remarked in 1850, following the poisoning of a farmer's dogs, that 'a man who would be guilty of such an act would probably feel few scruples against taking a human life to gratify his

Patrick J. Corish (ed.), *Radicals, Rebels and Establishments*, Appletree Press, Belfast (1985). 52–3.

[83] *HJ*: 16 August 1809.

[84] *HJ*: 16 September 1818.

[85] *HJ*: 29 May 1839 and 3 June 1857.

[86] *HJ*: 30 October 1839.

[87] *HJ*: 29 July 1857.

[88] Archer, 'By a Flash and a Scare'. 199.

revenge'.[89] Archer, however, argues that it is a 'misconception on the part of historians' to view 'animal maiming as an act of social protest rather like incendiarism', because the crime 'was not always committed by the working class against members of the ruling class'.[90] Although this may have been the norm in East Anglia the evidence from Herefordshire suggests the opposite was true. Of the twenty-six reported cases of animal-maiming, 56 per cent of the attacks were aimed at the stock and pets of tenant farmers and a further 32 per cent of maimed animals were the property of landowners. In short, 88 per cent of all the reported cases of animal maiming were aimed at the employers of agricultural labour. Indeed, there was only one reported attack to an animal owned by an 'unoffending labouring man' in the period 1800 to 1860: a pig, which had its tail hacked off in 1847.[91]

While Herefordshire was less likely to experience outbreaks of animal-maiming than East Anglia, when it did occur it was directed against agricultural employers and not the rural poor. Moreover, although the poor conviction rate does little to clarify the social status of animal-maimers in Herefordshire, it seems likely that they came from the ranks of the embittered agricultural workforce. Israel Draper and Lucas Locke were each transported for seven years in 1853 for poisoning two pigs belonging to a Llangarren farmer. Under examination they claimed to have killed the pigs because the farmer had refused them employment.[92] A 66-year-old labourer, employed at hedge-cutting in 1844, hamstrung one of his employer's bullocks. Despite a history of 'bad feeling' between the employee and the employer the Assize judge, taking his age and lack of previous criminal record into account, sentenced him to only one year's hard labour.[93] Pet swans belonging to an Allensmore landowner, E. B. Patshall, were successively poisoned, shot and beaten to death on three separate occasions and on another occasion a cart-horse was stabbed to death with a dung fork.[94] Clearly someone had a grudge against Patshall; however, the attack upon his swans can only be seen as an attack upon his wealth.

There were also occasions when the victim knew who was responsible for an attack, and presumably the reason why, but lacked the vital proof for a prosecution. In 1804 a Mr Byrdges, a farmer from Colwall, placed the following advertisement in the *Hereford Journal*:

Whereas some evil-minded and malicious person, or persons, did . . . between the hours of ten and five the following morning, kill and destroy a broken-haired black

---

[89] *HT: 31 August 1850.*

[90] Archer, *'By a Flash and a Scare'*. 201–2.

[91] *HJ: 15 December 1847.*

[92] HRO: BG/11/8/9. *Lent Assize 1853.*

[93] HRO: BG/11/8/9. *Summer Assize 1844.*

[94] See *HJ: 21 November 1821, 19 September 1832, 13 February 1833* and *25 January 1837.*

terrier bitch, and also did at the same time very much injure and wound another very old terrier bitch. . . . A reward of one guinea is hereby offered to any person, or persons, who will make a discovery of the offender, or offenders . . . Two persons are strongly suspected of being implicated in committing the above, the one a person under Mr Byrdges own roof, the other a servant to a tenant of Mr Brydges, residing near Colwall.[95]

Like incendiarism, animal maiming was a difficult crime to prove. As the advertisement above clearly illustrates, simply knowing who committed the crime was not enough. For a conviction to be assured a maimer either had to be caught in the act or caught out when being examined by a magistrate. Moreover, because the act of maiming was likely to be a solitary crime carried out at the dead of night, convictions were unusual. Despite the low numbers of animal-maiming cases we can be sure that the object of the attack was the animal's owner rather than the animal itself. The poor animal was merely a substitute for the farmer. Animal-maiming was, indeed, symbolic murder and the cruelties inflicted upon these beasts were a reflection of the extent of the hatred the maimer harboured for the animal's owner. While theft of crops, wood, game and sheep satisfied a need to survive, animal-maiming and incendiarism satisfied a desire for revenge, and both crimes were the ultimate display of bitterness.

[95] HJ: 13 June 1804.

Conclusion

The rural poor in Herefordshire, c.1800–60 – assertive criminals or silent victims?

As we have seen, the condition of the Herefordshire agricultural labourer during the first half of the nineteenth century was largely dependent upon the availability of employment, his wage rate and the price of basic provisions. To all intents and purposes these matters, although they affected his very livelihood, were outside his control. He was at the mercy of his employer's prosperity, generosity and compassion. All too often he was paid barely enough to keep body and soul together, hired and fired at will and generally exploited. Essentially, then, he was a victim: a victim to the greed of employers, agricultural change and poor harvests. Outwardly, to contemporaries at least, he seemed to accept these hardships with a philosophical shrug, yet it would be a mistake to assume that because he suffered in silence he was stupid, peaceable or content. Faced with grinding poverty and an awareness of his exploitation he often turned to crime either to supplement his income or to express his discontent.

The men and women who silently suffered hunger behind cottage doors or the hardships of workhouse discipline were indeed victims. To cast all of the rural working class into the same mould, however, is to rob those who chose not to starve or to accept the tyranny of the workhouse of their identities, their personalities and their pride. Their class identity is illustrated clearly by their solidarity, in their refusal to aid the authorities when they sought to apprehend criminals, even when large sums of money were available to those who were prepared to do so. Their pride, in many cases, drove them to criminal acts. Both men and women committed crimes not only to escape the humiliation of having to apply for relief but it was also pride that put food on tables and wood on the fire. Moreover, contemporary newspapers and, occasionally, court records illustrate that the men and women who fell foul of the law were individuals, each with their own personality. Some, such as Ann Perkins the sheep-stealer, who was so hungry that she could have 'ate the wool of its back', were sad, vulnerable figures. Others, such as Price, the supposed 'Madley Fire-King', were alleged to be mad, and the Jones family from Ledbury were seen as simply bad. Despite their differences they all had one thing in common; they were marginal figures who broke the law. Admittedly it was respectable society which marginalized them because they either refused to, or could not, fit in with the way the elite wished; and in this sense they were victims. However, they were men and women who reacted to their poverty in a positive, if not strictly legal, way. Price, the Jones family and Perkins may have been mad, bad and sad but they sought to retain their independence and pride. Perkin, after all, could have entered the workhouse and the Jones family could have submitted to the discipline of regulated employment.

Research has also shown that, in Herefordshire at least, a greater number of crimes than hitherto suggested by historians can be embraced by the concept of social crime. While the poacher and incendiarist have, for some time, been afforded a degree of respectability by social historians the Herefordshire evidence suggests that there is a case for categorizing the sheep-stealer and those found guilty of wood- and crop-theft as social criminals. The evidence clearly suggests that sheep-stealing, for example, was, in some areas of the county and by some occupational groups, a community-sanctioned crime. Moreover, the very numbers of men, and especially women, engaged in the theft of wood and crops suggests that there was no social stigma attached to the crimes by the county's rural poor. Although it would be wrong to assume that simply because a particular crime was frequently committed it automatically enjoyed popular support research has failed to discover any intra-class hostility towards sheep- or crop-thieves. This was not the case for sexual offenders and murderers who were quickly informed upon or delivered up to the authorities. While it is clear that rapists and murderers stepped outside the boundaries of what was considered morally acceptable, the position of the crop-, wood- and sheep-thief was less clear-cut. We cannot doubt that the rural poor of Herefordshire were aware that the thefts of wood, crops and sheep were, in the legal sense, criminal acts yet we can be sure that their concept of property was not as clearly defined as that of the local elite. The rural poor and the rural elite had a different set of values and while the agricultural labourer did not condone property-theft any more than the landowning gentry they could, under certain circumstances, justify it; something the property owning classes could, or would, never do.

Although the county's farmers and landowners did not condone rural crime the evidence has also suggested that they often showed a great deal of restraint when dealing with certain offences. Poachers and sheep-stealers, as we have seen, were occasionally either given the benefit of the doubt or, if found guilty, had their sentences reduced. The punishment did not always fit the crime in the first half of the nineteenth century, and jurors and victims alike were aware of this. Moreover, it has been possible to show that the former, on occasion, found poachers, who were clearly guilty, innocent and for the latter to ask an Assize judge for mercy on behalf of the criminal. It has also been possible to show that even the magistrates themselves reduced fines, charged court costs only and generally took the delinquent's circumstances into account when sentencing. It was not, of course, only their consciences that discouraged them from carrying out the full letter of the law: there were sound social and economic reasons for them to be merciful.

Sentences of transportation and hefty fines put dependants on the parish or swelled the numbers of inmates at the Union Workhouse. The dispensers of criminal law understood that to be malicious and cruel was to invite hostility. Rural order continued intact and the Herefordshire countryside remained relatively peaceful; however, if the magistrates had hanged every sheep-stealer and transported every armed poacher, the history of the nineteenth-century agricultural labourer would be a more bloody chapter.

Although, as we have seen, it was their hunger and anger that justified their criminal acts there was a primitive sort of socialism in their actions. Indeed, at its most basic level theft is simply a redistribution of wealth. Moreover, it is not difficult to see how an agricultural labourer, when faced with hardship and hunger, could justify the theft of crops, sheep or whatever, by arguing that it was morally unjust for one man to have so much when he should have so little. He could also reason that the theft of one sheep or lamb from a flock or a few handfuls of peas from a field would not be missed by someone who owned so much. This is not to argue that they were consciously anti-capitalist. Indeed, a Marxian criminologist might argue that criminals are merely reflecting the capitalist ideology: the pursuit of property wealth and economic self-aggrandizement. Arguably, as long as stomachs were full, cottages were warm and employment was assured the majority of the agricultural population were blissfully unaware, or concerned, with such abstract concepts as capitalism. It is debatable if the average agricultural worker could, given his impoverished position, spare much thought for anything other than satisfying his and his family's everyday needs.

The growth of agrarian capitalism, although not particular to the nineteenth century, was mirrored by the growing number of statutes designed to protect farm property. A great deal of nineteenth-century criminal law was formed primarily to protect the property of the landed elite and not the property of the landless rural labourer who to all intents and purposes had very little worth stealing, if he had anything at all. Admittedly the law had to be seen to be there to protect the rural labourer as much as his employer, yet the evidence illustrated in this book clearly suggests that it was usually a member of the rural working class who stood in the dock while it was a member of the employing class who acted in the role of prosecutor. It suggests either that the poor did not steal from one another or that they did not use the legal system, or that they were in some way excluded from using the courts. Clearly the poor did steal from one another; however, their absence from the courts of Quarter Session as victims remains a puzzle. Admittedly, before Peel introduced a reform of the administration of the criminal justice system, poverty was the greatest deterrent but after the 1820s the courts, in theory, should have been accessible to all. Arguably, and there is some evidence to support this case, the rural poor policed their own communities by using more traditional methods of justice. Wife-beaters were ridiculed, fights were organized, compromises were reached and informers were hanged in effigy. They had no need to resort to the courts to gain satisfaction.

Admittedly, by the end of the period, prosecution expenses were reimbursed, whether the prosecutor won or lost the case; however, it has to be remembered that the aggrieved party still had to invest both money and time in advance in a court case before any refund was given. To expect men who were paid between 7s and 10s per week for much of the period to have the resources to bring often lengthy court cases over trivial offences was unrealistic. It was much cheaper and less time-consuming to settle matters out of court.

What is clear, though, is that the county's farmers and landowners were familiar with the law and felt comfortable about using it to protect their property. Indeed, the growing number of criminal offences, coupled with Peel's reforms of the criminal law system, which promoted 'fast track' justice, was reflected in the growing numbers of convictions. It would be fair to argue that the rationalization of the criminal system led to the criminalization of large sections of the rural poor. Because it became easier to bring prosecutions for trivial offences, such as 'stealing a handful of peas' or 'stealing a stick', offences that once never reached the courts became commonplace. These acts, although illegal before the reforms, were not, in terms of time and money, worth bringing to court unless the farmer suffered persistently from the attention of wood- or crop-thieves. In all probability, farmers once turned a blind eye to many criminal acts, the result being that the rural poor had come to see wood- and crop-'gleaning' as a customary perk of living in the countryside.

It is also possible to suggest that the increase in the numbers of criminal offences, the growth of policing and a more efficient method of dealing with offenders reflected the insecurity of the rural elite. Quinney argues that 'unemployment simultaneously makes necessary various actions of survival by the unemployed surplus population' (in this case theft); moreover, it 'requires the state to control that population in some way' (by increasing the number of criminal offences, police and so on).[1] Essentially, during periods of agrarian depression in Herefordshire the employers of rural labour, namely the farmers and landowners, were forced to release part of their workforce in order to survive. This created a surplus pool of unemployed labour which was a potential, and real, threat to property; thus more and more control was given over to the criminal justice system and policing.

Over the past thirty years social historians have made great strides in attempting to reconstruct the lives of those who have been 'hidden from history'. Despite these advances further research needs to be carried out both in the study of particular criminal activities and the attitudes of contemporary plebeian society. In doing so it will be possible for historians to illustrate the depth, and nature, of the conflict that existed in rural

---

[1] Richard Quinney, *Class, State and Crime: On the Theory and Practice of Criminal Justice*, McKay, New York (1977). 149.

England during the first half of the nineteenth century. The rural working class of Herefordshire have left us very little to suggest they even existed, and it is only through the pages of the contemporary press and the court records that we can begin to understand how they reacted to their poverty, exploitation and alienation. That reaction, as this thesis has shown, was often against the law, and, as agricultural production became increasingly rationalized and intrusive, the numbers of men, women and even children who appeared before an Assize judge or magistrate grew.

Appendices

Appendix I Petty Session Returns: Convictions, 1822–60[1]

Year	Epiphany	Easter	Trinity	Michaelmas	Total
1822	3	7	10	1	21
1823	9	7	7	6	29
1824	19	13	10	2	44
1825	20	13	8	9	50
1826	20	7	10	14	51
1827	20	10	4	18	52
1828	24	20	15	37	96
1829	46	44	16	55	161
1830	29	52	25	32	138
1831	26	37	33	54	150
1832	42	45	35	36	158
1833	32	45	37	46	160
1834	34	68	41	78	221
1835	40	62	39	65	206
1836	72	0	4	7	83
1837	2	32	34	65	133
1838	94	67	68	68	297
1839	101	60	63	49	273
1840	52	64	40	95	251
1841	90	35	21	71	217
1842	69	47	76	86	278
1843	46	80	75	148	349
1844	129	117	85	149	480
1845	100	68	81	80	329
1846	78	64	72	75	289
1847	61	44	138	85	328
1848	80	99	108	82	369
1849	100	77	89	82	348
1850	84	82	120	120	406
1851	101	117	115	113	446
1852	104	74	122	130	430
1853	70	71	193	147	481
1854	93	82	80	84	339
1855	199	130	81	139	549
1856	137	86	101	153	477
1857	113	158	67	55	393
1858	80	93	175	237	585
1859	78	147	88	111	424
1860	96	64	140	189	363

[1] HRO: Q/CM/4. *Petty Session Returns: Convictions, c1822–51* and HRO: Q/CE/1. *Petty Session Returns: Convictions, c1852–60*.

Appendix II Petty Session Returns: Convictions for wood- and crop-theft, trespass, wilful or malicious damage and Game Law infringements, 1822–60[1]

Year	Epiphany	Easter	Trinity	Michaelmas	Total
1822	3	7	0	8	18
1823	8	5	2	3	18
1824	11	7	4	0	22
1825	7	8	6	7	28
1826	13	6	3	9	31
1827	12	5	1	15	33
1828	12	19	10	14	55
1829	32	18	7	27	84
1830	15	34	10	23	82
1831	12	14	14	29	69
1832	24	27	7	16	74
1833	15	23	8	18	64
1834	12	36	4	29	81
1835	21	40	11	23	95
1836	47	0	0	0	47
1837	0	22	13	13	48
1838	28	28	18	15	89
1839	45	22	10	14	91
1840	34	32	11	47	124
1841	39	13	5	23	80
1842	25	16	18	20	79
1843	24	31	16	26	97
1844	46	64	18	70	198
1845	38	31	12	23	104
1846	27	26	12	23	88
1847	29	25	22	46	122
1848	38	22	17	23	100
1849	53	50	39	20	162
1850	37	39	33	23	132
1851	46	69	30	30	175
1852	44	16	40	31	131
1853	23	30	49	55	157
1854	34	24	26	15	99
1855	56	65	16	34	171
1856	38	29	34	60	161
1857	30	44	25	8	107
1858	14	17	37	38	106
1859	12	34	17	21	84
1860	20	27	38	39	124

[1] HRO: Q/CM/4. *Petty Session Returns: Convictions, c1822–51* and HRO: Q/CE/1. *Petty Session Returns: Convictions, c1852–60*.

Appendix III Petty Session Returns: Convictions for wood-theft, 1822–60[1]

Year	Epiphany	Easter	Trinity	Michaelmas	Total
1822	1	0	0	0	1
1823	2	1	0	0	3
1824	5	2	0	0	7
1825	0	0	1	0	1
1826	6	0	1	0	7
1827	0	1	0	3	4
1828	1	9	8	4	22
1829	13	7	1	1	22
1830	7	5	1	2	15
1831	2	6	0	5	13
1832	3	13	4	3	23
1833	6	5	4	3	18
1834	0	14	1	3	18
1835	1	8	6	1	16
1836	7	0	0	0	7
1837	0	10	2	0	12
1838	7	6	3	8	24
1839	11	6	3	2	22
1840	10	1	1	5	17
1841	11	8	1	3	23
1842	7	7	7	1	22
1843	8	8	7	3	26
1844	4	2	2	5	13
1845	7	3	2	0	12
1846	2	0	0	0	2
1847	1	2	0	0	3
1848	2	5	1	0	8
1849	7	2	2	2	13
1850	1	2	3	0	6
1851	0	6	2	1	9
1852	2	3	0	5	10
1853	0	0	1	1	2
1854	1	1	0	0	2
1855	1	1	0	0	2
1856	2	7	1	1	11
1857	0	0	1	0	1
1858	1	2	3	1	7
1859	0	6	1	0	7
1860	2	1	3	1	7

[1] HRO: Q/CM/4. *Petty Session Returns: Convictions, c1822–51* and HRO: Q/CE/1. *Petty Session Returns: Convictions, c1852–60*.

Appendix IV Petty Session Returns: Convictions for crop-theft, 1826–60[1]

Year	Epiphany	Easter	Trinity	Michaelmas	Total
1826	0	0	0	2	2
1827	0	0	0	5	5
1828	1	0	0	0	1
1829	1	0	0	7	8
1830	4	8	0	0	12
1831	0	0	0	7	7
1832	0	0	0	2	2
1833	1	0	2	8	11
1834	5	0	0	4	9
1835	1	0	0	1	2
1836	7	0	0	0	7
1837	0	3	0	5	8
1838	2	3	1	3	9
1839	9	0	2	7	18
1840	3	3	0	27	33
1841	5	0	0	8	13
1842	0	0	0	4	4
1843	2	0	0	9	11
1844	3	2	0	6	11
1845	5	4	1	7	17
1846	5	1	0	7	13
1847	0	0	2	10	12
1848	6	1	3	5	15
1849	9	2	1	6	18
1850	1	6	1	3	11
1851	5	10	0	4	19
1852	7	0	6	3	16
1853	3	4	6	8	21
1854	3	1	0	5	9
1855	8	8	0	4	20
1856	1	1	8	2	12
1857	5	6	0	1	12
1858	2	5	0	5	12
1859	0	1	0	4	5
1860	1	1	2	6	10

[1] HRO: Q/CM/4. *Petty Session Returns: Convictions, c1826–51* and HRO: Q/CE/1. *Petty Session Returns, c1852–60.*

Appendix V Petty Session Returns: Convictions for wilful and malicious damage, 1836–60[1]

Year	Epiphany	Easter	Trinity	Michaelmas	Total
1836	16	0	0	0	16
1837	0	2	4	1	7
1838	4	7	3	1	15
1839	4	1	3	2	10
1840	6	9	8	7	30
1841	10	2	0	4	16
1842	8	4	2	6	20
1843	0	7	5	7	19
1844	17	41	11	36	105
1845	19	14	4	7	44
1846	6	12	8	7	33
1847	14	10	13	19	56
1848	11	7	11	10	39
1849	20	28	28	3	79
1850	10	11	4	11	36
1851	16	22	14	14	66
1852	12	4	16	9	41
1853	7	6	15	19	47
1854	10	8	14	2	34
1855	15	26	1	19	61
1856	13	12	14	29	68
1857	9	9	13	2	33
1858	2	2	11	14	29
1859	1	10	2	2	15
1860	1	4	14	9	28

[1] HRO: Q/CM/4. *Petty Session Returns: Convictions, c1822–51* and HRO: Q/CE/1. *Petty Session Returns: Convictions, c1852–60.*

Appendix VI Petty Session Returns: Convictions for Game Law offences, 1822–60[1]

Year	Epiphany	Easter	Trinity	Michaelmas	Total
1822	2	6	0	6	14
1823	6	4	1	3	14
1824	6	4	1	0	11
1825	7	8	3	7	25
1826	7	5	2	6	20
1827	10	4	0	7	21
1828	10	8	0	3	21
1829	8	11	6	5	30
1830	4	6	7	4	21
1831	6	4	0	13	23
1832	19	7	3	6	35
1833	8	17	1	5	31
1834	6	14	2	15	37
1835	10	20	2	16	48
1836	17	0	0	0	17
1837	0	7	7	7	21
1838	10	10	11	3	37
1839	19	15	2	2	38
1840	15	18	2	7	42
1841	13	3	4	8	28
1842	10	5	9	9	33
1843	12	16	4	7	39
1844	22	19	5	23	69
1845	7	10	5	9	31
1846	14	12	4	9	39
1847	14	13	7	17	51
1848	19	9	2	8	38
1849	17	18	8	9	52
1850	19	7	17	9	52
1851	25	19	14	9	67
1852	23	9	14	14	60
1853	7	12	27	25	71
1854	16	4	9	8	37
1855	17	15	9	11	52
1856	16	5	7	22	50
1857	9	19	4	2	34
1858	5	1	13	11	30
1859	3	1	9	4	17
1860	3	4	14	4	25

[1] HRO: Q/CM/4. *Pety Session Returns: Convictions, c1822–51* and HRO: Q/CE/1. *Petty Session Returns: Convictions, c1852–60.*

Appendix VII Petty Session Returns: Convictions for trespass, 1822–60[1]

Year	Epiphany	Easter	Trinity	Michaelmas	Total
1822	0	1	0	2	3
1823	0	0	1	0	1
1824	0	1	3	0	4
1825	0	0	2	0	2
1826	0	1	0	1	2
1827	2	0	1	0	3
1828	0	2	2	7	11
1829	10	0	0	14	24
1830	0	15	2	17	34
1831	4	4	14	4	26
1832	2	7	0	5	14
1833	0	1	1	2	4
1834	1	8	1	7	17
1835	9	12	3	5	29
1836	0	0	0	0	0
1837	0	0	0	0	0
1838	2	2	0	0	4
1839	2	0	0	1	3
1840	0	1	0	1	2
1841	0	0	0	0	0
1842	0	0	0	0	0
1843	2	0	0	0	2
1844	0	0	0	0	0
1845	0	0	0	0	0
1846	0	1	0	0	1
1847	0	0	0	0	0
1848	0	0	0	0	0
1849	0	0	0	0	0
1850	6	13	8	0	27
1851	0	12	0	2	14
1852	0	0	4	0	4
1853	6	8	0	2	16
1854	4	10	3	0	17
1855	15	15	6	0	36
1856	6	4	4	6	20
1857	7	10	7	3	27
1858	4	7	10	7	28
1859	8	16	5	11	40
1860	13	17	5	19	54

[1] HRO: Q/CM/4. *Petty Session Returns: Convictions, c1822–51* and HRO: Q/CE/1. *Petty Session Returns: Convictions, c1852–60.*

Appendix VIII Cases of incendiarism: Reported in the *Hereford Journal* and *Hereford Times*, 1800–60

Year	Month	Time	Target	Farm or parish
1800	Oct		Barn, barley & wheat rick	Malborough
1801	Apr		Wheat rick (500 bushels)	The Parks (nr Tenbury)
	May		Hedge and Hurdles	Hampton Bishop
1807	Jun		Hay and corn ricks	Whitbourne Court
1811	Oct		2 barns	Much Cowarne
1814	Apr	1–2 a.m.	Wheat rick (250 bushels)	Middle Sarnesfield
	May		Barn and outbuilding	The Crumme (Hundington)
1818	Mar		Hay-house**	Munsley
1820	May		Coppice wood*	Brockhampton
1825	Jan		Farm property	Nr Ross
1828	Oct		Barn of wheat and barley	The Park (nr Ross)
1829	Jan	2–3 a.m.	Barn, cow-house and ricks	Lliadarary (nr Hay)
1830	Dec		Barn	The Stow (Kenchester)
1831	Jan		Farm property	Whitecross
1833	Sep		Barn	Much Dewchurch
1834	Feb		Wheat rick*	Yarpole
	Mar		3 faggot ricks	Pipe and Lyde
	Apr		Barn	Bolstone
	Jul		Barley rick (300 bushels)	Madley
1837	Feb	11–12 p.m.	Farm buildings	Withers Farm (nr Ledbury)
1839	Oct	1–2 a.m.	Corn mill (300 sacks of flour)	Hoarwithy
1840	Apr	8 p.m.	Wheat rick (250 bushels)	Weir End Farm (nr Ross)
	Oct	3 a.m.	Barn (600 bushels of barley)	Llangarren
1841	Mar	Night	Wheat rick (14 loads)	Showell (nr Madley)
1843	Mar	1.30 a.m.	Ricks, barn, beest-house	Cannon Bridge (nr Madley)
	Mar/Apr		Farm property	Madley
	Mar/Apr		Farm property	Madley
	Mar/Apr		Farm property	Madley
	May	12–1 a.m.	Farm buildings	Cannon Bridge (nr Madley)
	Aug		Cow-house and stock	Barges Farm (Madley)
	Aug	12 a.m.	Hay-house	The Wegnalls (nr Leominster)
	Nov		4 hay and 2 corn ricks	Eaton Bishop
1844	Jan		Farm buildings	Brinsop
	Jan		Wheat rick	Lye Court (nr Kington)

continued . . .

Appendix VIII *continued*

Year	Month	Time	Target	Farm or parish
	Jan		Stables	St Martin's (nr Hereford)
	Feb		Barns and wheat & hayricks	Upper Hill
	Feb		5,000 faggots	Abbey Dore
	May		Farm outbuildings	Scar Farm (Staunton on Wye)
	Sep	Night	Wheat ricks (500 bushels)	Pipe and Lyde
1845	Jan		2 wheat ricks	Tressack (nr Ross)
	Feb		900 faggots**	Pipe and Lyde
	Apr		35 acres woodland	Nash Wood (Presteigne)
1846	Apr		3 wheat and hayricks*	Pool Farm (Blackmarston)
	Jul		Wain-house (27 tons of clover)	Rotherwas (nr Hereford)
1847	Feb		Clover rick	Whitcliffe
	Apr	Night	2 wheat ricks	Apostiles Farm (nr Kington)
	Sep	Night	16 stooks of wheat	Nr Kington
	Sep		Wheat and hayricks*	Fullower's Farm (Kimbolton)
	Sep	Night	14 ricks, barns and stable	Verry's Farm (nr Ross)
1848	Jun		40-ton hayrick	New Barn Farm (Stretton Court)
	Nov		Corn stacks	Yarpole
1849	Feb	12 a.m.	Hay and straw ricks	Ullingswick
	Mar	12–1 a.m.	Barn and outbuildings	Church House Farm (Madley)
	Mar	11 p.m.	Barn and wheat rick*	Madley
	Mar		Hayrick*	Little Marcle
	Apr		2 barns and threshing machine*	Newtown Farm (nr Hereford)
	Apr		Stables	Newtown Farm
	Apr	7–8 p.m.	Farm buildings**	Preston Court (Stretton Sugwas)
	Sep	12–1 a.m.	Hayricks	Stretton Sugwas
	Oct		Barns and stable	Pantile Farm (nr Bromyard)
	Nov		Barns	Bromsberrow (nr Ledbury)
	Dec	2 a.m.	2 barns	Shenmore (nr Madley)
1850	Jun		Wheat rick*	Old Forge Farm (Goodrich)
	Nov		Barns	Mansel Gamage
1851	Jan	9 p.m.	2 wheat ricks	Allensmore

continued . . .

Appendix VIII *continued*

Year	Month	Time	Target	Farm or parish
	Jan	10–12 p.m.	Farm buildings	The Lakes (Stretton Sugwas)
	Feb	9 p.m.	Clover and hayricks	Stretton Sugwas
	Jun	1–2 a.m.	Farm outbuildings	Bishop's Stone
1852	Feb	8 p.m.	Wheat and barley ricks**	Hanley Court (Kingstone)
	Mar	8 p.m.	Stables and sheds	Shenmore (Madley)
	Mar		Gorse	Orcop Hill
	Apr		Wheat rick (250 bushels)	King's Pyon
	May		Underwood*	Dinmore
1853	Sep		Hay and clover ricks	Garway
	Nov		Load of straw	Moraston Farm (nr Ross)
1854	Feb		2 sacks of oats*	Upper Sapley
	Mar		Straw rick	Wormelow Tump
	Mar	Night	Uninhabited farm cottage	Middlewood
	Oct	3 p.m.	Barn (350 bushels of wheat)	Sutton Court
	Nov	10 a.m.	Barn (200 bushels of wheat)	Parish unknown
	Dec	Night	Corn stacks and clover ricks	Holme Lacy
	Dec	12 a.m.	Cottage and cider mill	Shenmore (Madley)
1855	Jan	2 a.m.	Wheat rick	Callow Hill
	Feb		Oat and clover stacks	Upper Sapley
	Jun		Barn holding straw*	Whitchurch
	Jun	11.30 p.m.	1,200 bushels of wheat**	Weston Under Penyard
	Aug	11.30 p.m.	Fodder rick	St Weonards
	Dec	2 a.m.	7 ricks	Little Cowarne
	Dec	Night	Several ricks	Little Cowarne
1856	Apr	Night	Coverts*	Kingswood (nr Kington)
	Jul	Night	Barns	Norton Cannon
	Jul	11 p.m.	Hayrick (5 tons)	Dorstone
1857	Apr	Night	Wheat, straw and clover ricks	Weston Under Penyard
	Apr	Night	Fodder rick	Sollers-Hope Court Farm
	June		Barn	Alton
	Jul		Barn and hayricks	Merryvale Farm (nr Ross)
1858	Feb	3 a.m.	Barn and wheat and straw ricks	Upper Michaelchurch
	Mar		Gorse**	Goodrich
	Mar	Night	Ricks, barn and livestock	Old Court Farm (nr Goodrich)

continued . . .

Appendix VIII *continued*

Year	Month	Time	Target	Farm or parish
	Jul		Hayricks	Lugg Bridge (nr Hereford)
	Aug	5 p.m.	Barn	Stockley Hill Farm (Madley)
	Aug	10.30 p.m.	Large hayrick	Nr Kington

Notes
* Indicates a committal.
** Indicates a committal and a conviction.

Appendix IX Cases of animal-maiming: Reported in the *Hereford Journal* and *Hereford Times*, 1800–60

Year	Month	Target	Method	Victim	Parish
1804	Jun	2 dogs	Cut	Farmer	Colwall
1809	Aug	2 mares	Cut	Farmer	Bodenham
1816	May	Horse	Cut		Walford
1818	Sep	Mare	Cut	Farmer	The Callow
1821	Nov	3 swans	Poison	Landowner	Allensmore
1826	Jun	13 horse's manes	Cut	Farmers	Breinton/Broomy Hill
	Aug	14 horse's manes	Cut	Farmers	Nr Hereford
1828	Apr	2 cart-horses	Beaten	Landowner	Bishopstone Court
1830	Dec	Horse's manes	Cut		Westmancote
1832	Jan	Horse	Cut		Bullingham
	Sep	Swan	Shot	Landowner	Allensmore
1833	Jan	Swan	Beaten	Landowner	Allensmore
1837	Jan	Cart-horse	Cut	Landowner	Allensmore
1839	Apr	Sheep	Cut	Farmer	Much Birch
	May	Cow	Cut	Farmer	Wellington
	May	Horse	Cut	Landowner	Barrs Court
	Aug	Lamb	Cut	Farmer	Nr Hereford
	Oct	Sheep	Cut	Butcher	Nr Hereford
1840	Jan	9 horse's manes	Cut	Landowner	Yarkhill Court
1841	Sep	9 Cows	Cut	Farmer	Nr Kington
1842	Jul	2 Rams	Cut	Landowner	Pencoyde
1843	May	7 horse's manes	Cut	Farmers	Much Cowarne
1844	Aug	Bullock**	Cut	Farmer	Luston
1846	Mar	6 pigs	Poison	Farmer	Eyton
1847	Sep	Cow	Poison	Farmer	Dewsall
	Dec	Pig	Cut	Labourer	Withington
1850	Aug	2 dogs	Poison	Farmer	Holmer
1853	Mar	2 pigs**	Poison	Farmer	Llangarren
1856	Jul	Horse	Cut	Farmer	Dorstone
1857	Jun	Colt's ears and tail	Cut	Farmer	Marden
	Jul	4 sheep	Cut	Landowner	Chandois Estate

Note
** Indicates a committal and a conviction.

Bibliography

Sources

Hereford Record Office (Hereafter abbreviated to HRO): Q/SR/88–148. *Hereford Quarter Session Rolls, c1800–60.*

HRO: BG11/8/9. *Summary of Cases at Various Courts, 1837–69.*

HRO: Q/014/253. *Hereford Quarter Sessions: Game Convictions, c1815–21.*

HRO: Q/CM/4. *Petty Session Returns: Convictions, c1822–51.*

HRO: Q/CE/1. *Petty Session Returns: Convictions, c1852–60.*

HRO: Rsc/1. *Hereford Quarter Sessions: Convictions, c1855–60.*

HRO: Q/SMc/1. *County Gaol Calendar of Prisoners, c1848–60.*

HRO: A95/V/W/C/30. *Calendar of Prisoners: Lent Assize, 23 March 1839.*

HRO: A95/V/W/C/31. *Calendar of Prisoners: Summer Assize, 27 July 1839.*

HRO: A95/V/W/C/98. *Cause List: Spring Assize 1827.*

HRO: Q/SO/8. *County of Hereford Orders of Sessions Relating to County Business: 1825–39.*

HRO: Q/SO/9. *County of Hereford Orders of Sessions Relating to County Business: 1839–47.*

HRO: Q/SO/10. *County of Hereford Orders of Sessions Relating to County Business: 1847–56.*

HRO: Q/SO/11. *County of Hereford Orders of Sessions Relating to County Business: 1857–66.*

HRO: AF/67. *Minute Book of Magistrates Meetings: Wormlow Hundred, c1810–1811.*

HRO: BB/88/1. *Magistrates Examination Book, of the Reverend Henry Gorges Dobyns Yate (Rector of Bromesbarrow) c1801–1803.*

HRO: Q/R1/1-59. *Herefordshire Enclosures.*

HRO: E41/75/110. *Hampton Court Estate Accounts.*

HRO: T70/36. *Digest of Game Laws (1783).*

HRO: *Directories and Gazetteers of Herefordshire, c.1816, 1817, 1830 and 1835.*

Littlebury's Directory and Gazetteer of Herefordshire (1867), Collingridge.

HRO: A/33/8. *Rules and Regulations of the Ganarew, Whitchurch, Marstow and Goodrich Association for the Prosecution of Felons and Other Offenders (1818).*

HRO: A/33/9. *Rules and Orders of the Wormlow Association for the Prosecution of Felons.*

HRO: A/33/10. *Association for the Protection of Property (Lower Part of the Hundred of Wormlow).*

Hereford City Library (Hereafter abbreviated to HCL): *Hereford Journal*, 1800–50.

HCL: *Hereford Times*, 1832–60.

HCL: John Clarke, 'General View of the Agricultural State of Hereford (1794)', *Board of Agriculture*.

HCL: John Duncumb, 'General View of the Agricultural State of Hereford (1805)', *Board of Agriculture*.

HCL: John Duncumb, 'General View of the Agricultural State of Hereford (1813)', *Board of Agriculture*.

HCL: FALC343.2 Broadside, c1832, *Executions at Hereford, Commencing (sic) with the Year 1770*.

HCL: Local Collections, Pamphlets, Vol. 21. *Articles of the County of Herefordshire Association for the Discovery and Prosecution of Felons and Other Offenders (1825)*.

HCL: The Davies Collection, Vol. 3. *The United Parochial Association for the Prosecution of Felons and the Prevention of Crime in the Parishes of Bishopstone, Bredwardine, Bridge Sollers, Brobury, Byford, Kinnersley, Letton, Mansell Gamage, Moccas, Monnington, Norton Canon, Staunton-on-Wye and Yazor (1841)*.

British Parliamentary Papers

1851 Census of Great Britain, Volume 6. Irish University Press, Dublin.

Crime and Punishment, Volume 8. Irish University Press, Dublin.

Population (1871–73), Volume 18. Irish University Press, Dublin.

Royal Commission on the Poor Laws (1834), Volume 27. Irish University Press, Dublin.

Population (1851), Volume 45. Irish University Press, Dublin.

Books

John Archer, *'By a Flash and a Scare': Arson, Animal Maiming and Poaching in East Anglia, 1815–1870*, Clarendon Press, Oxford (1990).

Alan Armstrong, *Farmworkers: A Social and Economic History, 1770–1980*, Batsford, London (1988).

J. M. Beattie, *Crime and the Courts in England: 1669–1800*, Clarendon Press, Oxford (1986).

J. Briggs and C. Harrison, *Crime and Punishment in England: An Introductory History*, University College London Press, London (1996).

Milton Briggs and Percy Jordan, *Economic History of England* (12th edn) University Tutorial Press, Slough (1978).

E. J. Burford and Sandra Shulman, *Of Bridles and Burnings: The Punishment of Women*, St Martin's Press, New York (1992).

Bob Bushaway, *By Rite: Customs, Ceremony and Community in England, 1700–1880*, Junction Books, London (1982).

J. Caird, *English Agriculture in 1850–1851* (2nd edn), Frank Cass, London (1968).

Albert Camus, *The Rebel*, Penguin, Harmondsworth (1962).

J. D. Chambers and G. E. Mingay, *The Agricultural Revolution: 1750–1850*, Batsford, London (1966).

Andrew Charlesworth (ed.), *An Atlas of Rural Protest in Britain: 1548–1900*, Croom Helm, London (1983).

Garth Christian (ed.), *James Hawker's Journal: A Victorian Poacher*, Oxford University Press, Oxford (1979).

J. S. Cockburn (ed.), *Crime in England: 1550–1800*, Methuen, London (1977).

Patrick J. Corish (ed.), *Radicals, Rebels and Establishments*, Appletree Press, Belfast (1985).

W. R. Cornish (ed.), *Crime and the Law in Nineteenth Century Britain: Commentaries on British Parliamentary Papers*, Irish University Press, Dublin (1978).

T. Critchley, *A History of the Police in England and Wales: 900–1966*, Constable, London (1967).

J. P. D. Dunbabin (ed.), *Rural Discontent in Nineteenth Century Britain*, Faber, London (1974).

Clive Emsley, *Crime and Society in England: 1750–1900*, Longman, London (1987).

Friedrich Engels, *The Condition of the Working Class in England*, Penguin Classics, Harmondsworth (1987). First published 1844.

Lord Ernle, *English Farming: Past and Present* (6th edn), Frank Cass, London (1961).

Frances Finnegan, *Poverty and Prostitution: A Study of Victorian Prostitution in York*, Cambridge University Press, Cambridge (1979).

H. L. V. Fletcher, *Herefordshire*, Robert Hale, London (1948).

V. A. C. Gatrell (ed.), *Crime and the Law: The Social History of Crime in Western Europe Since 1500*, Europa Press, London (1980).

V. A. C. Gatrell, *The Hanging Tree: Execution and the English People, 1770–1868*, Oxford University Press, Oxford (1996).

Anthony Giddens, *Sociology*, Polity Press, Cambridge (1991).

David Grigg, *English Agriculture: An Historical Perspective*, Blackwell, Oxford (1989).

Rider Lilias Haggard, *The King of the Norfolk Poachers*, The Norfolk Library, Boydell Press, Woodbridge (1974).

J. L. and B. Hammond, *The Village Labourer*, Longman, London (1966).

M. Haralambos (ed.), *Sociology: Themes and Perspectives*, Unwin Hyman, London (1988).

Douglas Hay and Francis Snyder (eds), *Policing and Prosecution in Britain: 1750–1850*, Clarendon Press, Oxford (1989).

Douglas Hay, P. Linebaugh and E. P. Thompson (eds), *Albion's Fatal Tree: Crime and Society in Eighteenth Century England*, Allen Lane, London (1975).

Bridget Hill, *Women, Work and Sexual Politics in Eighteenth Century England*, University College London Press, London (1994).

Eric Hobsbawm, *Primitive Rebels*, Manchester University Press, Manchester (1963).

Eric Hobsbawm and George Rudé, *Captain Swing*, Pimlico, London (1969).

Harry Hopkins, *The Long Affray: The Poaching Wars in Britain*, Secker and Warburg, London (1983).

Pamela Horn, *Life and Labour in Rural England: 1750–1850*, Macmillan, London (1987).

Pamela Horn, *Labouring Life in the Victorian Countryside*, Macmillan, Basingstoke (1995).

David Jones, *Rebecca's Children: A Study of Rural Society, Crime and Protest*, Clarendon Press, Oxford (1989).

David Jones, *Crime, Protest, Community and Police in Nineteenth Century Britain*, Routledge & Kegan Paul, London (1992).

David Jones, *Crime in Nineteenth Century Wales*, University of Wales Press, Cardiff (1992).

M. S. Kimmel, *Revolution: A Sociological Perspective*, Polity Press, Cambridge (1990).

John Knott, *Popular Opposition to the 1834 Poor Law*, Croom Helm, London (1986).

Peter Linebaugh, *The London Hanged: Crime and Civil Society in the Eighteenth Century*, Allen Lane, London (1991).

Frank McLynn, *Crime and Punishment in Eighteenth Century England*, Oxford University Press, Oxford (1991).

Linda Mahood, *The Magdalenes: Prostitution in the Nineteenth Century*, Routledge, London (1990).

Steven Marcus, *'Engels': Manchester and the Working Class*, Weidenfeld & Nicolson, London (1974).

Trevor May, *An Economic and Social History of Britain: 1760–1970*, Longman, London (1987).

B. R. Mitchell and P. Deane, *Abstracts of British Historical Statistics*, Cambridge University Press, Cambridge (1962).

Clifford Morsley, *News From the English Countryside*, Harrap, London (1979).

P. B. Munche, *Gentlemen and Poachers: The English Game Laws, 1671–1831*, Cambridge University Press, Cambridge (1981).

J. M. Neeson, *Commoners: Common Right, Enclosure and Social Change in England, 1700–1820*, Cambridge University Press, Cambridge (1993).

Keith Nield (ed.), *Prostitution in the Victorian Age: Debates on the Issue from Nineteenth Century Critical Journals*, Gregg International, Farnborough (1973).

Stanley Palmer, *Police and Protest in England and Ireland: 1750–1850*, Cambridge University Press, Cambridge (1988).

A. J. Peacock, *Bread or Blood: The Agrarian Riots in East Anglia, 1816*, Victor Gollancz, London (1965).

David Philips, *Crime and Authority in Victorian England: The Black Country, 1834–1860*, Croom Helm, London (1977).

Ivy Pinchbeck, *Women Workers and the Industrial Revolution: 1750–1850*, Virago (1981).

Leon Radzinowicz, *A History of the English Criminal Law and its Administration from 1750*, Vol. 1: *The Movement for Reform*, Stevens & Son, London (1948).

Leon Radzinowicz, *A History of the English Criminal Law and its Administration from 1750*, Vol. 2: *The Enforcement of the Law*, Stevens & Son, London (1956).

Mick Reed and Roger Wells, *Class, Conflict and Protest in the English Countryside: 1700–1880*, Frank Cass, London (1990).

George Rudé, *Ideology and Popular Protest*, Lawrence and Wishart, London (1980).

George Rudé, *Protest and Punishment: The Story of the Social and Political Protesters Transported to Australia*, Oxford University Press, Oxford (1985).

George Rudé, *Criminal and Victim: Crime and Society in Early Nineteenth Century England*, Oxford University Press, Oxford (1985).

J. G. Rule (ed.), *Outside the Law: Studies in Crime and Order, 1650–1850*, Exeter University Press, Exeter (1982).

J. G. Rule, *The Labouring Classes in Early Industrial England: 1750–1850*, Longman, London (1986).

J. G. Rule and Roger Wells, *Crime, Protest and Popular Politics in Southern England: 1740–1850*, Hambledon Press, London (1997).

K. Sayer, *Women of the Fields: Representations of Rural Women in the Nineteenth Century*, Manchester University Press, Manchester (1995).

J. A. Sharpe, *Crime in Early Modern England: 1550–1750*, Longman, London (1987).

R. M. Smith and K. Wrightson (eds), *The World we have Gained: Histories of Population and Social Structure*, Blackwell Press, Oxford (1986).

K. D. M. Snell, *Annals of the Labouring Poor: Social Change and Agrarian England, c1660–1900*, Cambridge University Press, Cambridge (1987).

John Stevenson, *Popular Disturbances in England: 1700–1832* (2nd edn), Longman, London (1992).

W. E. Tate, *The English Village and the Enclosure Movements*, Victor Gollancz, London (1967).

E. P. Thompson, *Whigs and Hunters*, Penguin, Harmondsworth (1990).

E. P. Thompson, *The Making of the English Working Class*, Penguin, Harmondsworth (1991).

E. P. Thompson, *Customs in Common*, Penguin, Harmondsworth (1993).

F. L. M. Thompson (ed,), *The Cambridge Social History of Britain: 1750–1950*, Vol. 3, Cambridge University Press, Cambridge (1993).

J. Tobias, *Crime and Industrial Society in the Nineteenth Century*, Batsford, London (1967).

J. Tobias, *Crime and Police in England: 1700–1900*, Gill & Macmillan, Dublin (1979).

J. Walkowitz, *Prostitution and Victorian Society*, Cambridge University Press, Cambridge (1980).

E. G. Walsh (ed.), *The Poacher's Companion: An Anthology*, Boydell Press, Woodbridge (1983).

Roger Wells, *Wretched Faces: Famine in Wartime England, 1763–1803*, St Martin's Press, New York (1988).

Merryn and Raymond Williams (eds), *John Clare: Selected Poetry and Prose*, Methuen English Texts, London (1986).

E. A. Wrigley (ed.), *Nineteenth Century Society: Essays in the Use of Quantitative Methods for the Study of Social Data*, Cambridge University Press, Cambridge (1972).

Lucia Zedner, *Women, Crime and Custody in Victorian England*, Clarendon Press, Oxford (1991).

Harold Zehr, *Crime and the Development of Modern Society: Patterns of Criminality in Nineteenth Century Germany and France*, Croom Helm, London (1976).

Articles

William Albert, 'Popular Opposition to Turnpike Trusts in Early Eighteenth Century England', *The Journal of Transport History*, Vol. 5 (1979).

John Archer, 'A Fiendish Outrage?': A Study of Animal Maiming in East Anglia, 1830–1870', *Agricultural History Review*, Vol. 33 (1985).

Alan Armstrong, 'The Influence of Demographic Factors on the Position of the Agricultural Labourer in England and Wales: 1750–1914', *Agricultural History Review*, Vol. 29 (1978).

J. M. Beattie, 'The Pattern of Crime in England: 1660–1800', *Past and Present*, No. 62 (1974).

John Bohstedt, 'Gender, Household and Community Politics: Women in English Riots, 1790–1810', *Past and Present*, No. 118–21 (1988).

A. Booth, 'Food Riots in the North West of England: 1790–1801', *Past and Present*, No. 77 (1977).

David Brooke, 'The Lawless Navvy: A Study of Crime Associated with Railway Building', *Journal of Transport History*, Vol. 10 (1989).

Anthony Brundage, 'Ministers, Magistrates and Reformers: The Genesis of the Rural Constabulary Act of 1839'. *Parliamentary History*, Vol. 5 (1986).

Bob Bushaway, 'Grovely, Grovely, Grovely and all Grovely: Custom,

Crime and Conflict in the English Woodland', *History Today*, Vol. 31 (1981).

Stephen Caunce, 'Farm Servants and the Development of Capitalism in English Agriculture', *Agricultural History Review*, Vol. 45 (1997).

Andrew Charlesworth, 'Comment: Morals, Markets and the English Crowd in 1766', *Past and Present*, No. 116 (1987).

E. J. T. Collins, 'Migrant Labour in British Agriculture in the Nineteenth Century', *Economic History Review*, No. 29 (1976).

Philip Dodd, 'Herefordshire Agriculture in the Mid-Nineteenth Century', *Transactions of the Woolhope Naturalists Field Club*, Vol. XLII (1980).

Ian Dyck, 'William Cobbett and the Rural Radical Platform', *Social History*, Vol. 18 (1993).

Clive Emsley, 'The Bedfordshire Police, 1840–1856: A Case Study in the Working of the Rural Constabulary Act', *Midland History*, Vol. 7 (1982).

Trevor Fisher, 'The Open Secret of Victorian Britain', *Local History Magazine*, No. 63 (1997).

Allan Fletcher, 'Game Laws in the Late Nineteenth Century: A Case Study from Clwyd', *The Local Historian*, Vol. 26 (1996).

R. E. Foster, 'A Cure for Crime? The Hampshire Rural Constabulary: 1839–1856', *Southern History*, Vol. 12 (1990).

Douglas Hay, 'War, Dearth and Theft in the Eighteenth Century: The Record of the English Courts', *Past and Present*, No. 95 (1982).

Eric Hobsbawm, 'Distinctions Between Socio-political and Other Forms of Crime', *Bulletin of the Society for the Study of Labour History*, No. 25 (1972).

Pamela Horn, 'The Employment of Children in Victorian Oxfordshire', *Midland History*, Vol. 4 (1977).

J. Humphries, 'Enclosure, Common Rights and Women: The Proletarianization of Families in the Late Eighteenth and Early Nineteenth Centuries', *Journal of Economic History*, Vol. 50 (1990).

Joanna Innes and John Styles, 'The Crime Wave: Recent Writing on Crime and Criminal Justice in Eighteenth Century England', *Journal of British Studies*, Vol. 25 (1986).

Richard Ireland, 'Eugene Buckley and the Diagnosis of Insanity in the Early Victorian Prison', *Llafur*, Vol. 6 (1993).

David Jones, 'Thomas Campbell Foster and the Rural Labourer: Incendiarism in East Anglia in the 1840s', *Social History*, Vol. 1 (1976).

David Jones, 'The Poacher: A Study in Victorian Crime and Protest', *History Journal*, Vol. 4 (1979).

Peter King, 'Decision-Makers and Decision-making in the English Criminal Law: 1750–1800', *Historical Journal*, No. 27 (1984).

Peter King, 'Gleaners, Farmers and the Failure of Legal Sanctions in England: 1750–1850', *Past and Present*, No. 122–5 (1989).

Peter King, 'Customary Rights and Women's Earnings: The Importance of

Gleaning to the Rural Labouring Poor, 1750–1850', *Economic History Review*, Vol. 44 (1991).

Peter King, 'Locating Histories of Crime: A Bibliographical Study', *British Journal of Criminology*, Vol. 39 (1999).

Penelope Lane, 'Work on the Margins: Poor Women and the Informal Economy of Eighteenth and early Nineteenth Century Leicestershire', *Midland History*, Vol. 22 (1997).

Peter Linebaugh, 'Eighteenth Century Crime, Popular Movements and Social Control', *Bulletin of the Society for the Study of Labour History*, No. 25 (1972).

P. Muskett, 'The East Anglian Riots of 1822', *Agricultural History Review*, Vol. 32 (1984).

P. Muskett, 'The Suffolk Incendiaries: 1843–45', *Journal of Regional and Local Studies*, Vol. 7 (1987).

Roy Palmer, 'Herefordshire Street Ballads', *Transactions of the Woolhope Naturalists Field Club: Herefordshire*, Vol. XLVII (1991).

Mick Reed, 'The Peasantry of Nineteenth Century England: A Neglected Class?', *History Workshop Journal*, No. 18 (1984).

Graham Rogers, 'Custom and Common Right: Waste Land Enclosure and Social Change in West Lancashire', *Agricultural History Review*, Vol. 41 (1994).

J. G. Rule, 'Social Crime in the Rural South in the Eighteenth and Early Nineteenth Centuries', *Southern History*, Vol. 1 (1979).

J. A. Sharpe, 'The History of Crime in England, c1300–1914: An Overview of Recent Publications', *British Journal of Criminology*, Vol. 28 (1988).

R. Swift, 'The English Magistracy and the Administration of Justice During the Early Nineteenth Century: Wolverhampton, 1815–60', *Midland History*, Vol. 17 (1992).

E. P. Thompson, 'The Moral Economy of the English Crowd in the Eighteenth Century', *Past and Present*, No. 50 (1971).

E. P. Thompson, 'Patrician Society, Plebeian Culture', *Journal Of Social History*, Vol. 7 (1974).

Clifford Tucker, 'William Cobbett's Monmouthshire', *The Journal of Monmouthshire Local History Council*, Vol. 35.

Roger Wells, 'The Revolt of the South West, 1800–1801: A Study in English Popular Protest', *Social History*, Vol. 5 (1977).

Roger Wells, 'Sheep-Rustling in Yorkshire in the Age of the Industrial and Agricultural Revolutions', *Northern History*, Vol. 20 (1984).

Roger Wells, 'Mr William Cobbett, Captain Swing and King William IV', *Agricultural History Review*, Vol. 45 (1998).

Dale Williams, 'Morals, Markets and the English Crowd in 1766', *Past and Present*, No. 104 (1984).

Richard Williams, 'Securing Justice in Eighteenth Century England: The Example of Berkshire', *Southern History*, Vol. 18 (1996).

Sydna Ann Williams, 'Women's Employment in Nineteenth Century Anglesey', *Llafur*, Vol. 6 (1993).

J. R. Wordie, 'The Chronology of English Enclosure: 1500–1914', *The Economic History Review*, Vol. 36 (1983).

Susan Wright, 'Holding up Half the Sky': Women and their Occupations in Eighteenth Century Ludlow', *Midland History*, Vol. 14 (1989).

Index

Aconbury 88, 139
agriculture 4, 78–9
  and depression 36–9, 47, 51
  and enclosure 28, 46–9
  growth of agrarian capitalism 18–19,
    21, 203
agricultural labourers
  alternative employment opportunities
    39, 45–6
  day labour 43
  disparate experiences of 93
  living-in 40–2
  migrant labour 39–40
  migration 39–40
  poverty 36–53
  radicalism 27–9
  rejection of capitalism 2
  as a revolutionary class 23–4
  wages 13, 38–9
Allensmore 99
animal-maiming 176–200
  and the criminal law 176–7
  hair docking 196
  extent of 195
  and protest 192, 197
  as a social crime 177
  victims of 197–200
anonymous letter 13, 168
Aston 13
Aymestrey 135, 163

Barrs Court 198
Barton 138
Berrington Hall 13, 167
Bill Mill 110
Bishopstone 121
Black Acts (1723) 163, 176
Boatside 102
Bodenham 125, 166
Bolstone 148, 183
Bosbury 135
Bradlow 131
Brampton Abbots 134
Breinton 15, 67, 196
Bridge Sollers 125

Brinsop 187–8
Brockhampton Court 168
Bromsberrow 155
Bromyard 66, 69, 100, 103, 133, 134
Broomy Hill 196
Burghill 67, 107

Chepstow (Monmouthshire) 57
Clun (Shropshire) 103
Cobbett, William 26–9
Colwall 199–200
community justice
  informers 14, 128–9, 161
  scolds 25
  wife-beaters 25
Corn Laws 188
court records 33–4
Cradley 17, 49
Credenhill 124, 131, 140, 187–8
crime
  extent of in Herefordshire 4, 30–6, 51
  and poverty 30–53
  as a sign of modernity 21
  victims of 22–3, 52–3
criminals
  ages of 42
  fatalism of 129
  as social bandits 22
criminal law and the courts
  cost of bringing prosecutions 74–7
  extension of summary powers for
    magistrates 76
  granting of expenses 75–6
  numbers of petty crimes reaching courts
    135–6
  reform of 73–7
crop theft 33, 43, 50, 113–40
  and children 133–4
  cost of prosecution for 135
  extent of 114–17, 120
  farmers wanting protection from 136
  and grain theft 137–9
  petty nature of 135
  and poverty 132–3
  as protest 131–2

and seasonality 122
and violence 139–140
and women 123

Dewchurch 58, 88, 92
Dilwyn 125
Donnington 156
Dormington 104, 105
Dorstone 192
Doward 68, 91, 97, 99–100, 104, 110,
    112

Eaton Bishop 100, 183
Eye 13

farmers
    attitudes towards policing 58
Fownhope 89

gamekeepers 165–6, *see also* poaching
Game Laws *see also* poaching
    attitudes towards 153–6, 158, 175
Ganarew 48
Goodrich 191

Hampton Bishop 131
Harewood End 174
Herefordshire
    and population growth 38
Holme Lacy 83, 145, 151
Holmer 33, 63, 134
Hope Under Dinemore 131, 166
Huntington 100

incendiarism 8, 176–95
    community support for 190
    and the criminal law 176–7, 185–7
    extent of 177–8, 180, 184, 187
    fear of 181–2
    insurance against 182
    and Lucifer matches 184–5
    and poverty 186, 188
    and the press 180–1, 187, 190
    and protest 176–7
    and Rebeccaism 187–8
    as revenge 191
    and seasonal unemployment 189–90
    and social crime 177
    targets of 182–3
    unpopularity of victims of 190
Ivington 166

Kimbolton 184
Kingsland 163

Kingstone 164, 169, 172, 187
Kington 65, 100, 184, 189
Kivernoll 125
Knighton (Radnorshire) 69

landowners
    and charity 5
    and wage cuts 38
leasing 114
Ledbury 129, 148, 150, 155–6, 201
Leominster 52, 102, 129, 163, 174
Lingen 121
Linton 92, 138
Little Cowarne 189, 191
Little Dewchurch 100
Llangarren 100, 190, 199
Llanrouthal 100
Lyonshall 146

Madley 180, 181–2, 183, 187, 192–4, 201
Madley Fire-King 192–4
Monnington on Wye 139
Mordiford 82, 166
Moreton 13
Moreton on Lugg 100
Much Cowarne 149, 171
Much Marcle 126
Munsley 107, 185

Newport Rising (1839) 64
newspapers
    and attitudes towards criminals 127–8
    and crime 1–2
    and reward advertisements 12–13, 80,
        91, 106
Newton Warton 166
Newtown Farm 184, 191, 194

Ocle Pritchard 99

parish constables 55–8, 72
    Commission of Rural Constabulary
        Report (1839) 56–8
Pengethley 106
Pipe and Lyde 186, 194
Pixley 111
poaching 16, 17, 43, 75, 76, 89, 90–1,
        141–75, *see also* Game Laws
    animal-maiming and incendiarism 17
    attitudes towards 153–6, 158, 175
    community support for 156, 161, 168
    and the criminal law 142–8, 161–3,
        170–4
    and cross-dressing 169

extent of 144, 146–8, 151–2
and food prices 151–2
and gamekeepers 165–7
at night 162
poachers as petty criminals 155–6,
  168–9
poachers as social bandits 159–60
as a profession 20, 148–9, 150–1
as protest 160, 167–70
as a social crime 160
and unemployment 152–3
and violence 161, 163–5
and women 148
police 54–77
  assaults on 70–2
  attitudes towards 69–72
  County and Borough Police Act
    (1856) 68
  County Police Act (1840) 63
  and farmer's subscriptions 68–9
  Municipal Corporations Act (1835)
    62
  resistance to policing by magistrates
    63–5, 72–3
  resistance to policing by ratepayers
    65–6
  rural special constables 66–7
Pontrilas 84
poor law 14–15, 37, 42, 93
Preston on Wye 182
Preston Wynn 181
prices
  bread 45, 85–6, 188
  fuel 123
  potatoes 45
  sheep 85–6, 88
protest
  as a community-sanctioned act 12–14,
    17, 22, 91
  definition of 9–10
  ideology of protesters 24–9
  as an individual act 11
  Luddism 21
  Pentrich Rising 27
  against poor law 129–30
Putson 50

Rebeccaism see incendiarism
Redhill 69
riot
  against encroachers 17, 49
  over grain prices 137–8
  against injustice 17, 128–9
  at Ross election 27

Ross 12, 57, 66, 69, 70, 75, 96, 100, 106,
  107, 109, 123, 134, 174, 182, 183,
  186, 196

St Weonards 60, 124
sheep-stealing 78–112
  Associations for the prosecution of
    felons 60
  and bargees 82–5, 91, 97, 110
  and community sanction 91–2
  and the criminal law 80, 94–6, 97–101,
    108
  extent of 87–9, 101
  by families 89–90
  methods of 92–3, 109
  methods of detection 91
  police apprehensions 43, 58, 62–3,
    106–8
  and poverty 86, 89, 101–2, 104
  professionalism of 88
  as protest 93–4
  as rustling 81–2, 87–8, 101–4
  as a social crime 90–1, 97
  and wheat prices 85–6
  and women 88–9
Shelwick 14
Shobdon 163
social crime 15–17, 19–20
Stapleton 65
Stoke Edith 68
Stoke Prior 164, 166
Swing (1830–1), 7, 10, 21
  as backward-looking 24
  in Herefordshire 4
  as protest 10, 78
  and radicalism 27

Tarrington 55, 104
Tenbury (Worcestershire) 103, 109

Upper Sapey 109
Upton Bishop 17, 128–9

Walford 70, 115
Wellington 49, 57, 132, 136
Welsh Bicknor 99
Weobley 129, 150, 164
Westhide 165
Weston Beggard 99
Whitchurch 68, 91, 97, 99, 100, 104, 110,
  112, 120, 191
Whitney 100, 110
Wigmore 48, 120, 133
Withington 136

Wolferlow 133
wood-theft 43, 50, 89, 113–40
  and children 133–4
  and the criminal law 117–20
  expense of prosecution for 135
  extent of 114–17, 120
  farmers wanting protection from 136
  petty nature of 135
  and poverty 132–3
  as protest 130–2

  and violence 139–40
  and women 123
Woolhope 93
work
  changing customs 18–19, 40–2
  wages for women and children 123–4
Wormlow 139, 161

Yarkhill 63
Yarpole 145, 194